THE
STANFORD
LAW
CHRONICLES

THE
STANFORD
LAW
CHRONICLES

Doin' Time on the Farm

ALFREDO MIRANDÉ

University of Notre Dame Press
Notre Dame, Indiana

Library of Congress Cataloging-in-Publication Data

Mirandé, Alfredo.
The Stanford law chronicles : doin' time on the farm / Alfredo Mirandé.
p.   cm.

ISBN 0-268-02283-6 (cloth : alk. paper)
ISBN 0-268-02284-4 (pbk. : alk. paper)
1. Mirandé, Alfredo.   2. Hispanic American lawyers—
California—Biography.   3. Lawyers—
California—Biography.   I. Title.
KF373.M567A3   2005
340'.092—dc22

2005021972

∞This book is printed on acid-free paper

Para mis hermanos queridos,

Alejandro Rovíer Mirandé González ("Alex")

Héctor Xavíer Mirandé González ("Gordo")

CONTENTS

THREE L

ACKNOWLEGDMENTS

I have published a number of books over the years, but this one has been the most difficult to write. I did not set out to write a biography, but from the moment I prepared my law school application and personal statement, I found myself relating back to my family and my early childhood experiences. It is to them, then, that I owe my greatest debt. Law school seeks to strip you of your identity and sense of self. I found myself resisting and, in the process, rediscovering and reaffirming a core identity, which was deeply rooted in my childhood, family, and culture.

Three former students and good friends, Enrique López, David López, and Walter Martínez, deserve special recognition. Enrique read early versions of the manuscript and consistently provided support and friendship. David, an accomplished trial lawyer, read the entire manuscript and provided valuable insights and encouragement. Walter read the final manuscript and provided invaluable input and guidance at a critical stage in the process. Edith Vásquez proofed and corrected the final manuscript. Finally, I would like to acknowledge and thank University of Notre Dame Press editors Jeff Gainey and Rebecca DeBoer and the anonymous reviewers for their editorial support and assistance.

I want to thank my children, Michele, Lucía, and Alejandro Xavier ("Mano"), for their love, support, and tolerance in permitting me to pursue my dreams and for their patience and indulgence. The only regret that I have about attending law school and pursuing my dream to become a lawyer is that it took precious time from my children at a time when I think they most needed a father.

Sadly, the people who deserve most of the credit for this book, and for anything that I might accomplish, are deceased: my parents, Xavier and Rosa María; my beloved brothers, Alex and Héctor Xavier; my paternal grandparents, Ana María and Alfredo; and grandfather Alfredo's sisters, *las tías*, Lupe and Carmela, who played a critical role in my development. This book is dedicated to their strength, spirit, and memory, which are unending.

The faculty and my fellow students at Stanford Law School shared their experiences and made this book possible. The incidents described in the ensuing pages are real, but the people are not. To preserve their anonymity and privacy, except for my family and my friend Enrique López, all of the names in this book are pseudonyms. I have also combined and altered background information and changed the circumstances surrounding events, and any resemblance to any person, living, or dead, is coincidental.

THE
AWAKENING

PROLOGUE

This is a book about law school. Several years ago I left my job as a professor in the Department of Sociology at the University of California, Riverside, and enrolled as a first-year law student, or "One L," at Stanford Law School (SLS). Like any good ethnographer, I kept a journal in which I recorded my observations, responses, and reflections. I did not realize at the time that I was embarking on an unforgettable journey that would force me to reevaluate not only law and the law school experience but also my early childhood, my family, and the core of my identity. My law school days proved significant and exciting. It was the most rewarding and intellectually stimulating period of my life and at the same time the most painful and alienating.

Rereading my field notes and reflecting on the experience, I am struck by the breadth and range of my alienation. Although I loved the law and was excited intellectually, I was frustrated by the pretentious hierarchies and hurdles I encountered. I have tried to tell my story as it happened, in its raw, uncensored form.

This book is written in different tenses and voices. I often retain the first person and present tense that I used in my field notes, to describe certain events as they transpired or to describe my memories. When I reflect on the law school experience, I normally use the second person and the past tense. I also sometimes unwittingly objectify myself and use the third person, or "Alfredo."

Like other total institutions such as prisons, boot camps, monasteries, and concentration camps, law school systematically strips students of their previous professional (student, doctor, journalist, priest, professor), cultural and ethnic (Mexican, African, Asian), and personal and familial identities. The first-year law student is taught to abandon previous moral and ethical standards, to be skeptical, to approach law in an objective and dispassionate

3

manner, and to focus on efficiency rather than justice. Law school education is training for hierarchy.

Although the values and ethos that law school imparts are presented as apolitical, objective, neutral, value-free, and universal, they are at their core the values of elite white male culture. Racial minorities, women, and working-class whites who enter law school, then, are seeking admittance into an elite white male club. Admission requires not only that one learn a new language and the substantive law but also that one adopt the values and ideologies of privileged groups.

One cannot undergo the law school experience without having one's psyche altered in a fundamental way. In retrospect, I believe that I was lucky. I emerged from the experience wounded but relatively unscathed and, in the end, able to think like a lawyer without having to surrender my previous identities or value system. This account of the law school experience is written by a law student who resisted indoctrination and the stripping of his culture and personhood and survived to write about it. One of the things that enabled me to endure the unrelenting assault on my psyche and personhood is the fact that I was a successful Chicano[1] professor and author with a solid identity as teacher, sociologist, and father when I enrolled. I had long been curious about law and had considered law school before deciding to pursue a career as a sociologist.

Stanford is one of the top two or three law schools in the United States, although distinctions are made even among elite schools. Harvard is the oldest, most revered, and most hierarchical and presumably the standard against which other law schools are gauged.[2] Ironically, it is said to be closely connected "to both big business and radical legal thought."[3] Yale is also prestigious but less hierarchical. It is often described as philosophical. The University of Chicago Law School is conservative and closely identified with the law and economics movement. Stanford is at the other extreme: it is considered one of the most progressive law schools in the country.[4]

While the setting for this book is Stanford, it is about the law school experience generally. Despite differences in the prestige, rankings, and influence of law schools, legal education is remarkably similar, uniform, and unchanging across space and time. Harvard is the prototype of the elite hierarchical law school and the oppressive and intimidating Socratic method. Although Stanford prides itself on being diverse, open, and nonhierarchical, I encountered hierarchies at every turn: in the classroom, at the Stanford Law Review, in recruitment by elite law firms, and in clerking for a U.S. district court judge. But the most unexpected hierarchies were those that emerged among the students enrolled in the progressive poverty law curriculum (called "Lawyering for Social Change"), which attracted nontraditional students who wanted to use the law as a vehicle for helping racial minorities, the poor, and the oppressed.

This book is unique in a number of ways. First, it is the first book about law school written by someone who was not already a member of the elite white male club. John Jay Osborne's *The Paper Chase* is a popular fictional account of the first year of law school at Harvard.[5] Scott Turow's *One L* is not supposed to be fiction, but the book is remarkably similar to *The Paper Chase and* reads like a novel.[6] Turow attended Harvard Law School in 1976 and published a classic on the experience. Written before Turow gained fame as a novelist, *One L* was subsequently reissued by a major press and is now required reading for anyone interested in law and legal education.

Chris Goodrich's *Anarchy and Elegance* is a more recent firsthand account by a journalist who enrolled in a one-year Master of Law program at Yale. Goodrich faults Turow because he is critical of legal education "not because it changed students' understanding of the world—and thus their notions about justice—but because it didn't prepare them to operate within the existing legal system."[7] However, in the end, both books provide top-down views of legal education. Goodrich received a fellowship to study the first year of law school and to write a book about the experience. He took the same first-year classes as other entering students but did not graduate and did not intend to become a lawyer.

Both Turow and Goodrich come from privileged backgrounds. Turow observed that many of his classmates were the children of privilege but sheepishly admits that "those observations applied just as well to me—eastern-educated, a son of the well-to-do—and if advantages became a basis for exclusion then I might well have been the first to go."[8] Goodrich's elite roots run even deeper than Turow's. He was a Yale College undergraduate, and some of his college friends and a number of relatives had attended Yale Law School.[9] His grandfather Elizur Goodrich was a law professor and is buried in the family plot at the Grove Street Cemetery.[10] Goodrich describes the Grove Street Cemetery as "to the east, out of the Law School's back door," with "its crypto-Egyptian gateway announcing 'the Dead Shall Be Raised.'"[11]

Despite their elite lineage, both Turow and Goodrich claim to identify with the underprivileged. Turow was alienated by the elite background of many of his classmates, who, by obtaining a Harvard law degree, were now acquiring additional advantages. Although Turow is painfully aware of his privileged background, on several occasions he goes out of his way to note that his progressive, 1960s liberal political ideology set him apart from most of his classmates. In law school he was put off by the emphasis placed on the Law School Admission Tests (LSAT) in admissions decisions and by the intense competition over grades, making the Harvard Law Review, and landing a lucrative firm job: "In College, at Amherst, in the era of Vietnam and the civil-rights struggle, the law had seemed to me the instrument by which the people in power kept themselves on top. When many of my friends had decided to go to law school, I had been openly critical of their choices."[12]

Goodrich was also turned off by the way law school dehumanizes students. It provided people with many masks—counselor, advocate, cross-examiner, coach, confidant—but the most pervasive was "the neutral, lawyer persona, a mask that was difficult, once affixed, to remove."[13] Goodrich felt that his grandfather, in particular, would have disapproved of his views on legal education and "at [that] very moment was probably spinning in his grave."[14]

This book is also unique because it is the first book on law school written by a person of color.[15] I was born in Mexico and did not come from an elite background, so I offer an outsider's perspective on law school and legal education.

Like other students, especially students of color, I experienced culture shock during the first-year indoctrination and beyond. I especially resented being labeled one of the best and the brightest and identifying with the dominant privileged culture and ideology. The prototypical "reasonable man" in the law school curriculum is objective, detached, unemotional, and always rational. No one in my family or community, it seemed, acted like the reasonable man. In fact, my father was the prototypical authoritarian father and the paragon of unreasonableness and arbitrariness. I came to law school with a strong sense of family pride and identified strongly as a Mirandé and as the youngest of three brothers. My father always pushed his sons to excel in their endeavors, and we were high achievers.[16] I also knew only too well that whatever I did in my life, positive or negative, would ultimately reflect on my family.

I underwent the same brainwashing and stripping processes as other entering law students, but I believe that my age and the many layers of identity enabled me to resist them more readily. Like Brother Remy, a monk who wrote an account of life in a Cistercian monastery where the monks had taken a vow of silence,[17] I was able to resist indoctrination and the stripping of my identity by objectifying myself and analyzing the law school experience from afar. I unconsciously came to observe law school and the trials and tribulations of "Alfredo" from the vantage point of a detached, neutral third party. I came to observe and describe "Alfredo's" law school experience in the same way I might observe and describe the experiences of others. Over time and before my very eyes, Alfredo was transformed from a vibrant, charming, and affable professor to an old, alienated, angry Mexican.

Finally, this is the first book that focuses on the entire law school experience. I write about topics ranging from Law Review to the Lawyering for Social Change curriculum and to representing my first client in the Immigration Clinic. In chapter 12, I describe my return to law school several months after graduation: like a repressed nightmare, any trace of "Alfredo's" existence had been erased from the collective memory of Stanford Law School.

Training for Hierarchy

Law school has been aptly described as training for hierarchy. According to the progressive Harvard Law professor, Duncan Kennedy, although many law students enter law school with visions of changing the social order and using law as a vehicle for social change, most end up adopting an ideology that helps to maintain and support the status quo.[18] Law schools appear on the surface to be theoretically barren and nonpolitical, but they are in fact "intensely political" places.[19] Despite the "trade school mentality" that focuses on the trees at the expense of the forest and avoids any discussion of politics or ideology, law schools perpetuate an ideology that directly and indirectly maintains prevailing hierarchies and patterns of domination.[20] According to Kennedy:

> To say that law school is ideological is to say that what teachers teach along with the basic skills is wrong, is nonsense about what law is and how it works, that the message about the nature of legal competence, and its distribution among students, is wrong, is nonsense; that the ideas about the possibilities of life as a lawyer that students pick up from legal education are wrong, are nonsense. But all of this is nonsense with a tilt; it is biased and motivated rather than random error.

What it says is that it is natural, efficient, and fair for law firms, the bar as a whole, and the society the bar serves to be organized in their actual patterns of hierarchy and domination.[21]

Like many other students, I entered law school with the hope of using law to bring about significant change. Many students enter with a vision of using law, like Brandeis did in an earlier generation, as a progressive force.[22] Others enter law school thinking that law can be used as an effective tool that in the hands of a skilled technician can be turned against the system. In this view, "the student imagines herself as part technician, part judo expert, able to turn the tables exactly because she never lets herself be mystified by the rhetoric that is so important to other students."[23]

One of the reasons that the socialization of first-year law students is so effective is that much of it is insidious and covert, so that law students think they are simply learning the law and how to think like a lawyer without realizing that they are also being socialized to adopt a distinct ideology and political and ethical system. In fact, law students learn precious little about law or the skills that are required for effective law practice in law school. This is not to say that students do not learn valuable skills during the first year.

They learn to retain large numbers of rules organized into categorical systems (requisites for a contract, rules about breach, etc.). They learn "issue spotting," which means identifying the ways in which the rules are ambiguous, in conflict, or have a gap when applied to particular fact situations. They learn elementary case analysis, meaning the art of generating broad holdings for cases so they will apply beyond their intuitive scope, and narrow holdings for cases so that they won't apply where it at first seemed they would.[24]

But mostly they learn how to be compliant and to accept the system as it is.

Law students learn how to argue both sides of an issue effectively and how to dissect and break down logical arguments. They learn how to turn feelings on and off like a faucet and to mask emotions. When Goodrich visited friends on his first break from law school, for example, he found himself "addicted to law" and suddenly empowered so that law became like "an artificial high."[25] Instead of wanting to share a moment of friendship or engage in trivial conversation or quiet reflection with his old friends, he wanted to lock horns and strut his stuff, perhaps even intimidate.[26] Very quickly, he found that law had changed him: he was arrogant, self-centered, and unable to engage in meaningful conversation on nonlegal topics.[27] He found himself becoming the kind of person he had previously despised.

In the formal law school curriculum, students are taught legal rules and legal reasoning, and they come to be convinced by teachers that legal reasoning exists independently of values and policy analysis. Kennedy notes that in a given subfield of law, teachers are likely to group cases into three categories: the relatively large number that are treated as routine exercises in legal logic and used to demonstrate legal reasoning; the exceptional, outdated, or anomalous cases that are either antiquated or wrongly decided; and the small number of cutting edge cases that illustrate policy issues and growth or change in the law.[28] Significantly, in discussions of cutting edge issues, the discourse is open and freewheeling, with students' comments receiving "pluralistic acceptance."[29]

The ground rules of the law school curriculum are those of late-nineteenth-century laissez-faire capitalism.[30] Liberal professors teach limited interference where the market makes sense and is grounded in statutes, whereas conservatives teach that "much of the reform program is irrational or counterproductive, or both, and would have been rolled back long ago were it not for 'politics.'"[31] In addition to the basic courses, there are peripheral courses in areas such as legal philosophy or legal theory and clinical courses such as those in the Stanford Lawyering for Social Change curriculum. These are presented as "soft" courses that are not part of the objective, serious, analytical core of law.[32] They are viewed as "a kind of playground or finishing school for learning the social art of self-presentation as a lawyer."[33]

The law school classroom has been described as "culturally reactionary."[34] From the first day, law students learn that the law is hierarchical from the way the first-year classroom is structured. The teachers are overwhelmingly white, traditional, and "deadeningly straight and middle class in manner" and receive a degree of deference and fear that is more reminiscent of high school than college.[35] As undergraduates, students are used to being anonymous and sitting passively through lectures, but in law school there is an expectation of pseudo-participation in which one struggles to avoid being humiliated in front of a large number of people.[36] Students quickly learn that the Socratic method is an insidious game in which it has been said there is only one winner.[37] *The Paper Chase* begins with the famous law student folkloric tale about the daunting Professor Kingsfield.

In the few days between arrival at Harvard Law School and the first classes, there are rumors. And stories. About being singled out, made to show your stuff.

Mostly, they're about people who made some terrible mistake. Couldn't answer a question right.

One concerns a boy who did a particularly bad job. His professor called him down to the front of the class, up to the podium, gave the student a dime and said, loudly:

"Go call your mother, and tell her you'll never be a lawyer."

Sometimes the story ends here, but the way I heard it, the crushed student bowed his head and limped slowly back through the door, his anger exploded. He screamed:

"You're a son of a bitch, Kingsfield."

"That's the first intelligent thing you've said," Kingsfield replied. "Come back. Perhaps I've been too hasty."[38]

The law school classroom appears to be a combination of "the patriarchal family and a Kafkalike riddle state."[39]

My Early Training in Resisting Hierarchies

Ironically, perhaps what best prepared me for dealing with law school was not my extensive schooling or experience as a professor and community activist but growing up in a hierarchical, patriarchal Mexican family. I was the youngest of three boys—Alexandro, Héctor Xavier, and Alfredo Manuel—born to Xavier Ándres Mirandé Salazar and Rosa María González Ochoa.

My father did not attend college and had never been anywhere near a law school, but strangely he was a Mexican counterpart of the legendary Professor Kingsfield. Like Kingsfield and God, he was all-powerful, all-knowing, and ever-present. I learned early in life that right or wrong, my dad was always right. One questioned what he did or what he said at great risk. When we dared to ask for an explanation for his arbitrary and capricious conduct, his response typically was to retort, "Porque sí! Porque yo lo digo!"—Because! Because I say so!—or, more commonly, to ignore the question.

My father was a strict disciplinarian, and we were subjected to numerous beatings either for misbehaving or because there was a perception or possibility of misbehavior. When he was in a good mood, *papá* used to say things like "Si se portan bien, los voy a llevar a ver comer helado" (If you behave, I'm going to take you to watch people eat ice cream). Although he was kidding, it reflected his primitive view of child rearing and the value of disciplining one's sons. The implication was that getting to eat ice cream would be done in steps, and the first step, naturally, was to watch. In my law school application personal statement, I wrote:

> My father was a violent person. He didn't believe in justice, civil rights, and didn't seem to know or care that in this country one is said to be presumed innocent until proven guilty. He always beat us fairly and in chronological order. I, therefore, had to watch my older brothers get thrashed as I waited my turn. Unlike my older brothers who accepted their fate like *machitos* (little men), I generally tried to reason with my father and to plead my case. Amazingly, I sometimes convinced him and was spared. As an adult my dad would tell me how much he admired and respected not only the fact that I dared to question his actions but my ingenuity in coming up with explanations or reasons why a beating was not justified. He would say, "Ese muchacho debe ser abogado!" (That boy should be an attorney).

My interest in justice, equity, and cross-cultural differences surfaced at a very early age. When I was nine or ten I thought that I wanted to be a lawyer. I would later decide that my calling was teaching sociology, but law was like an old sweetheart I never forgot.

I was struck by another interesting parallel between the prototypical authoritarian law professor such as Osborne's Kingsfield at Harvard and Professor Hazard, his counterpart at Yale, and my father.[40] As a first-year law student, Goodrich came to the realization not only that "only one world view—hyperrational, adversarial, and positivistic—was acceptable in law school" but also "that law valued *appearing* to be right more than actually *being* right."[41] My father also valued appearing to be right more than he did actually being right. Although I sometimes was convinced that both my professors and my father were wrong, the truth is that in the game we were playing, they were always right. However, Goodrich adds, "the professor's aggressive assurance about the law masked a deep and abiding ambivalence."[42]

Because I was the youngest in my family and my father and brothers were larger and stronger, I learned early that my survival was predicated on my ability to think on my feet. I was not large enough or strong enough to challenge them physically, nor was I inclined to do so. I loved and respected my father and my brothers. Even as I grew larger and stronger, I did not challenge their authority, although I attempted to reason with them. I recall pleading with my father to let me explain before he beat me unfairly, telling him that I was doing this for his benefit because I knew that he would feel badly once he learned the truth of what had happened and my innocence was revealed.

Hunger for Memory

It is commonly assumed that exposure to higher education inevitably results in assimilation into the dominant culture, loss of one's native language, and alienation from one's family, community, and culture. Richard Rodríguez is perhaps the primary exponent of this view. Rodríguez, one of the few persons of Mexican descent to have written an autobiography and published books that became national best-sellers, has gained a great deal of notoriety for his controversial, conservative stance on a number of issues. He is opposed to affirmative action and to bilingual and bicultural education. He remarks, "I have become notorious among certain leaders of America's Ethnic Left. I am considered a dupe, an ass, the fool—Tom Brown, the brown Uncle Tom, interpreting the writing on the wall to a bunch of cigar-smoking pharaohs."[43]

Despite having a Spanish surname and parents who are working-class Mexicans, Rodríguez has become so Americanized and distant from them that they are no longer his parents in a cultural sense. He is not Ricardo but Richard, and he pronounces his name as he hears it, "Rich-heard Road-ree-guess."[44] According to the book jacket, *Hunger of Memory* is "the poignant journey of a 'minority student' who pays the cost of his social assimilation and academic success with a painful alienation—from his past, his parents, his culture—and so describes the high price of 'making it' in middle-class America."

Rodríguez claims to have known only fifty words of English when he entered an all-white Catholic school in Sacramento, California. Today his language and culture have been eradicated so that he writes not as a Mexican or a Chicano but as an educated middle-class American. His dark skin and Indian features make him so exotic and enigmatic that a Mexican woman carrying a tray of hors d'oeuvres wonders what he is doing at a cocktail party in Bel Air.[45] Richard, the scholarship boy, has entered a world that his parents cannot understand. They wonder why he stayed in school for such a long time and why he cannot find a regular job. In the end, Rodríguez is "a tragic figure caught as the comic victim of two cultures."[46]

Despite his humble origins, Rodríguez has much in common with the children of privilege: "Perhaps because I have always, accidentally, been a class-mate to children of rich parents, I long came to assume my association with their world; came to assume that I could have money, if it was money I wanted. But money, big money, has never been the goal of my life."[47] Rodríguez's ultimate goal is to have the privilege of being a writer. But in choosing to become a writer and pursue higher education, he became increasingly distant and alienated from his family and uncomfortable with his Mexicanness.

The comparisons between Rodríguez and Turow are obvious. Turow rejects his privileged white background and seeks to align himself with activist politics, civil rights, and affirmative action and to become an advocate for the underprivileged. Rodríguez, on the other hand, rejects his Mexican underprivileged background and is more comfortable with the rich and famous. He relishes white culture, and white bread, opposes affirmative action, and wants to shed his Mexicanness. Despite their obvious political differences, in the end, Rodríguez and Turow are both successful writers who seek to distance themselves from their class, cultural, and familial roots. It is as if each wishes to shed his own skin and enter the skin of the other, but this is difficult to do in a society where race definitely matters.[48]

In rereading my law school admissions personal statement, I am struck by how I drew from my early childhood experiences to interpret and augment my law school candidacy. I downplayed my academic accomplishments and publications,[49] which were substantial, and focused instead on my childhood and place in the family.

When I was nine years old my father decided to seek a new life in the United States. He held an assortment of jobs as a laborer in the steel mills and in various factories such as Cracker Jack, Nabisco, and Derby Foods. I attended elementary school and high school in a working-class "redneck" neighborhood on the outskirts of Chicago.

Without knowing a word of English, or having the benefit of a bilingual or English as a Second Language (ESL) Program, I was immersed in an alien culture and language. The first two words I learned in English were "upstairs" and "downstairs." My regular classroom was upstairs and the first grade class was downstairs. Each day during the reading program I had to shift classrooms so that I could take reading with the first graders. Since I already knew how to read, I was humiliated to have to sit with the first graders. It was here that I was introduced to the pristine, white, sanitized world of "Dick, Jane, and Spot."

I recall that in graduate school I felt somewhat isolated from my family and childhood friends, as though I had entered a world that my family would never know. Although for a time communication with my older brothers was strained and awkward, I continued to love them and my parents and I gained a deeper understanding of my place in the family pecking order. I wrote in my law school application personal statement:

My life in the United States could be characterized as a truly bilingual/bicultural experience. My family was Mexican and Spanish speaking; the outside world, American and English speaking. As I went on in school this caused some distancing from my family, but unlike Richard Rodríguez in *Hunger of Memory*, I did not reify myself or become synonymous with my education. I learned very early in life that one's place in the Mexican/Chicano family is largely determined by age and gender. As the youngest of three sons, I would occupy a subordinate and deferential position relative to all other family members. With or without a Ph.D., I was destined to be the kid brother; the one who has to "go out and get the beer" during family gatherings. As a result of numerous beatings at hands of my father and older brothers, I learned respect, humility, and, most importantly, diplomacy. . . .

Del Altar a la Tumba (From the Altar to the Grave)

I don't know about other families, but Mexican families possess a wealth of folk knowledge, which is transmitted from generation to generation and used indirectly to perpetuate a moral and ethical code. I was blessed with a rich family folklore, which was maintained and transmitted through *dichos, cuentos, y leyendas* (sayings, stories, and legends). Much of our family interaction, especially at weddings, funerals, and other events that brought us together, consisted of telling and retelling the same stories. They are based on real events and constitute parables that convey a moral lesson or truth. But in the continual telling and retelling, they are inevitably embellished and, of course, exaggerated.

When I applied to Stanford Law School, I was asked to identify the person I most admired. Although I considered a number of prominent historical and political figures such as Gandhi, Martin Luther King, Jr., and Emiliano Zapata, I quickly realized that the person I most admired and respected was my paternal grandfather, Alfredo Ignacio Mirandé. Although don Alfredo died when I was about two years old, I have always identified with him and have sought to model my life after his.

While growing up in Mexico City, I was very close to my paternal grandfather's two sisters. *Las tías* (the aunts) lived in the same apartment building we did, and I visited them virtually every afternoon. One was a retired teacher; the other an artist of sorts. Neither one had married or had children. Because I was named after my grandfather Alfredo and because *las tías* spoke so highly of him, I always begged them to tell me stories about him. I spent hours listening to stories about my grandfather and the Mexican Revolution. Apparently, Alfredo's family did not have a lot of money. He had worked hard, studied, and graduated as a civil engineer. During the Mexican Revolution, he volunteered as a civilian under Zapata. He joined the revolution committed to bringing about social justice and distributing the land held by the large landowners among the Mexican *peones*. According to the historian John Womack, Alfredo Miranda [sic] was one of Zapata's key assistants and worked as a spy in Puebla for some time under the code name DELTA.[50]

One of my favorite stories involved a pickpocketing incident. My grandparents were apparently strolling after Sunday Mass when a thief tried to pick my grandfather's pocket. Alfredo was a large, powerful man, and he caught the thief in the act. Rather than beat the perpetrator or have him arrested, he grabbed the man's hand and continued undaunted, walking with my grandmother with the thief in tow. Onlookers laughed and ridiculed the thief as they realized what had happened and saw him stumbling behind my grandfather.

The values that I learned directly from my *tías* and indirectly from my grandfather were that while you should stand up for your principles, you should attempt to avoid war and personal conflicts if at all possible. You should also be on a higher moral plane than your adversaries. He was intelligent and principled, but what impressed me most is that he was said to be just and judicious. He treated people of all educational and economic levels equally and with dignity and respect.

This book is no hunger of memory. Higher education in general and law school in particular, rather than distance me from my family and culture, intensified my ties to them. Regardless of my education, training, or success, my status in the family remained fixed and immutable. My parents, brothers, and other family members were extremely proud of my accomplishments. They knew only too well that other than my grandfather Alfredo, I was the first person in the family to attend a university. I was also the first and only one to obtain a Ph.D., the first to write a book, the first to attend law school, and the first to attend an elite institution like Stanford. But these accomplishments did not alter my place at the bottom of the Mirandé pecking order as *el Bebo* (the Baby).[51] Indeed, that I was the baby made my accomplishments that much more remarkable, since I was not expected to do anything better than my siblings.

I do not pretend to present the last word on law school or legal education. This book is nothing more or less than an old Mexican's view of an experience that has remained remarkably stable since the Socratic method was introduced to Harvard Law School by Dean Christopher Columbus Langdell in 1882.[52] I read about Langdell's legal formalism in my second semester of law school in legal theory. I recall thinking that, other than that the students were no longer exclusively white men, the law school classroom and the case method had remained essentially the same. Like *One L,* this is simply "one person's perspective on an experience that is viewed in widely varying ways."[53]

I also do not pretend to present a view of law school that is completely objective, impersonal, and detached, for what I saw, and didn't see, was surely shaped by my background and experience. As a *mexicano* who came from a working class background, I was undoubtedly an outsider, and I present an outsider, non-elite view of law school and legal education.

When I thought about my grandfather and my background, I could not help but contrast it with the experience of Chris Goodrich and others with close links to elite law schools. My grandfather Alfredo never lived in the United States, did not speak English, and was far removed from Yale, Harvard, or Stanford. I wondered what it would have been like if several members of my family had attended the law school and if my grandfather had been a law professor and was buried in the family plot nearby. My father, grandfather, and *las tías* are buried in *el Panteón Francés* (the French Cemetery) in Mexico City. In fact, when my father was buried, I recall how the remains of *Tía* Lupe were removed from the family plot by one of the grounds-keepers and placed in a large, green plastic leaf bag to make room in the grave for my father.

As I reflected back on my law school experience, I came to the strange realization that although affirmative action had created the illusion of equality, it was nothing more than that, the illusion of inclusion. There is a sense in which all of us who had the opportunity to attend a good law school were privileged because we were given opportunities that other members of society did not have. But the fact that we were privileged certainly did not make us equal.

CHAPTER ONE

El Día de Los Muertos
(The Day of the Dead)

The phone rings in the middle of the night. It is my sister-in law, Nili. She is hysterical, sobbing. "It's Héctor. He's had a massive stroke. . . . It's bad. He's in intensive care and on life support. The doctors are hopeful. . . . But it is bad." Within an hour I was on an American Airlines flight from Southern California to Chicago. I slept briefly and woke up thinking it had been a dream, but it was not.

In Chicago I was met by second cousin Bill Neebe, *Tía* Tere's son. *La Tía* was the magnet that drew us to the United States. She was the sister of my paternal grandmother Anita, my father's mother and Grandfather Alfredo's wife. During World War I, at around the age of eighteen, she had gone to France to serve as a Red Cross Volunteer. On the return voyage she met an American couple from Detroit, and they offered her a job as a seamstress in their home. She worked in Detroit for a while before moving to Chicago, where she married a young man named Rudolph (Rudy) Neebe. After my parents divorced, when I was about six or seven, my father came to the United States as a *bracero* and lived with them, while my two brothers and I were placed in a military school in Querétaro for a year.

Uncle Rudy, who was of German descent, was a salesman. What I remembered most about him was that he slept on the couch a great deal and snored loudly. As a child, I also had a vague recollection that his father was an important man. Much later, while doing research on labor activist Lucía Gonzáles Parsons and her husband, Albert Parsons, I discovered that *Tío* Rudy's father, Oscar Neebe, was a German immigrant who had been one of the famous Haymarket Square Martyrs.[1] The Martyrs, or "anarchists" as they were called at the time, were labor leaders who were falsely accused of setting off a bomb that killed several Chicago policemen and led to the so-called Haymarket Square Massacre of 1882. Parsons, Neebe, and the others were sentenced to hang. Parsons, the leader of the group, was hanged, but the governor of Illinois pardoned Oscar Neebe. It was difficult to believe that my uncle was the son of a historic figure. Uncle Rudy had been dead for many years, but I wondered why I had never heard him talk about his famous father. I would have loved to know more about Oscar Neebe.

Cousin Bill later told me it was my grandfather Alfredo who had told him that his own grandfather was famous. When he was fifteen, Bill had gone on vacation to Mexico City. Alfredo asked him whether he wanted to learn about his grandfather and took him to the Diego Rivera Mural, which honors the Haymarket Square Martyrs. Bill had since developed an intense interest in his grandfather and had done research on the Martyrs. In fact, he became an expert on the Haymarket Square Massacre, and as a descendant of one of the Martyrs he was often asked to speak at the yearly ceremony in Chicago on May 1, commemorating the event.[2]

On the plane I had hoped against all hope that my brother Héctor had made a miraculous recovery. But the moment I saw Bill's face, I knew. Bill told me that my brother had been suffering from migraine headaches for several weeks. The headaches had become more severe, and Héctor decided to check into the hospital where he worked as an emergency room doctor. The doctors conducted numerous tests but could not isolate the cause of the headaches. My brother was experiencing excruciating pain and becoming increasingly frustrated. He demanded that the doctors do something, and they scheduled an angiogram—a dangerous procedure, but one that he authorized and approved. In fact, the doctors claimed, he "insisted on it."

Shortly after the procedure was performed he began to panic, after losing control of the left side of his face. Nili was with him when it happened. Héctor suffered a massive brain hemorrhage. He was now on life support, and while there was an outside chance that he might recover, the damage to his brain was probably extensive.

On the drive from the airport to the hospital I felt as if I was getting to know Bill for the first time. Bill and his brother Jim were considerably older than my brothers and me. The Neebe boys were actually my father's cousins. I always saw them more as uncles than as cousins. Bill was an interesting, sophisticated, talented, and articulate man. He had attended the Chicago Art Institute and was largely self-educated. His hair was now white, and he had a large white mustache; like my father, he was a good-looking man with deep blue eyes. I thought he looked a bit like Porfirio Díaz, who ruled Mexico with an iron fist for thirty-three years before the Mexican Revolution.

Both of *Tía* Tere's sons were commercial artists. Bill had been a successful artist and businessman, but he encountered financial difficulties and his business failed. Bill blamed it on capitalism and on his salesmen. In any event, he became quite radical, especially in the 1960s. I regretted the fact that we had not had much contact as adults, whereas my brother Héctor had grown close to Bill after moving back to Chicago. Héctor and Bill were intelligent, intense, type A personalities. They would often get into heated intellectual discussions that sounded like arguments but were simply intense exchanges. I suspect they both loved the stimulation and each other.

———

When my brothers and I first arrived from Mexico, my brothers entered school but my enrollment was delayed. I was to spend several weeks with Bill's mother, *La Tía*, and learn proper English. Alex already knew English because he had spent a year in Chicago five years earlier. He had lived with the Neebes and returned to Mexico speaking flawless English. In retrospect, the thought of having *Tía* Tere as my language tutor was frightening, if not comical. She had lived in the United States all her adult life and claimed to speak perfect English. Actually, she had a distinct, thick Mexican accent that sounded like the Count on Sesame Street. *Tía* Tere taught me how to count in this accent, like the Count—"ONE, TWO, THREE, FOUR, FIVE, SIX!" She also diligently taught me the English alphabet, which sounded to me a lot like the Mexican alphabet.

My aunt had bought into the American Dream. She and Uncle Rudy lived in a comfortable middle-class neighborhood on the north side of Chicago, near Cub's Park, Wrigley Field. Except for her accent, my aunt was an American in every sense of the word. She cooked American dishes like hot dogs and hamburgers and made delicious pancakes on the top of her stove. The people in the area were not rich, but it was a nice, clean neighborhood with pleasant bungalows. It was the kind of neighborhood that my aunt's commercial artist sons and other Americans were "selling" in the glossy magazines.

In retrospect, I think that *Tía* Tere was also the first person who made me realize that I was Mexican and different from American boys. Race and nationality were not issues for me before coming to the United States. I thought everyone was Mexican. My aunt would talk about "Mexicans" in a way that suggested that she wasn't one, and this confused me. She thought that people in Mexico were not very "clean," and she clearly favored the American way of life.

One incident that stands out in my mind was going to the movies with the boy next door, Roger Schroeder, a tall redhead about my age. I guess I was not as sociable as my brother Alex, because all of the neighborhood kids "loved" Alex, and I certainly did not get a sense that they loved me. I felt intimidated by them and preferred to play by myself. Roger invited me to the movies. I was reluctant at first, but *La Tía* thought I should go, and so I went at her urging.

We took the bus to the movie theater, which was far from the house, and saw a horrible science fiction film. During the movie, Roger ate like crazy. He consumed what seemed to be massive quantities of popcorn, ice cream, candy, and soda. He finally asked, in a tone that suggested that not eating massive quantities of food was odd or abnormal, why I wasn't eating anything. I responded in my limited English that I barely had enough money for the bus fare. Roger said not to worry because he would take care of the bus, so I went ahead and spent the little I had. After the show, Roger was very upset when he found out I did not have money for the bus. We had to walk home, and my aunt was worried and upset. I tried to explain what had happened, but she didn't believe me. *Tía* Tere asked Roger whether he had told me that he would pay for the bus. He looked at her with his baby-blue eyes and said, "No!" My aunt punished me severely. It was here that I first learned that "American boys do not lie." This statement bothered me not only because I knew it to be untrue but also because it implied that Mexican boys do lie.

The Neebe boys were set up as role models for us to emulate. They seemed very much like other American boys. They did not speak Spanish, and there was nothing especially Mexican about them. As Bill and I drove to the hospital, I thought about my brother Héctor and the fact that he had grown close to Bill. Bill now seemed like a role model to me. Ironically, I was back where I started when I came to the United States. My brother had recently returned to the place where he had started; in a sense, he had never left.

El Velorio (Vigil)

For the next forty-eight hours we participated in a continuous vigil. Everyone came: my mother, who had remarried after her divorce, and my half-brother (Gustavo) and half-sister (Sylvia) from Mexico; nieces and nephews from California, Georgia, and West Virginia; childhood friends from Chicago; doctors and nurses who worked with my brother. The power of death over life was overwhelming. Death was capable of uniting a family that had long been divided and fragmented. Death would bring together a broad assortment of people. Héctor's Mexican mother and Nili's Israeli mother were holding hands and praying together. Nili's father and her daughter, Ayala, with her long-haired Berkeley boyfriend, Jim, stood embracing and comforting each other, crying unabashedly. The Mexican custom is to never leave the corpse alone until burial. Héctor was not dead, but we never left him alone. We took turns, going to stand by him, conferring with the doctors, getting reacquainted, recounting family stories, and wishing we did not need to be there.

The late-night phone call is a recurring nightmare. It is fifteen years earlier. The phone rings. It is my half-brother Gustavo. There has been an accident. It's bad. Alex was traveling from Guadalajara to Mexico City. His wife Rebeca was driving. They had a blowout, and the car went out of control and crossed the center divider. The car was broadsided on the passenger side by a semi-truck. I pressed Gustavo: "How bad is it?" There was a long pause. Alex, their fourteen-year-old son Alejandrito, and their ten-year-old daughter Gabriela are dead. Rebeca has a fractured collarbone but will recover. Miraculously, their twelve-year-old son Armando only has minor scratches. Gustavo asks, "Will you call Héctor and tell him?"

It had been fifteen years to the day since I got that call in the middle of the night. Even the date, April 9, is the same. Both brothers had died untimely deaths. I thought about the idea of an "untimely" death and wondered whether death could ever be timely.

The inevitable moment came. We had to decide whether to turn off the life support. The doctor felt we should. Nili felt we should, and the children, Raúl and Ayala, apparently agreed. I would have waited. My mother would have waited. It is strange how such life and death decisions are made in this country. I couldn't understand how the woman who had brought this person into the world was not consulted in this decision.

Héctor would be cremated. There would be a memorial service in the hospital chapel. Héctor had recently told Nili that he wanted to be cremated and to have his ashes spread over *Popocatepel,* the volcano outside Mexico City. There was a meeting to plan the service. It would include a priest and the rabbi who had married Nili and my brother. Two medical colleagues would speak, a close Jewish friend from medical school and an Asian doctor who worked with Héctor in the emergency room. My cousin Bill, who had grown so close to Héctor, would also speak. My nephew Raúl asked me if I wanted to say something. I said I could not. In the end, it was agreed that after the service anyone who wanted to could come up and speak.

I sit and watch as each person pays tribute to my brother. They were touching, wonderful tributes. I thought about the last time that I saw Héctor. It was February 22, about seven weeks before he died, ironically at a testimonial dinner held in my honor at the Casa Blanca Community Center, a barrio in Riverside, California. At first I was hesitant to invite my brother. He and Nili were living in San José at the time, and he was about to move back to Chicago. Nili would stay behind until their children finished school: Ayala was a junior at the University of California, Berkeley, and Raúl was in his last year of medical school at the University of California, San Francisco. Finally, I decided to invite my brother because I remembered that in the previous year he had attended an autograph signing party for the publication of one of my books, and he had had a ball. Héctor called and told me he couldn't believe that I would consider not inviting him. The dinner was attended by several hundred people, and I was honored by the tribute. I remember sipping a glass of wine on the porch that evening and talking to my brother about a recurrent dream that I have had since childhood, in which I am attending my own wake. The dinner reminded me of the dream—it was a little like attending my own wake. It felt as if I had cheated death. Héctor smiled, shook his head, and agreed.

The most lasting memory that I have of my brother is the look on his face when I introduced him to the audience during the testimonial dinner. He stood, looked embarrassed but proud, and waved one arm in triumph, like boxers do when they are introduced at ringside. (He had been a Golden Gloves boxer.) His face was beaming. He was as proud as one could be at the accomplishments of his baby brother.

Now I sat and listened as each person, one after the other, stood to pay tribute to my brother. I was sad but proud. This was Héctor's testimonial farewell. Unfortunately, he had not cheated death. Dr. Meyer talked about the respect that he had for Héctor as a doctor and friend. The Mexican cleaning woman said that my brother was very kind, treated her with dignity and respect, and always talked to her in Spanish. Cousin Bill was eloquent. He told the story of how at age fifteen Héctor had run away from home, hitchhiking from Chicago to Matamoros, México, in search of my mother, who was living with her second husband, Gustavo, on a ranch near Matamoros. As Bill told the story, my brother had reached a point of desperation in his young life. He was walking along the highway, wondering where he would get money to eat, when he found a brown paper bag along the side of the road. He opened the bag and discovered that it contained money, enough money for him to eat and continue his journey.

I remember that night very clearly. My father was upset over something Héctor had done or had not done, it didn't matter. As punishment, my brother was told to keep working all evening, digging the basement that my dad had planned, using his sons as free labor. My father, Alex, and I went to the drive-in to see the movie *Treasure Island*, returning to find the outside light on an extension cord, shining brightly. The shovel was stuck in a large mound of freshly excavated dirt. My brother was gone. He would hitchhike more than fifteen hundred miles without money or food, would be stopped and chained to a post by *la migra* (Border Patrol), and would cross the border, only to be turned away by a mother who could not take him in.

When the speakers finished, we were asked whether anyone else wanted to come forward. It was silent. I looked around, waiting for someone else. The testimonials had been beautiful, but the service still seemed incomplete. Surely, there was more to be said. I thought, it could not end like this. I glanced toward my mother and my half-brother and sister. They could not speak, not only because of their emotion but because they did not speak much English. Héctor's wife, Nili, and children, Ayala and Raúl, also could not speak. It was too painful to speak. A strange force came over me. I felt as though I was in a trance. I walked slowly to the podium. I felt as though each eye in the chapel was riveted on me. At first, it was difficult to speak. I felt as if I would break down. I opened my mouth, wondering whether words would come forth. I felt as if I was no longer in control, yet I must have been in control.

I can't remember much of what I said. Many people came up afterward and told me it was one of the most powerful and moving testimonials they had ever heard, a melding of mind and emotion. Further, the other testimonials were beautiful, but there was something missing because no one from the family, except Bill, had spoken. Those who were closest to Héctor were the ones least able to speak.

It is interesting to contrast those we honor at death with our own images of them. Every family is a victim of its own folklore. Within our family, Héctor was viewed as bad-tempered and difficult to get along with. I remember talking with my nephew Armando, Alex's surviving child, the night before the memorial service. Armando told me that when he was little he feared uncle Héctor, especially when he stayed with him.

My oldest brother, Alex, somehow always stole Héctor's thunder. Alex was the one who was loved by the American children in *Tía* Tere's neighborhood, the one who had lots of friends, the one who was the captain of the baseball team, the one who got the pretty girls, the one who was always the leader, the one who was my grandparents' and my mother's favorite. In a short story Héctor wrote, he described Alex: "He was special. It was not just the blue eyes, a significant trait in a brown-eyed country, he was well liked by adults and peers, a born leader. He had charm, controlled aggression and the gift of knowing when to use them. . . . He was a people person; I was books. I was tolerated; he was loved, even by me."[3]

My mother was only sixteen when she married, and she didn't know much about being a mother or raising a child. When Alex was an infant, his feet were badly scalded when my mother failed to check the water before putting him in a *tina* (tub) of boiling water. Grandfather Alfredo, the patriarch, was incensed, and he and my grandmother took Alex to live with them when my father accepted a new job as a physical education instructor that would force the family to leave Mexico City.

In the same short story, Héctor described meeting his older brother for the first time:

I can recall meeting him. How many of us can remember the exact moment when they "met" their siblings? I was brought up the stairs to his room, and left staring over the bottom half of a Dutch door at the wonders inside. A beautiful oriental carpet dominated the center while electric trains whistled, smoked and lit up in continuous arcs . . . and in the middle of it all sat my blue-eyed brother in a genuine silk Pinocchio costume. He turned his head toward the door and smiled. He was gorgeous in a blaze of Disney colors. He came out, carefully closing the door behind him, took my hand, and our life as brothers began.[4]

At the memorial service I felt I had met my brother Héctor for the first time. He was sensitive, loving, and had a big heart. He was always trying to help people, but he did it in a brusque way and often did not get credit for the wonderful things that he did.

Camino a Palo Alto

Fifteen months after my brother Héctor's death, his son Raúl got married. Raúl had just graduated from medical school, and Kari, his fiancée, had graduated from the nursing program at the University of California, San Francisco.

I had not seen most of the family since the memorial service. Although this was a happy occasion, one could feel Héctor's absence—or was it his presence? Cousin Bill and his wife, Betty, were in attendance with their younger son, Mark. My half-brother Gustavo and his family traveled all the way from Mexico. A number of close family friends flew in from Chicago.

Raúl and Kari had apparently planned the entire ceremony themselves and had incorporated members of the family and friends. A close friend of the bride sang several songs during the service. Another friend had choreographed a humorous dance routine for the reception, set to the song "Going to the Chapel." The service was a Jewish service, held outdoors and conducted by a progressive young rabbi. Raúl was nominally Jewish, and Kari was Protestant.

Nili had mentioned to me on the phone that Raúl and Kari might ask me to say a few words during the service. I had thought about what I might say but had drawn a blank. As the day of the wedding approached, however, I concluded that the couple had decided not to ask me to speak after all. I could relax and have a good time.

At the reception I was struck by the mix of people. There were Nili's Israeli friends and family, the guests from Mexico, lots of medical and nursing students, and a large contingent of western-style folk from the bride's family. Several of Kari's uncles were wearing Wrangler jeans, cowboy boots, and leather vests. Following the Israeli tradition, the bride and groom were lifted in their chairs and paraded around the room to sound of "La Hora," the traditional Israeli dance. The music stopped. All of a sudden the musicians started playing "good ol' country music." The bride's relatives and friends came alive. They stormed onto the dance floor and broke into this "shit-kickin'" country dance. It was a scene to behold. I thought about my brother Héctor and smiled. I knew that he really liked Kari, but I don't think he would have expected this. I could just see the look on his face. It would have been culture shock. But I also thought about how much he would have enjoyed the event and how proud he would have been of his son.

Just before the couple were to cut the cake, Raúl came up and said, "We're going to play 'The Boxer' by Simon and Garfunkel. It was one of dad's favorite songs. I wonder if you could introduce the song and say a few things about him?"

Raúl was cool and low-keyed, like it wasn't a big deal, but I panicked. I hadn't prepared anything. What would I say? The reception hall at the Lucy Stern Center in Palo Alto is next to a public park, Rinconada Park. I stepped outside and walked along the sidewalk on the perimeter of the park. I was surprised to discover that the patrons at the park were Mexican. The vast majority of the people inside the reception hall were white, and Palo Alto itself is very white, yet as I walked along the park I was faced with a sea of brown faces. Mexican families were eating, drinking, and playing. To my left, a group of men were huddled together around a guitar, singing. I thought about my brother, who also played the guitar, about the people inside the hall, and about my family and how far we had traveled: Mexico, Chicago, California, Palo Alto. I felt comfortable walking among these people.

It is hard to describe how I felt: not only comfortable but also strangely proud and inspired. I felt proud to be Hector's brother, proud that I was asked to say something on his behalf, proud to be *mexicano*, but mostly, proud to be a Mirandé. I felt that whatever I said, I had to make Héctor proud, and I wanted to make my people proud. Back inside, as I stood to introduce the song, I thought about Héctor's memorial service, and the words flowed effortlessly. I began by relating that when we first walked into the reception hall, we did not know where we were supposed to sit until my young son, Alejandro, spotted our table. It was a small table near the dance floor with a hand-made ceramic vase that said "Mirandé." After we had been seated for several minutes we noticed that the table next to us also had had a vase that said "Mirandé." In fact, my children were thrilled and excited to discover that all of the tables had our surname.

Next I talked about an amazing American Indian woman, Katherine Sauvel. She is a Kawai Indian, probably in her seventies, and is a very accomplished person: an ethno-botanist, historian, linguist, author, and community elder. She has written several books and made tapes of the Kawai language. Her major concern, and a driving force in her life, is that her native language is in danger of becoming extinct. Because Indians in the reservation schools were not permitted to speak their native tongue, and because younger generations are being subjected to assimilation and acculturation, only a few remaining elders now speak the language. Sauvel's fear is that with language goes culture, and the next step will be the extinction of her own people.[5]

As I stood before the guests, I began to understand how Sauvel felt. My concern was not so much with language as with culture and heritage. I realized I feared that the "Mirandés" might also die out. As I toasted the young couple, I told them if I could think of a single thing that characterized my brother's life, it was that he lived every moment with incredible passion and intensity. He had lived as though he knew that it would not last, dying prematurely yet living a full life and experiencing more than many people twice his age. I urged the couple to live their lives and to love one another, as he had—fully and with passion. And I urged them to raise their children to carry on the Mirandé family heritage, traditions, and folklore.

On the return flight, as I thought back on the events of the last few months, I realized that I was beginning to look at myself in a new light—not only in terms of how my family defined me. I was reevaluating my own life. I had also discovered a new voice. I began to wonder if I could use it to a new end.

CHAPTER TWO

Las Mañanitas

Revelations

Today is my birthday, four months after my nephew Raúl's wedding, and I am sitting in a university ethnic studies class listening to an animated discussion of career goals and aspirations. It reminds me of when I first came to the United States and had to sit in the tiny chairs with the first-graders. I am in the audience sitting at a desk surrounded by other students and taking notes. We are listening to a presentation by a panel of Latinas about factors that have encouraged or impeded their career and educational achievement. It is an impressive group that includes a dentist, a teacher, a businesswoman, and a mother and daughter.

I am moved by the mother and her young daughter. The daughter, Dena, is a twenty-two-year-old university student; the mother, Mariana, an upbeat forty-year-old single parent who has had to overcome traditional gender role expectations and an abusive, alcoholic husband who abandoned the family when Dena was five. Over the past fifteen years Mariana has dedicated herself to raising Dena and her other children and is very proud that Dena is in college and plans to go to law school.[1] Mariana sacrificed so that Dena could attend Catholic school. Dena is the first person in her family to have attended college. Mariana is relieved that her daughter has had more opportunities and will not have to struggle, as she did. Yet what strikes me most is that Dena is just as proud of her mother. Her mother has worked hard to maintain the household and has a good job with the county of Los Angeles. But what makes Dena most proud is that her mother has recently decided to go back to school and has started taking classes at a community college. She plans to get an Associate of Arts degree and eventually transfer to California State University, Los Angeles.

Another panelist is a fifty-year-old woman who started college and became a successful dentist after her children were in school. Her husband works for Pacific Gas & Electric and is very supportive. The panelists are diverse in terms of age, generation, and education. They have different stories and different goals, but their message is the same. They are telling us not to give up, to pursue our life goals, but mostly they are saying that it is never too late to pursue your dreams. Through their words and deeds they are telling us, "Sí se puede!" (You can do it!). They are brown, vibrant, alive, and hopeful.

What I found most inspirational at the panel discussion was a comment by a student in the audience. The student, Camille, a young woman of about thirty with two preschool children, went back to school after a painful divorce. Though it was difficult being a single mother and a full-time student, she did not regret her decision to go back to college. It had been influenced by an anonymous caller to a talk-show radio program who said that he couldn't go to school because he was going to be forty on his next birthday. The talk-show host responded: "Well, you are still going to be forty, whether you go to school or not!"

I thought it was amazing that something that simple could be so profound. I wondered how many people used their age, their job, their marital status, their race or gender, or even their children as a justification or excuse for inaction, as an excuse for not pursuing their dreams.

I kept thinking about the panel and about the revelation that you would keep getting older, regardless. Going to law school was something I had considered before. I often pondered the newspaper ads by local, mostly unaccredited law schools. The ads were seductive: "Earn a law degree at night in only three years"; "Become a lawyer in your spare time"; or a testimonial with a photograph of an ex-gang member who said, "Law Changed my life!" I had previously taken a two-and-a-half-year sabbatical leave from my teaching position to do research and to write. When I came back from the leave, I realized that I could have virtually finished law school in that time. Here I was several years older and, I hoped, a little wiser, but I still had not started law school and could not stop thinking about it.

A few days after the panel discussion, I finally got enough nerve to make what would prove to be an important phone call. I had been thinking about calling Rick Romo, a law professor at Stanford, but it was not an easy call to make. I had met Romo during my sabbatical leave in the Bay Area several years earlier and felt he could give me good advice about law school. We were not close friends, but he was someone I trusted, respected, and felt comfortable sharing my secret with. In fact, for the next seven or eight months, he would be one of only two people (the other was my close friend Enrique López) who knew I was planning to take the LSAT and apply to law school.

After a brief exchange of greetings and a little small talk, I got straight to the point. "Rick, this probably sounds strange, but for a long time I have had this crazy idea about going to law school. It comes and goes. I thought I would get over it. But it won't go away." I waited for his response, hoping he would not laugh. He didn't. In fact, he didn't even sound surprised. I think what I appreciated most is that he made me feel normal. He said, "Hey, don't be embarrassed! We all have secret ambitions. I've always wanted to be a playwright. I sit at home writing this stuff and thinking how much I would love to write plays. The thing is that most of us never do anything about it. The difference is that you are trying to do something."

Romo did not offer to send me an application or even encourage me to go to law school. He talked about law school and the law in a candid and straightforward way to give me a realistic assessment of what it might be like. He told me the first year would be tedious and probably not intellectually stimulating. But once I got beyond that first year, there would be things that would be really interesting and challenging. He seemed to know a lot about me and my interests and was able to discuss those things about law school that I would probably find especially exciting. We also discussed different schools, including Stanford. At first Romo encouraged me to consider the University of California, Los Angeles, because it had a large, diverse law school, and he felt I could work with more people of color there than at Stanford. There would be more African Americans, Chicanos, Asians, and progressive white faculty who could serve as mentors. I think Romo was too modest to suggest Stanford and the progressive curriculum he was developing there. But I felt immediately that he was someone I would love to work with.

Something magical happened during the conversation with Romo. I began to see Rick differently. He was no longer simply Rick Romo the smart lawyer and colleague. This was Romo the teacher and mentor. We spoke for a long time, and as the conversation progressed, I began to feel more like a prospective law student than a colleague. I began to see him as a mentor. I began to see the possibility of going to law school, perhaps being one of Romo's students.

I was energized after the conversation with Romo. Law school no longer seemed like an idle idea or a fantasy. It was real. I frankly did not understand this for a long time, but I think the most important thing about the phone conversation with Romo is that I had unknowingly started the transition from professor to student and in the process taken the first step toward making law school a reality. I was changed.

La Vida—Life

It is hard to imagine anything good could come from death. I didn't make the link at the time, but in retrospect I believe my brother Héctor's sudden death a year earlier gave me a new lease on life. I began to live every day as though it was my last. It was like I was experiencing life for the first time. I began to see, to feel, and to smell the flowers and other things around me. I began to notice the incredible sunsets and the magnificent California weather. I started to notice and to appreciate people around me more, especially my family and children. At the same time, I grew increasingly demanding of life and of people. I deserved to be happy, I thought. I needed to follow my dreams, to be without limits or boundaries. I was destined to float, to fly, to soar. Héctor's death was like a revelation. One moment you were alive, vibrant, and full of passion, hope, and ambition; the next moment you were on life support, clinging to life, and then you were dead.

I knew my brother was a bit overweight, but who wasn't? Most people in this country are overweight. I knew there was a family history of high blood pressure and strokes. Grandfather Alfredo (*Tata*) was significantly overweight. The doctors warned him to cut down on his eating and stop smoking cigars. He felt life was not worth living without good food and fine cigars and continued to eat and smoke. He died at age fifty-two. My dad was athletic and never overweight, but he had high blood pressure and, eventually, a stroke. After he died, my mother cleaned up his apartment. She shook her head and said that all of his *medicina* was in the *ropero* (armoire) in his bedroom, unopened. We often die the way we have lived. Octavio Paz was right, I think, when he said, "Tell me how you die and I will tell you who you are."[2] My brother Héctor also had high blood pressure and suffered from recurrent headaches, and I sometimes worried about his lifestyle and work schedule. He was a doctor in a trauma center with erratic hours and seventy-two-hour shifts, and it seemed as if he hardly slept. But I knew he was a very good doctor and I believe that, unlike my father and grandfather, he would have guarded his health.

Mexicans have a cult of death, it seems. We have a national holiday, *El Día de Los Muertos*, to honor the dead, celebrated on November 1 and 2. I have vivid childhood memories of the celebration. A special bread is served on this day, called *pan de muerto*. There are also little candy skulls made of sugar, skeletons, and devils. It is customary for people to set up *altares* (altars) in their homes to honor deceased relatives, putting out for display personal articles and food as *ofrendas* (offerings) in memory of the dead. If a deceased loved one drank beer, for example, you might put out a can of that person's favorite beer, say, Budweiser or *Tecate*, or you might put out a picture, ring, or a favorite bread or other food. The belief is that even after death the spirit persists. During the night the spirits will come out and enjoy the offerings. They don't consume them, but they somehow partake of them. At night people will go out to the cemetery, eating, drinking, and carousing with the dead.

The cult of death reflects an intense passion for life. Ironically, although solitude is an inextricable part of Mexican culture, "the solitary Mexican loves fiestas and public gatherings."[3] For the ancient Mexicans, "life, death, and resurrection were part of a cosmic process which repeated itself continuously," as "life had no higher function than to flow into death."[4] "Our deaths illuminate our lives."[5] Héctor's life was certainly illuminated by his death, and so was mine. I got to know him for the first time at his memorial service, it seems. But what was unexpected is that his death helped to define and to give meaning not only to his life but also to my life.

My brother Héctor's death was unlike any other death I had ever experienced. My brother Alex's death and the deaths of his two children fifteen years earlier were tragic, incomprehensible, anomalous. It was a horrible unexpected accident. I never really connected Alex's death with my own life. I was much younger then and suffered from the arrogance of youth that makes one feel invulnerable and immortal. I grieved Alex's death, but I did not connect it to my life or my own mortality. The police report on the accident said it all. The accident was "caused by a blowout and the front tires were *lisas*" (bald). On the morning of the accident, my mother had a premonition. She called Alex in Guadalajara to bless him and to tell him to drive carefully. His son, Alejandrito, took the call and told her Alex had gone out to get tires for the car. If anything, I saw Alex's death as an accident that could have been prevented by checking the vehicle's tires and avoiding dangerous two-lane toll roads.[6]

It was at the memorial service for Héctor that I began to see myself for the first time. I began to see myself as others might see me. When I gave the eulogy, it was like an out-of-body experience. This Alfredo was a confident, articulate, and powerful speaker; I was someone who had always been an advocate for people and who was wondering whether I could be a good lawyer. My brother's death had uncovered a special force that had previously been untapped. I was the oldest surviving Mirandé. There was no one to guide me, to counsel me, to protect me. I experienced an increased sense of responsibility. Because my brothers had died prematurely, I felt I had to do as much with my life as I could. I had to use whatever talents I might have to help those people who were less fortunate and to advocate on their behalf. It was as a result of my brother's death that I began to think seriously about law school. I knew my fallen brothers and my father would have wanted me to pursue my dreams.

Life Comes Full Circle

I am driving to Los Angeles to meet with Cristina Marín. It is a hot summer day, and the air-conditioning does not work on my 1980 Chevy Caprice Classic. I am thinking about how I had first met Cristina, several years ago when I was a visiting professor at the University of California, Davis, and several years before I seriously considered attending law school. She was enrolled in one of my undergraduate classes and had been admitted to a number of elite law schools, including Harvard and Stanford. Deciding on the right law school proved a difficult decision. Cristina was from Woodland, a small town near Sacramento. She had attended a community college in the area before transferring to Davis and had never been far from home. Her parents wanted her to continue to live at home and attend the law school at Davis. When she was growing up, her parents did not speak to her in Spanish because they felt she had to know English to be successful in the United States. She was one of those Chicanas who was very talented but felt an obligation to be near her family. She also feared moving out of state might make the transition to law school more difficult. But Harvard was Harvard, and it was hard for a Chicana from a poor farmworker background to pass up the opportunity.

Cristina was leaning toward Harvard when she came to me for advice on the various law schools. I asked her whether she had visited Stanford or talked to anyone there. When she said that she had not, I suggested that she contact Rick Romo, whom I had recently met. I took the liberty of giving her his telephone number and urged her to call him. I felt that he would be especially knowledgeable and helpful because he had graduated from Harvard Law School and had taught at Yale before taking a teaching position at Stanford.

When I saw Cristina a couple of days later, she was beaming. She said that Romo was wonderful and that after talking to him for several hours on the telephone, she was sold on Stanford. He had made it an easy decision. Romo felt that in her area of interest, public interest law, Stanford would provide training that was certainly as good as and probably better than Harvard. Stanford was also much smaller, had a more supportive environment for students of color, and provided more personal attention. He felt that she would be less likely to get lost in the crowd than at a place like Harvard.

As I approached Cristina's apartment, I felt a strong sense of irony. The tables had turned. She was a recent Stanford graduate, the one with the knowledge and experience, and I was now a prospective law student. I liked the reversal. It made me feel like the possibilities in life were limitless. I felt there was a cosmic circle, so that when you helped others, they would eventually help you.

The previous December I had run into Cristina at a Mexican American Legal Defense and Education Fund (MALDEF) dinner in Los Angeles. She was sitting at a table with a group of friends, and we only spoke for a few minutes. I was glad to see her and very curious about her law school experience. However, at this point I didn't know whether I would be admitted and had not made my interest in law school public. I tried to probe, while pretending to have only a casual interest in law school. I tried to act like I would have acted with any of my students who had gone to graduate or professional school. But my interest was now more intense and more personal.

Cristina told me Stanford had been a wonderful experience, and Romo was an "awesome" teacher, mentor, and person. Cristina added that there had been a group of progressive students at Stanford who were very close and supported one another. The group was multiracial and included progressive white, African American, Asian, and raza (Latino) students. However, there was tension because many of the advanced courses are by invitation only, and some of the white students were upset because they had not been allowed into Romo's course while several students of color had been accepted. Cristina was thrilled when she learned Romo had let her into one of his trial practice classes. I wanted very much to share my secret with Cristina, but I resisted the temptation. It would wait for another day.

I didn't talk to Cristina for several months after that. It was not until I had been admitted by several law schools and was trying to decide whether to go to law school and, if so, which one to attend that I decided to call and consult with my old student. After graduation, she first went to work for a large firm, but she hated it. It didn't take long for her to realize that she was not cut out for this kind of work. After a brief stint with the firm, she decided to go into public interest law.

Cristina was surprised but thrilled when I told her I was applying to law school. My choice was not between Stanford and Harvard, as hers had been, because I had not applied to any out-of-state schools. I had narrowed the choice to Stanford and UCLA. She felt that UCLA was a very good law school and that there would be a lot of advantages to being in Los Angeles. She mentioned a woman of color who had been a visitor at Stanford and was now at UCLA. This person was an excellent scholar in the areas of feminist jurisprudence and critical race theory. In the end, it was my decision, but she would definitely choose Stanford.

Cristina lived in a modest neighborhood with small, wooden houses. It was a quiet, mixed neighborhood, but there were a lot of Mexican children playing in the area. The house Cristina was renting was old but nice. The lawn was overgrown and had several large bamboo shoots growing in the middle. They had apparently spilled over from the fence separating her house from the one next door. Cristina's shiny new black automobile was parked in the middle of the lawn, Chicano style. I felt embarrassed about my old Chevy and parked several houses down, where it was out of sight. Although the neighborhood was not what I expected, I was pleasantly surprised. I guess I expected Cristina to live in a modern condo or a new apartment complex with a pool, a sauna, a jacuzzi, tennis courts, and a security system.

When I appeared at the screen door, Cristina greeted me with a warm smile. She was dressed casually in shorts, lying on the sofa reading a biography of Sor Juana Inés de la Cruz by the Nobel Prize laureate Octavio Paz. She later mentioned that after Stanford, which had been a very white experience, she was now in her Latino period and was reading all she could about her culture, learning to dance salsa, and dating Latino men. She was now part of a women of color consciousness-raising group that met regularly, read feminist literature, and talked about common areas of concern.

When I asked her if she could see me as a law student at Stanford, she said, "Oh yes, definitely, you would be great. I think, with your background and experience, you would have a lot to offer. You would blow people away." Cristina told me that I would be learning a new way of thinking and of analyzing problems and a new language, which would be very useful in anything that I might do after law school. Even if I returned to teaching, I would look at things differently. Her confidence in my abilities and her unqualified endorsement of Stanford and Rick Romo reinforced my decision to go to law school and to attend Stanford.

I had been reading *One L* and asked Cristina whether she had read it before she went to law school. She replied, "Everyone reads *One L,* and Stanford was nothing like that." She had been intimidated initially, but it didn't last. Cristina reflected on her first day there. She attended a reception for first-year students at an outdoor garden at the law school. It was intimidating because people came up to her and asked her stock questions: "Where did you get your undergraduate degree?" "What was your score on the LSAT?" "What other schools did you consider?" "Yale, Harvard, Chicago?" "What kind of law are you interested in?" She felt embarrassed because although Davis was a good school, it wasn't Harvard. Most of her classmates had gone to Brown, Penn, Princeton, Harvard, or Yale, and it seemed that all had graduated summa cum laude and had perfect LSAT scores. But still, Stanford was nothing like *One L.* It turned out that people were pretty open and generally very friendly. The professors called on you, and you were nervous at first, but many of them called you by your first name and no one was as intimidating as the prototypical professor in *One L,* or the one in *The Paper Chase.*

"What about competition?" I asked. "In the literature I got when I was admitted, they said that students at Stanford do not compete with each other. Is this true?" She responded, "It's true there isn't that much competition. You are sort of in competition with yourself. That's true." I noted that Turow found that at Harvard, behind the noncompetitive facade, there was fierce competition over grades, clerkships, and placements with prestigious law firms. She thought for a moment and smiled.

> Well, there was one group that was extremely competitive. We use to call them "the Brain Trust." That's not what they called themselves but what we called them. They studied together, sat together in a group, and were always raising their hands to answer questions in class. It included this one guy who was a history professor and had decided to get a law degree. They were extremely competitive. It was all white males of course. But I think they were the exception.

Next I asked Cristina about study groups. I wondered whether study groups were an essential part of legal education, as Turow maintains. Cristina felt it depended on the person. She had not been in a study group because she learned better on her own, but there were people who preferred to study in groups. Cristina later confided that one of the reasons she had not participated in the study groups was because she had always been very quiet:

> I don't know if it's cultural, but one of the obstacles that I have faced is passivity. Whether in grade school, high school, college, or law school, I have always been very quiet. I don't know if it's cultural, but I also think if I ask someone for help, it will be taken as a sign of weakness, so I'm afraid to ask for help. At Stanford we called it "silenced in the classroom." That's when people of color and women do not feel free to speak and think they are being silenced.[7]

I asked, "What advice would you give someone just going into law school?" She responded immediately and said it was very important to get "Gilberts." These are commercial course outlines that provide course overviews. "The professors will tell you not to use them, but don't pay any attention to them. Buy them when you buy your other books. They really are important." The Gilberts contain what she called the "black letter law," the agreed-on understanding of the principles underlying the common law. Cases, in contrast, represent the application of the law. Without Gilberts it was easy to get lost in the cases because the professors used the Socratic method, and they didn't come out and tell you what the bottom line, black letter law was. You had to figure it out for yourself.

As I looked back on the meeting with Cristina, it is clear that we weren't really having a conversation. I was interrogating her. I was acting like a sociologist studying perceptions of law school, and Cristina was one of my respondents. I didn't tape record the conversation, but I might as well have, because I had a notepad and took detailed notes of the meeting. Incredibly, I had made the transition from teacher to student. I had been Cristina's teacher, but now she was the mentor. I was thrilled: the possibilities in life seemed endless. I realized that there was no turning back. I was driving my old Chevy east on the 60 freeway toward Riverside, but soon I would be heading north on El Camino Real to Palo Alto.

ONE L

CHAPTER THREE

One L, Chicano Style

The Journey

Life is a journey. I have vivid childhood memories of the Pullman train rides from Mexico City to Guadalajara to visit my aunt and uncle. I am sitting on the top bunk of the tiny *gabinete* (compartment) staring into the night, mesmerized by the stars, the lights, and the dark. I remember a feeling of solitude and peace. It is like the world is moving and I am standing still, or is it the other way around? Is it that I am moving as the world stands still? I am hypnotized by the sound of the moving train and the mystery of the night. Life is good. I feel protected and secure as I peer down at my mother and my brother Héctor, asleep in the bunk below. The rhythmic movement of *el tren* rocked me to sleep. Then *la madrugada* (dawn) would come, filling the empty void with amazing sights: an old man wearing a sombrero and walking a burro carrying *leña* (kindling) on its back; *marchantas* carrying baskets filled with wondrous foods; a *panadero* on a bicycle, effortlessly balancing a large *canasta* of bread on his head. People are moving briskly in the cold morning mist. We pass *jacales* (huts) and tiny rainbow-colored houses, pigs, horses, and cows, and merchants transporting their wares to the *mercado*.

As a child of the city, I am overwhelmed by the sight. It is like a walking *nacimiento* (Nativity). Each December we would put up a small, scrawny, dry Christmas tree. We decorated the tree, but the centerpiece of our holiday celebration was not the tree or the presents; not Santa Claus, reindeers, or Christmas lights; but *el nacimiento*. A good *nacimiento* was an elaborate undertaking that took planning and preparation. First, we had to select the best location, somewhere near the tree but not under it. We covered a small table or box with a sheet or cloth and then covered the area for the *nacimiento* with *heno* (Spanish moss). A mirror became a lake, complete with ducks, and tinfoil was magically transformed into a majestic waterfall. In addition to José, María, *los tres reyes magos* (wise men), and *"el niño"* (baby Jesus), we added shepherds, sheep, cows, horses, mules, and pigs. The landscape was dotted with red, pink, and purple houses, and more clay *campesino* figures. We even had an *ermitaño* (hermit) with a white beard, nestled in the mountains.

———

Now I was traveling in a twenty-four-foot U-Haul truck, cruising into Palo Alto at approximately 2:00 p.m on Friday, August 30, and headed down El Camino to the Stanford campus. The truck didn't make a rhythmic sound like *el tren* or purr like my old Chevy, but I was glad to have reached my destination. It had been almost two years since that memorable birthday when I was inspired by the panel of Latinas to change the direction of my life. I reflected on the initial conversation with Rick Romo about my dream of attending law school. I was about to fulfill my life's dream. In preparing for this day, I felt like a groom who is about to take the trip down the aisle and make a lifetime commitment.

It had been difficult to give up my teaching job. I was passionate about teaching and research. It wasn't as if I was an unemployed engineer or furloughed airline pilot. I had a wonderful job as a professor in sociology and ethnic studies and was in my intellectual prime. I loved writing and teaching. I was used to running a classroom, to being in control; I was used to having my opinions count, both in the classroom and in my research. But I couldn't stop thinking about law. As I packed the things in my office, I came to the frightening realization that I would literally have to put my old life in boxes while I attended law school.

My teen-age daughter, Lucía, and I would be living in family housing at Escondido Village on the Stanford campus. My youngest child, Alejandro ("Mano"), would remain with his mother in Riverside, where I also had a grown daughter. My son and my good friend Enrique had accompanied us on the trip. We had fun, but I would be lying if I didn't say it was stressful. In fact, everything that could go wrong did go wrong. Enrique had agreed to help me pack the truck on August 29 and vowed he would be to my apartment before 10:00 a.m. As usual, he was late. He showed up at 5:00 p.m. Apparently he was tied up with errands like taking his daughter to a doctor's appointment in Los Angeles.

As the hours passed, we began to panic, frantically throwing clothes and other articles into large plastic garbage bags. A couple of nice college students who lived in the apartment complex took pity on us. They pitched in and helped with the last-minute packing. Finally we left Riverside at about 11:00 p.m.

The two-bedroom apartment in Escondido Village was disappointing. I had called the Escondido Village Housing Office during the summer to make an appointment to see the apartment but was told that housing assignments would not be finalized until the last minute. I could not see the unit until the scheduled move-in date. It turned out to be a very small two-bedroom, with the living room, kitchen, and a small dining area on the first floor and two bedrooms and bath upstairs. The plastic tiles in the living room and dining area were badly warped and cracked. The apartment had a musty, offensive odor. It was depressing, but I tried hard to not show my disappointment so that my daughter would not be upset. No less depressing was the fact that units in Escondido were "furnished" with beat-up furniture that looked like rejects from the local thrift shop. Some residents bought furniture and stored the furnished furniture in their outside patios. I was lucky because I had my own things. Once we got rid of the old furniture and lamps and my things got unpacked and arranged, the apartment began to look like home.

Dos Mexicanos en Stanford: The Welcoming Reception

I anticipated a one-day orientation before getting down to business, but we embarked on a one-week orientation with countless receptions, parties, picnics, and other scheduled activities. It seemed like it was *puro* party, one reception or event after another.

The welcoming reception was set for 6:00 p.m. on Friday at the law school. Although tired, hot, and sweaty from the trip and from unloading the truck, Enrique and I decided to attend the reception. Unfortunately, we didn't have much time, but we cleaned up a bit and set out for the reception.

One of the first things we noticed when we arrived was that we were definitely underdressed. Enrique wore shorts, and I wore blue jeans and a polo shirt. The others were dressed in preppy attire. The welcoming remarks had ended and people were already lining up to eat. Most of the people in attendance were One Ls, but there were some second- and third-year students who were members of the welcoming committee sponsored by the Stanford Law Student Association (SLSA) and several administrators and staff. Although the atmosphere appeared festive and friendly, the students were not overtly friendly. Apparently many of the students already knew each other. They were sitting in small groups at the various tables. Some had been undergraduates together, and others lived in the law school dorm. Students were gathered around Crocker Garden, talking in small groups. We felt out of place and didn't understand why. Was it that we were older? Was it that neither one of us looked like a One L? Was it racism? The conversations we entered into and the comments we overheard were predictable. They were exactly the same questions Cristina had mentioned: "Where are you from?" "Where did you do your undergraduate work?" "What other schools did you consider?" "What sold you on Stanford?" Discouraged but undaunted, we tried to pierce the veil. Our persistence paid off, and we managed to talk to several groups of students, including a handful of Latino students.

The Stanford One L class was an impressive mix. Most had attended elite undergraduate schools. There was a top gun navy officer and jet pilot, a female commercial airline pilot, a handful of Ph.D.'s, several professors, journalists, and even a Roman Catholic priest. But other than Peter, the Catholic priest, there weren't many older students. We were immediately struck by how young and clean-cut everyone looked. Even the students of color struck us as incredibly preppy. What became clear very quickly is that many of the students of color had a white parent. Cristina had warned me that it was rare to find Mexican law students who were not biracial. In our class, for example, I could only identify four of us with two Mexican parents, Leo, Carmen, Rudy, and me. The same pattern existed in the other classes, so that only a handful of students were what Cristina had jokingly termed "pure-blooded" Mexicans. The Latino students appeared even more homogenized than the black students and except for their surnames and hue were largely indistinguishable from their white counterparts. It seems it's easier for Latinos to assimilate when they want to. I thought Richard Rodríquez would have felt at home.

We were greeted by a member of the welcoming committee, a small, blond Two L from Georgia who wore a University of Georgia baseball cap and spoke with a distinct southern drawl. He was very friendly and pleasant. I was shocked when I saw his nametag—Skip Sánchez. The point is not that he was fair skinned and blond, for there are many Mexican *güeros*, including my father, but that he was phenotypically, culturally, and linguistically the same as the other students.

Later that night we learned that there would be a party at the Pub in Crothers Dormitory, which housed many of the first-year students. It was an old dorm, but it seemed comfortable. Crothers had a lounge (Tapper) and a small law library and was recognized as the social hub of the law school, at least for One Ls. Second- and third-year students preferred to live in Rains, a newer, more modern dorm. When I took my daughter to a reception at Rains, she was impressed and commented that it seemed more like a nice motel than a dorm. She wished that we could live in a nice modern place like Rains instead of Escondido Village.

The next day, Saturday, would be the traditional annual excursion to the beach and boardwalk in Santa Cruz. Enrique and I were busy unloading the truck and did not seriously consider attending the beach party. One of the things that struck me was the irony of taking a bunch of privileged kids on a field trip to the beach. It reminded me of the types of self-help "cultural enrichment" programs for inner-city kids who have never been to the beach, the mountains, or a university. But this was different.

My friend and I would later kid about the reception. We were reminded of an old Mexican movie called *Dos Mexicanos en Nueva York* that chronicled the incredible adventures of two Mexicans in New York City. We joked about doing a sequel, but it would be called *Dos Mexicanos en Stanford*. We felt different but not in a bad way. We were self-assured and not easily intimidated or discouraged. There were some very interesting and talented people in the cohort. We met a pleasant, friendly woman who appeared to be in her thirties. She had worked as a television producer and seemed more mature than most of the people we met. Another interesting and friendly person was Leo, a young Chicano from Colton, a small predominantly Chicano community between Riverside and San Bernardino that was a stop on the Union Pacific Railroad. Leo had attended University of California, Santa

Barbara, had been active in Chicano politics, was from a working-class background, and seemed much like my students at University of California, Riverside. Carmen Montoya also seemed like a regular Chicana and did not act white or assimilated. She was from Martínez, a town between Sacramento and San Francisco. Rudy Rivera had been an undergraduate in Texas. He spoke Spanish and was bicultural. Rudy was charismatic and not shy about speaking up in class.

We worked all day unloading the truck and decided to go out for a drink in the evening. We first went to a popular hangout for Stanford students in downtown Palo Alto, a place called 42nd Street. It was nice, but the people seemed aloof, superficial, and, like the Stanford law students, not very friendly, so we went to a Mexican bar on El Camino Real. I had noticed La Cumbre when we first drove down El Camino to the campus. It was a nice restaurant and club with an informal family atmosphere, but it was relatively empty. There were only a few patrons in the place, and though we were Mexican, we were clearly outsiders. We drank a couple of beers and left. Although we knew we were outsiders, I felt less out of place at this working-class Mexican bar than at the law school.

After the Labor Day weekend, the orientation resumed on Tuesday morning with a welcome address by the dean of the law school and brief remarks by two associate deans. One of the associate deans, Lorraine Thompson, a very pleasant and warm African American woman, was in charge of minority recruitment and retention and served as the unofficial adviser for students of color. The other associate dean was a white woman named Betsy Mathews who was in charge of curricular matters. Mathews had been a partner in a large New York law firm before assuming her current post.

The dean, Jonathan West, was a pleasant-looking man in his late fifties. He had worked in the Civil Rights movement as a young attorney in the 1950s and clerked for the Supreme Court. He talked about the law school's commitment to excellence and the low-key noncompetitive climate. Its commitment to diversity, he said, was reflected in our class, the most diverse in the history of the law school. We were diverse in terms of occupational background, age, race, ethnicity, and sexual orientation, and the majority of the students in the entering class were women. The dean then proceeded to tell us how privileged we were to be a part of this great institution. He referred to us as the best and the brightest of our respective communities and predicted we would make lifelong friendships at the law school.

As I reflected on the dean's welcome, perhaps what bothered me most is that it seemed the remarks were directed primarily at people of color. What did the comments imply? If we were the best and the brightest, did this mean that we were different from the communities we represented? Did it mean that people of color are not generally that bright? Did it mean that our differences would alienate or distance us from our communities? Were we destined to follow the path of Richard Rodríguez and blend into the great American melting pot?

I knew that while I may have been more fortunate than many in the Mexican community, I was no brighter, better, or more meritorious. For a number of years I had taught a Chicano issues class at the California Rehabilitation Center in Norco, a prison in Southern California. Some of my undergraduate students came with me, and we met together with members of the Mexican American Youth Organization (MAYO), a prisoner self-help group. The class discussed important issues facing the Chicano community. What impressed me most about the experience was the tremendous wealth of talent within the prison walls. We found artists, poets, philosophers, self-made lawyers, and people with many other talents and great verbal fluency. Given the opportunity and training, I believe, some of these prisoners would have run circles around the Stanford students.

The days continued to be filled with receptions, parties, and presentations. One of the presentations, by Dean Mathews, focused on "alternatives" to the traditional law school curriculum. She began by talking about chaos theory and then segued into a discourse on diversity and how women and people of color were beginning to challenge dominant paradigms. Her focus on alternatives suggested that she was about to present a radical or progressive alternative to the traditional law school curriculum. I envisioned an attack on the Socratic method and hierarchies in legal education. I listened with interest. I agreed with her basic premises, but the presentation proved disappointing. In the end, we were subjected to a slick multimedia presentation. At the conclusion of the program, we were told how "special" we were, and each of us was given a rose as a special memento of the occasion. It struck me as empty rhetoric.

I was surprised that people seemed impressed with the associate dean's speech. It seemed incredibly superficial to me. Afterward, people were hugging each other and walking around carrying their roses. It was like they had already graduated. It was intended to make us feel good about ourselves, but

I didn't need this person to tell me I was special. It wasn't that I didn't agree with what she said but she had not gone far enough, and the presentation lacked substance. A couple of the third-year students agreed. One of them, a Chicano, dismissed the associate dean, saying she was unofficially known as the Shirley MacLaine of the law school because she liked to wear shawls and was sort of the resident mother. She apparently had been making the same speech for years.

"Better Get Rid of Your Accent": Meeting My Peers

The first week of classes was at once one of the most exciting and stressful weeks of my life. I had met a lot of people, and though I didn't know everyone, they all seemed to know me. It was strange and a little embarrassing. People greeted me on the stairway, in the hall, or the cafeteria: "Hi, Alfredo," "How's it going, Alfredo." It bothered me that I didn't know many of their names. Why? I guess I really stood out. There were other Latinos, other older students, and about a half a dozen Ph.D.'s and a few professors. I had not met any students with children, but I knew they were here. Apparently being older, having a Ph.D. and being a professor, being Chicano, and having a teenage daughter made me unique.

Peter, the Catholic priest, also stood out in our class. He had several masters' degrees and was a teacher and coach at a Catholic high school. He seemed to be a very nice person; I would say that he quickly became the most liked and respected person in our class. Everyone seemed to know Peter. Peter and I were obviously the oldest members of the One L: our age and unusual backgrounds set us apart.

During orientation we were divided up into small sections or groups for mock classes. The dean taught my section. We read and discussed actual cases as a prelude to the beginning of classes. We read a series of constitutional law cases, known as the "shopping center" cases that deal with the rights of owners of privately owned shopping centers to exclude protestors from their property. Shopping centers are unique. Though privately owned, they are open to the public, and serve public functions. The shopping center cases illustrate the tension between the constitutional rights of private citizens to peaceful assembly and protest and the private property rights of landowners to exclude people from their property. One of the cases involved a Jehovah's Witness, Mrs. Marsh, who was prevented from distributing literature in a shopping area in a company town.[1] Part of the rationale for the Supreme Court's ruling in her favor was that in the United States the downtown area of a community represents the center of communication. During the discussion, I raised my hand and commented that the rationale in the decision was antiquated because with the advent of the mass media and modern technology, the downtown area was no longer the principal mechanism for the distribution of information. Television is the way information is transmitted today. I said something to the effect that Mrs. Marsh could go on the cable network to distribute the message. The class roared. The dean looked up at me, turned his head, and called on the next person.

Afterward, Peter congratulated me for making an excellent point. He also mentioned it was clear that I was Hispanic because of my accent. He had good intentions, but this seemed to be one of those backhanded compliments to which you don't know how to respond.

On Friday the Stanford Latino Law Student Association (SLLSA) held the first Happy Hour of the year at Rosita's, a small Mexican restaurant in East Palo Alto. Afterward I gave two of the Chicano students a ride home, Leo, the fellow from Colton, and Jorge, a Texan who is half Mexican and half white. Both mentioned being worried about having to adapt to the Stanford environment. Jorge seemed especially anxious:

> It's really hard when you're used to being the smartest one in the class and thinking that you're the best. Then all of a sudden you're just average, maybe below average. I feel dumb. And every day I feel dumber. Every time I open my mouth in class, it comes out sounding awkward and stupid. I feel stupid!

Leo said he not only felt dumb but also felt that he was not permitted to express himself or raise critical questions. He was troubled because despite the liberal rhetoric, the whole system was very rigid, hierarchical, and based on conservative assumptions about society and people. It was based on things like cost/benefit analysis, social policy, and the concept of the reasonable man. Questions that challenged these assumptions were quickly discarded or ignored. Leo and Jorge had noticed that minority students' comments in class were either ignored or neutralized by the professor. A few minutes later a white student would say essentially the same thing, and the professor would be ecstatic over the point made. One of the more vocal young Chicano One Ls, Rudy Rivera, actually challenged his torts professor:

"Hey that is exactly what I said a few minutes ago!" The teacher was embarrassed and halfheartedly apologized to him in front of the class. Although I had experienced the same thing and commiserated with my young classmates, I told them they should not feel dumb. On the contrary, their presence at Stanford meant that they were undoubtedly as smart as and perhaps smarter than their classmates.

Silencing in the Classroom

I had a couple of experiences the first week that disturbed me a great deal. The first incident occurred in Civil Procedure on the first day of classes. This was my first class in the morning. At the end of the class, Professor Morton referred to a story that was in one of our readings and was intended to be humorous. "A Bedtime Story" is about a child who wants to stay up to watch a special television show that is to air after his bedtime. The babysitter was instructed by the parents to make sure he went to bed at the designated time. Each plan of attack or excuse used by the boy as a ploy to stay up to watch the television show was used to illustrate a rule of civil procedure. Morton asked that we read the story, assuring us that we would find it amusing if not hilarious. I raised my hand and said, "I read the story and I didn't think it was funny. Is there something wrong with me?" Morton paused for a moment, then said, "Yes, there is definitely something wrong with you!" Everyone laughed, and the class ended. After class I walked up to the front of the room, and before I could say anything she added with a wry smile, "I hope you will develop your sense of humor in law school." I responded that I felt like I had a very good sense of humor but had simply not seen the humor in the story.

The next day I arrived a few minutes early for the class. It was important to arrive early because Morton had warned us that whatever seat we occupied that day would become our permanent seat. Unfortunately, the classroom was almost full, and there were no good seats left when I arrived. I found one seat near the center and sat down, only to discover that it was broken and uncomfortable. I was forced to change seats at the last minute and had to sit in the third row at the extreme left side of the room.

Although some classrooms are larger than others, they are all basically the same. The seats rise in a semicircle, like an amphitheater. Goodrich describes the typical law school classroom as "a raised stage encircled by tiers of long, arcing tables that marched upward to the rear wall,"[2] with every seat clearly visible from the podium. Each person was in an assigned seat, and the name and picture of each student was placed on a seating chart. Morton had told us that class participation was very important and that it would count for 10 or 15 percent of the final grade, and she encouraged us to come prepared and ready to participate.

I was very frustrated in the class. I raised my hand for what seemed like ten or fifteen minutes at a stretch, but she never called on me or even looked in my direction. It was like I was invisible. After class I walked up to the podium and told Professor Morton, politely, that I had had my hand up for a very long time and that she had called on people who raised their hands at the last minute. She told me she had seen me, but it was difficult to call on everyone. I asked whether it was possible to change seats because it was hard to see the board from the side of the room. I also felt she might not be able to see me on the side because of limited peripheral vision. Without looking at me, she picked up her papers and said coldly, "I saw you, and I would *prefer* that you *not* sit in the back." This was difficult for me to accept because the only available seats were in the back row. I also could not understand why I could not sit in the back, given that other students were sitting in the back of the room. It seemed like Morton was responding very negatively to me and I did not understand why. Perhaps she saw me as some sort of a threat or as a problem student. It disturbed me. As I reflected on this experience and the experiences that had been related by Leo and Jorge, I thought about my student Cristina. I wondered if this was an example of silencing in the classroom.

I was scheduled to have lunch with my student adviser and Carmen Montoya, the Chicana from Martínez, California. Entering students at Stanford were assigned a second- or third-year student as a peer adviser or student mentor, and as it turned out Carmen and I had the same adviser, a Two L from southern California named Elena Adams. Other students, we learned, had been contacted by their respective advisers during the summer. We were not contacted until a couple of days before we had lunch. Not only was our adviser slow to contact us, but it seemed strange that she would see us both at the same time.

Elena Adams was a young woman with a medical degree. She had short, bleached blond hair and reminded me of the prototypical Valley Girl. As we walked toward the Student Center for lunch, Elena asked about our classes and professors. She began by telling Carmen that she could not have the person Carmen "thought she had" for torts "because he was dead." When

Carmen showed Elena the class schedule with the professor's name on it, Elena reluctantly acknowledged that she might be confusing him with another professor. She also told us that Morton, whom I understood had been teaching for several years, was new because she had "never heard of her."

Elena asked if we had any questions, but before we could respond she launched into a long discussion of the do's and dont's in law school. The lunch was uneventful until she asked how we were doing in our classes and I decided to share some of the experiences that were troubling me. I related that I had noticed, and other students had commented on, the phenomenon of the silencing of minority students in the classroom. Her response was immediate and negative. She admonished me to be careful about saying that the faculty is "racist," noting that "Stanford really goes out of its way to make sure that women and minorities are represented and treated fairly." I told her I had not called them racist and I was not saying that this was true of the entire faculty or that the silencing was intentional.

I said a few things about each of my classes and then told Elena about the two incidents that had occurred in Professor Morton's class. I asked Elena for her advice. Should I stay in my current seat or move to the back? Should I talk to Morton and try to figure out what is going on or should I forget the whole thing? Again, she responded very negatively. She felt that I was overreacting and that I should give the professor the benefit of the doubt; it must be something that was in my head only. I related that Morton had said that the safeguard against class and racial bias in the judicial system is the jury system. I disagreed with this view and had raised my hand, but Morton did not call on me. Elena's response was incredible. Rather than focus on the fact that Morton had ignored me, she defended the professor and attacked me. She said the jury system is far from perfect, but it is "the best we have." The discussion deteriorated into a nasty argument that ended with my standing up abruptly and ending the conversation. I didn't walk away, but I was visibly upset, as was Elena. Carmen was understandably embarrassed by the whole scene and said nothing.

I was distressed by the exchange with my adviser and wondered why they had paired me with her. The only thing we had in common was that we were both second career types from southern California. Elena had asked how it was going, and when I told her she attempted to negate the validity of my experiences and feelings. If this was an adviser, I didn't need or want one.

As time went by, people were developing friendships and socializing in small groups. Though it seemed that everyone knew me, I still felt isolated.

I had befriended a few students—a multiracial group that included Jim, an African American from Pennsylvania who is an ex-football player; Joy, an African American–Jewish woman from New York; Laura, who is part English and part Syrian and is from Connecticut; William, who is Haitian and white and is from California; and Kim, an Asian American woman from Washington, D.C. I liked the friendships I was developing. One thing that distinguished the people in my group is that they were a bit older than the average student. They had worked for two or three years after graduation and were more mature than those who went to law school straight out of college. Jim was soft-spoken and universally liked. Joy was known as the Salsa Queen because she loved to dance. She had joined SLLSA (pronounced "Salsa") not because she was Latina or political but because she had heard that they were organizing a group that went dancing on Thursday nights. Laura was exotic, with dark hair and beautiful hazel eyes. William had a beard and dreadlocks and dressed like a hippie. He sat in the back of Morton's class and did not attend class after the first week.

Treading Water

September 18.
I decided over the weekend to work on developing a more positive attitude toward my Civil Procedure class and the professor. She deserves the benefit of the doubt.

It seems as if we have been talking about one case, *Swann v. Burkett*, forever.[3] It is a housing discrimination case, involving a young black couple in Berkeley. I asked a question about the defendants' motion for nonsuit. Professor Morton asked me if I had read the case. I said that I had read it carefully, but she did not seem convinced. As it turned out, I had inadvertently misread Roman numeral VI as IV,[4] and my question did not make a whole lot of sense. I felt badly because I had read the case and simply transposed the numbers. What troubled me is that she had embarrassed me in front of the class by asking whether I had read the case. I didn't understand why. I read and brief all the cases. I felt the way I did many years ago with my seventh-grade teacher, an intimidating, white-haired old lady named Mrs. Price. She had a way of looking at me and responding to me that made me feel like a complete idiot.

I also noticed yesterday that when I ask a question, Morton never calls on me by my last name. When she acknowledges everyone else, it is always "Yes,

Mr. Roderick" or "Ms. Burton?" Yesterday when Morton turned to me and asked, "Yes?" I paused momentarily, then said, ". . . Mr. Mirandé?" before asking the question. Though it was an awkward moment, everyone laughed. I felt I had made my point.

We finally turned to another case, *Gómez v. Toledo,* which dealt with the issue of qualified immunity.[5] Gómez, an agent for the Bureau of Criminal Investigation, sued Toledo, the superintendent of police for the Commonwealth of Puerto Rico, alleging that he had fired Gómez without due process or a hearing in violation of his civil rights under U.S.C. 1983. The procedural issue is whether the burden is on the plaintiff or the defendant to note in the pleadings whether Toledo acted in good faith. The Supreme Court held that since only Toledo knew whether he was protected from prosecution by qualified immunity, the burden was on the defendant to claim good faith as an affirmative defense.

After class, I stayed to talk with Morton. When I first got to the podium, only one person was ahead of me, an Asian American male. As I waited, patiently other students started to gather around the teacher, waiting to ask a question. I couldn't help but notice that she took three or four people's questions ahead of mine and that she was essentially ignoring me. It seemed like she was hoping I would go away if she ignored me. But I waited patiently and was the last one to ask a question, as she picked up her notes and began to walk briskly up the stairs and out of the classroom.

I followed after her and asked my question: "If the statute does not make reference to bad or good faith or to qualified immunity, wouldn't the burden be on the plaintiff, rather than the defendant, to allege that the official acted in bad faith in order to state a claim for relief?" She said, "Yes, but you see the problem with you is that you have to learn to see both sides of an issue. What would you do if you were the attorney for the defense?" I told her I was sure I would come up with some innovative ideas, but in this instance I was looking at it as a third party, more like a judge than an advocate for one side or the other.

El Chambón (*The Bungler*)

My experience in the Civil Procedure class bothered me a great deal. I talked to several of my classmates, and most of them were very supportive but advised me not to worry about it. Peter suggested that I talk to Associate Dean Mathews. Romo thought I should try to put the whole thing behind me and move forward, since there wasn't much I could do.

After some reflection, I decided that the best person to talk to was Doris, my teaching fellow. The first-year students were divided into six small sections with roughly thirty students each. The section is your cohort, and you are all in the same courses together. Each course is composed of two sections. Section 1, for example, might be in Civil Procedure class with section 2, in Contracts with Section 5, and so on. Since there are six required courses in the first year, you end up being in at least one course with everyone in the first-year class. In addition, your small section has a one-unit pass/fail Research and Writing class taught by a graduate student, or teaching fellow.

Doris was a pleasant African American woman in her late twenties. I felt that she might be sympathetic and have some insights into the problem. Being silenced in the classroom is surely a problem that women, especially women of color, encounter more than men. Also, Doris was only a couple of years out of law school and had encouraged us to come to her about any problems that we might encounter during the first year.

As I expected, Doris was very receptive and sympathetic. After I explained the problem she said it could be racism, latent or overt, or it could simply be that Morton didn't see me as a young impressionable student and was threatened by my presence. I should add that Morton was up for tenure that year and she may have been eager to get good student evaluations. Doris advised me to talk to Morton directly, not necessarily to address the things that were bothering me but to let her know more about me as a person. I appreciated the advice but remained unconvinced that going to see the professor was the best route to take. Surely, I would not go to see her unless I had something substantive to ask. Also, I was busy with my other classes and didn't want to focus a lot of attention on all of this. I decided to follow Romo's advice.

My problems with Morton had become a running joke with my close friends. They thought it was humorous. Laura suggested it was probably a sexual thing. Kim commented that it had been rude of Morton to ask me whether I had read the material. Carmen noticed that Morton had not said my name. One day Morton confused two Asian American males in the class and rather than acknowledge the mistake, she insisted that they had switched seats. She then reprimanded them for not sitting in the correct seat.

As I reflected on my experience in the Civil Procedure course, it brought back feelings I had not had since high school and junior high school. My dad always seemed to time his vacations to Mexico so that they overlapped with the beginning of the school year. During my freshman year in high school, I missed the first week or so of classes and fell behind. My algebra teacher, Mrs. Hempell, grabbed me by the shoulders and literally shook me, saying, "Do you understand, Alfred!" It was déjà vu. I was reexperiencing the feelings I had in my youth when a teacher, my father, or some other authority figure made me feel like I was a real fuck-up and incapable of understanding something. As a child, when I couldn't do something right like driving a nail straight or learning to swim as quickly as my older brothers, my father would call me a *chambón*, sort of an endearing term for a clumsy person or bungler. It was hard going from being a college professor to being treated like a fuck-up who did not read the assignments and was a disruptive influence in class. What was ironic is that unlike a lot of students, I was conscientious about doing the reading and briefing the cases and always went to class prepared.

Talking to other people validated my feelings. Others in the class had noticed the way I was treated, though I was not the only person subjected to that treatment. Morton had her pets and was always nice to them; others, she treated disrespectfully. There was a running feud, for example, between Morton and Annie, who had been a journalist for a number of years and asked detailed questions. Annie began asking questions on the first day of orientation and never stopped. Since she was in my section, everyone groaned when she raised her hand. Yet Annie sometimes asked excellent questions and had the courage to stand up to the professor. Needless to say, Morton responded very negatively to Annie. It became clear that Morton would respond negatively to anyone who asked questions or challenged the narrow parameters of the class.

Outfoxing the Enemy

To make participation in the class more equally distributed, Morton introduced the panel system. There were eight panels in the class, each made up of about seven students. I was assigned to panel six. This means that although you could volunteer on any given day, you were responsible only for the material on the day of your panel. Morton would not call on you unless it was your panel day. None of my other professors used the panel system, and I wasn't sure I would like it. The obvious advantage was that there were no surprises; the disadvantage, that there was a disincentive to prepare when it was not your panel day.

Today was my panel. I prepared extensively, too extensively, and felt like I knew the material backward and forward. A critical tactical decision was whether or not to volunteer. Would she call on me if I raised my hand? Probably not. I devised a devious strategy. I would not volunteer. This would lead her to think that I was not prepared, and she would call on me, hoping to catch me unprepared. When class started and she did not call on me, I abandoned my game plan and volunteered. As usual, she ignored me throughout the class and only called on me to answer one short question and moved quickly to the next person. After class and for the rest of the day I felt a tremendous letdown. In the past I was used to preparing for class and for presentations. But here the preparation had not paid any dividends. I put in so much effort in exchange for ten seconds or so of glory, answering a fairly mundane question. I was wasting my time.

I had learned an important lesson: overpreparation does not pay off in law school. I resolved to be prepared every day and to not worry about whether or not it was my panel day or whether the professor would call on me. I concluded that the panel system was basically designed to accommodate people who were not typically prepared.

In Spanish there is a saying, "Cada vez que Dios cierra una puerta abre una ventana" (Every time that God closes a door, he opens a window). The anticlimax and disappointment in the Civil Procedure course led me to an important insight: the most difficult thing about making the transition to law school was not being a student, being poor, living in a dingy apartment, or losing status and prestige. All of that was easy. I concluded that what was really difficult and what I really missed was being a teacher. I realized that I needed a forum, a soapbox. Most of my adult life, after all, had been spent standing in front of people and telling them what I thought about a number of important issues. Amazingly, people paid to hear me talk. The most pervasive and frustrating feeling during my first year as a law student was being effectively silenced, and I wasn't sure whether I felt silenced because I was a person of color or because I was a teacher or both. This would have been difficult for anyone, I think, but it was especially difficult for someone who has been in front of the classroom most of his adult life. This may have been why it was so hard for me to just sit in class and listen. Except for the Civil Procedure course, I generally said at least one thing in each class. My comments were often brief but I'd like to believe they provided a different perspective. Apparently I had to learn to be a passive learner.

———

The routine of law school had begun to set in. I awoke at 6:30 a.m. or so and was in the law library by 8:00. The next hour and fifteen minutes were spent preparing for the Civil Procedure class. Except for an hour off for lunch, I was in class until 3:00 or 3:30 p.m. After class I returned to the library to study for about two and a half hours.

I generally took a break for dinner and relaxation, then returned to the library around 7:30 p.m. and studied until 11:00 p.m. The readings were detailed and tedious. On Thursdays and Fridays I was out of class by noon and would begin the reading for the following week, which continued into the weekend. Except for the Stanford football games and an occasional law school party, there was not much of a social life. I tried to stay in shape and go to the gym as often as possible, but as the semester progressed, it became more difficult to do this more than two or three times a week.

A Closed Forum

The Clarence Thomas Senate confirmation hearings abruptly broke the pace during the first year. During Professor Anita Hill's testimony, students huddled around a small television set in the law school lounge. The interest in the hearings was intense, and students were overwhelmingly in support of Hill. They hissed and made comments when a senator asked a hostile or unsympathetic question of Hill.

After the hearings started, the Civil Procedure class was devoted to a discussion of how judges are selected. Presumably, the format was intended to place the confirmation hearings in a broader and more meaningful context and to provide academic legitimation for the exercise. As in the orientation, all of the first-year students were given a special packet of reading materials by the instructors. Although the topic was supposed to be a broad discussion of the function of courts, it was understood that it would focus on the Thomas nomination.

I was terribly disappointed with the reading and with the discussion that took place in my section. At the start of the class, we took an anonymous poll to see how many students were in favor of the Thomas nomination: some 90 percent were opposed. I later learned that the vote was roughly the same in the other sections. The 10 percent of students who supported Thomas turned out to be a silent minority, because no one really came out against Hill or in favor of Thomas during the discussion. The discussion was a bust, and Morton seemed very awkward and ill at ease in her role as a non-authoritarian discussion leader who respected all views.

This experience reminded me of Duncan Kennedy's discussion of the way in which students are introduced to the Socratic method and taught to accept the idea that legal reasoning is distinct from other reasoning. In discussing the Thomas nomination, Morton suddenly abandoned the Socratic method of guiding us to the correct and inevitable result. Instead there was a laissez-faire atmosphere in which all opinions received equal acceptance.

On the day of the Senate confirmation vote, there was an open forum on the Thomas nomination. The room was packed. About 30 percent were men. The four speakers were three white female law professors, one African American female professor, and one staff person. The moderator was a liberal white male who taught Modern Legal Theory.

Since the Senate vote was only hours away, the "forum" looked more like a pep rally for Anita Hill. The first speaker talked about sexual harassment and how it had been a neglected area within the law. The second speaker, the first woman hired in the law school and an excellent criminal defense attorney, gave a persuasive lawyerly argument with regard to Hill's credibility as a witness. Using traditional criteria for judging the credibility of a witness, she found Hill's testimony extremely credible: Hill had absolutely nothing to gain from coming forth and a lot to loose; the argument that her testimony was less credible because she did not come forth earlier was a form of "blaming the victim." The speaker noted that women are often forced to work with men who have harassed them because they lack power or alternatives. Because men have the power, they cannot understand why or how women are sometimes forced to maintain a relationship with men who harass or abuse them or why they would be reluctant to bring charges. Finally, she felt, the president and the Republican senators were able to mobilize the media to discredit Hill. The last speaker, the African American professor, had also been a successful trial attorney and public defender. She began by admitting that she did not pretend to be neutral. She had known Hill for fourteen years and considered her a good friend. She sat behind Hill with family and close friends during Hill's testimony, and in her remarks she talked about "our" strategy when referring to Hill, as though she was one of Hill's legal advisers.

I felt ambivalent during the confirmation. Although I was one of the 90 percent who opposed the Thomas nomination, my opposition was based on his political ideology and the fact he was not qualified to be on the Court. Yet I was uncomfortable with the forum, because in fact only one point of view was presented. Also, the prevailing attitude at the law school was that if you did not believe or were skeptical of Hill's allegations, you somehow supported Thomas. I don't want to sound like a conservative critic of liberalism and political correctness, but I was shocked that the law school did not present both sides of the argument. It struck me as a strange way for lawyers to behave and as fundamentally unfair. If you didn't think that the charges against Thomas had been proven by a preponderance of the evidence, it was assumed that you condoned sexual harassment. It was as though we were to believe that no one had ever been falsely charged with sexual harassment. I would have opposed Thomas, even if there had been no sexual harassment. He was not competent to be on the Court. Sexual harassment was a separate issue.

Gender Wars

One doesn't have to be very observant to realize that gender is a salient issue at the law school. After the Thomas confirmation hearing, I felt a certain underlying tension between men and women. During lunch with my African American friend, Jim, we talked candidly about the hearings and the atmosphere at the law school. He confided that he too had felt the tension and heard the rumblings. He said the African American men talked about it themselves but felt intimidated about expressing their views publicly. It was simply not the politically correct thing to do and would not be well received. It would look like he condoned sexual harassment, which he did not. The conversations were going on within the African American community and outside the law school. At the school they took place behind closed doors. Jim said there were questions about Hill's testimony, especially the fact that she would follow a boss who had harassed her to another position when she had the opportunity to sever the relationship. It didn't make any sense.

For me, the issue was not so much Thomas or whether you supported him. The issue was whether a white nominee would have been subjected to this kind of treatment. I recalled that in Civil Procedure class it had come out that one member of the Supreme Court had been a member of the Klan. It was not as if Thomas was the first nominee with skeletons in the closet.

In my Research and Writing class, the issue of gender and political correctness surfaced in an indirect way. We had completed a legal memorandum. In the assignment, we were supposed to be law clerks for an appellate judge. Our task was to consider a case in which a woman who was a cocaine addict was charged with delivering drugs to a minor by transmitting the drug to the fetus after birth via the umbilical cord.

As in all assignments or law school exam questions, the facts were stated in such a way that there was no right or wrong answer, and you could argue either side of the issue. You could argue that she lacked the requisite mental state to commit the crime or that in drafting the bill, the legislature did not intend to prosecute pregnant crack cocaine addicts.

Though this was simply a class exercise and lawyers are trained to argue both sides of a question, the debate in the class was totally one-sided. The atmosphere in the room was electric. Many of the students were outspokenly outraged by the exercise and felt that prosecuting crack cocaine addicts was not the way to solve the problem. They argued that what was needed was more funding for drug treatment programs for low-income addicted women. Although women led the way in espousing this view, it was supported by a number of men. Interestingly, our teaching fellow, Doris, said that in their memos at least half of the class had argued that the woman should be prosecuted for the crime. However, no one came forth to publicly support this view during the class discussion.

The incident reminded me once again of Duncan Kennedy's discussion of the Socratic method and the fact that new cutting edge cases, where the black letter law is silent, are used to illustrate important policy issues and growth and change in the law. Significantly, such discussions tended to occur near the end of a course, or in classes like Research and Writing, which were taught by graduate student teaching fellows and were pass/fail one-credit courses.

Predictably, like a fool, I emerged as the devil's advocate. I took on the role so persuasively that I started to feel like the devil himself. I began by acknowledging that I was one of those evil persons who had felt that the defendant should be charged and proceeded to support my position. My statement unleashed the wrath of the class. The gist of the opposing view was that my position was not "morally" defensible. I was shocked by the response. Incredibly, I took the position that this was not a moral but a legal exercise.

It was a strange feeling: I found myself thinking and acting like a lawyer. In the past the old Alfredo, the progressive sociologist, would have been one of those who was morally outraged by the exercise and adopted a dismissive attitude. But Alfredo was now asking the class questions like who would serve as an advocate for the fetuses and the countless unborn children who would be born dependent on drugs. Though this Alfredo agreed that such legislation was not the way to address societal ills, once the law was passed he could see himself prosecuting someone for the crime.[6]

It was strange to be the bad guy, but I enjoyed taking on the class. I thoroughly enjoyed every heated moment. I think what mattered was not whether I was right or wrong but that I felt comfortable arguing either side of an issue and that I could do so effectively. It was scary. I was learning to think like a lawyer.

CHAPTER FOUR

The Age of Innocence

"En Esta Casa No Hay Duendes"
(There Are No Goblins in This House)

When we first came to the United States my father took me and my brothers to live in Oak Forest, a small, working-class town located about twenty-five miles from Chicago's downtown Loop. It had a population of about twenty-three hundred people, dirt streets, a volunteer fire department, two mini-markets, a barbershop, a restaurant/bar, and a gas station. The main social activities for adults were the Monday and Thursday night bowling leagues and the Friday night bingo at the Veterans of Foreign Wars Hall. I played first base for the win-less VFW Little League team. The favorite pastime for teens was cruising the A&W root beer stand. The mayor of the town, Ray Hall, was the local mechanic and owner of the only gas station in town, *La Texaco*. He was also the justice of the peace; he was a true Renaissance Man and did everything from fixing my dad's car to convicting or fining people for petty infractions.

I am back there, living in a small two-bedroom house, which my dad proudly declares, "Hice con mis propias manos" (I built with my own hands).

The house is quaint but crooked, and one doesn't have to be very observant to notice the slope in the living-room floor and ceiling. Our heater is an iron wood-burning stove in the kitchen. There is no insulation, and the pipes freeze in winter. We sleep with long johns, coats, warm Mexican blankets, and wool sailor caps. The outdoor pump is frozen, and we boys are sent to the neighbors for water, which we carry back in buckets. My brother "Gordo" (Héctor) takes a broomstick and skillfully balances two buckets of water on his strong, young shoulders. My little hands are red and itching from carrying buckets of water for several blocks. In the morning, we find a thin layer of ice covering the buckets of water in the kitchen.

In the spring of my eleventh year, things start to mysteriously disappear from the house. First it is loose change or dollar bills, then my father's watch. Finally, it is things like food, clothes, toys, and even a bag of grass seed from the garage. My father talks to us individually, and then we gather for a family council where my father has "a man to man" talk with his *tres mosqueteros* (Three Musketeers). He always begins our little talks by speaking softly and then slowly and deliberately building to a crescendo of emotion. He is like an evangelist preacher or a charismatic football coach giving an inspirational half-time speech, and he ends with incredible *fibra* (strength) and *ánimo* (spirit). We are told once again that we are blessed because we have the good fortune of having been born "Mirandés." It turns out the Mirandés are a special breed of people, almost like a different race, and unlike ordinary mortals. But privilege brings responsibility. Our destiny is to carry on the Mirandé name, and we must not do anything to shame the family or tarnish our good name. I come away from our sessions with renewed pride in being a Mirandé but also the feeling that I am carrying a heavy burden on my shoulders. With tears in his eyes, my father tells us he loves us and concludes by exclaiming, "Pero no se olviden de que en esta casa no hay duendes!" (But don't forget that there are no goblins in this house!). Things do not simply vanish into thin air. He goes around the room with each little *mosquetero* in turn proclaiming his innocence.

My father's vision of justice and due process is to interrogate us individually and collectively before inflicting punishment. Sometimes we are beaten, but more often he makes us do extra work around the house or write a thousand times in Spanish, "Prometo que no desobedeceré" (I promise I will not disobey), or "Prometo que no mentiré" (I promise I will not lie).

We know that none of us has taken anything, and yet things keep disappearing mysteriously from the house. I come home from school and notice our wooden ladder perched under my father's bedroom window. Several days later my brother Héctor spots a neighborhood boy with several watches on his arms. One of the watches belongs to my father, another is my trusted Westclox pocket watch. Héctor chases after him. The boy runs into his house with Gordo in hot pursuit. Héctor eventually finds him in the attic along with most of the stuff that had disappeared from our house. In fact, Héctor finds an attic filled with merchandise stolen from other people in the neighborhood.

Manny Dotson, the neighbor boy, whom we nicknamed "bug eyes" for obvious reasons, is always getting into trouble. (He eventually ended up in Joliet State Prison for the attempted rape of a sixty-five-year-old woman.) On a previous occasion Manny had come over to our house. We are not close friends, and I am a bit surprised. After visiting for a while, he invites me for an ice cream at Brozak's, the corner grocery store. Manny is uncharacteristically generous and buys me ice cream, candy, and soda. When I get home my father asks where I have been. I tell him that Manny and I went to the store. My father asks me whether I took a ten-dollar bill that was on the kitchen table, and I tell him I did not, and that Manny insisted on treating me. To make a long story short, Manny had taken the money from the kitchen table. My father did not believe me, and once again I am punished and forced to write a thousand times, "I will not steal money from my house."

A Gentler Form of Silencing

As second semester finals approached I found it increasingly difficult to write in my journal. It was ironic, in a sense, because I had more to write about but less time to do it. I resolved the problem by incorporating my journal observations into my class work as much as possible, so that my journal and the law school were not entirely separate, independent activities. I was often able to incorporate material from my journals in the required class essays.

The first few weeks of my second semester in law school had proved interesting and demanding. I took two required courses, Property and Constitutional Law, and two electives, Lawyering Process and Modern Legal Theory. The first-year curriculum is fixed at most law schools. Stanford is unusual in giving students two electives in the first year.

My Property professor, John Steadman, was an intelligent and personable man. I had met him at a cocktail party in December, and when I saw him several weeks later at a party, I was surprised he remembered me. Steadman was one of the few law professors I had met who seemed to take a personal interest in his students. Unfortunately, his class was boring. At first I thought he was doing an incredible job of making a mechanical topic relatively palatable and mildly interesting. I hoped the class would get better, but I felt he was doing the best he could.

The other required class, Constitutional Law, was being taught by a visiting professor from Yale, Peg Ryan. Ryan was a young, intelligent woman who seemed extremely knowledgeable. I have mixed feelings about Constitutional Law. In a sense, the professor seemed to mirror the student body: she was quick, confident, and technically competent but mechanical. She used the Socratic method: the professor, who presumably knows the answer, asks the question, there is a pause, she walks deftly behind the podium, looks down, and then looks up to a stream of hands raised by students eager to answer. There was a definite rhythm to the class. Although Ryan was supposed to be a feminist, I was surprised to learn in class that she believed in the Constitution and the American Dream.

With each passing day, I felt more and more like I was in an advanced high school Civics or American Government class. We started off the first class talking about *Marbury v. Madison,*[1] the landmark case that established the principle of judicial review, the authority of the Supreme Court to rule on the constitutionality of the actions of the other branches of government. Adams, a Federalist, had packed the Court before leaving office and made numerous last-minute appointments, including issuing Marbury's commission as justice of the peace. However, the appointment was never delivered, and President Jefferson had refused to recognize it when he took office.

The question faced by Supreme Court Justice John Marshall, who had been secretary of state under Adams, was whether the Court had the authority to order the president of the United States and his secretary of state, Madison, to deliver Marbury's commission. At issue was the separation of powers between the branches of government and the source of judicial authority.

I sat and I listened. I did not say anything until the third week of the course. I hadn't said anything because I had not been able to get a handle on the class so that I might ask an intelligent question. Then we began talking about the notion of "standing." This is an important concept in law in general and constitutional law in particular, but it's not a difficult one. In order to have "standing," as I understood it, a person had to show that he or she was directly or indirectly affected by the injurious act. It required, in other words, that the plaintiff suffer an injury in fact rather than a hypothetical or possible injury, that the injury could be traced directly to state action (causation), and that court action could reverse or remedy the injury (redressability).

I couldn't help but notice that one of the cases where standing was granted by the Court involved a white male, Allen Bakke.[2] Bakke was denied admission to the University of California, Davis, Medical School and challenged the Davis Affirmative Action Program, claiming that less qualified minority students were admitted ahead of him. As I read the standing cases, a disturbing pattern seemed to emerge: the Court essentially held that minorities and poor people lacked standing and that non-minorities and people who were not poor had standing. In *Allen v. Wright*,[3] black parents were denied standing to sue the Internal Revenue Service for failure to enforce the statutory mandate that tax-exempt status be denied to private schools that discriminate on the basis of race. And in *Simon v. Eastern Kentucky Welfare Rights Organization*,[4] low-income people lacked standing to challenge the government's denial of medical treatment. In another case, *Linda R. S. v. Richard D.*,[5] poor women wanting to enforce child support payments were also denied standing.

My question, directed at the professor and the class as a whole, was if you assume that the less power you have in society, the more difficult it becomes to identify the source of your lack of power and subordination, isn't there an inherent bias against people who lack power in the standing rules? If you are a elite man from a relatively privileged background, for example, isn't it easier to identify or isolate alleged injuries?

Ryan took a step back on her heels, rolled her bright blue eyes, and said something like, "That is a very interesting question, but it goes beyond the scope of the course." With a serious and concerned look, she pointed toward me and said, "I would love to sit down and talk to you about it more. Why don't you come by my office and we'll chat about it. OK?" She turned quickly, walked to the podium, and returned to the discussion.

I am not sure how I felt. I guess I was frustrated. I didn't ask a lot of questions, but I think I asked good ones. I liked and respected Ryan a great deal, and her command of the subject matter was awesome. She was certainly more responsive than Professor Morton. She smiled and said it was a good question, yet she never really answered. It seemed I was asking things that she had never considered. I felt that she liked and respected me, but it seemed that my queries were not on track. I felt sort of like a heckler and began to ask more and more of my questions after class or in her office. I was concerned because this was a kinder, gentler, more palatable form of silencing than I had experienced in Civil Procedure, but it was silencing, nonetheless.

The Honeymoon Ends

I thought things would get better in the second semester. Instead, I became more alienated. In the beginning, I felt that there were basically two types of people in the law school: (1) a large number with whom I had little or nothing in common, and (2) a few people that I could relate to. But as I came to know individuals in my section better, I concluded that I didn't really care to know most of them.

I began with the assumption that people were probably nice once you got to know them. I felt that I had been very open with and tolerant of people over the past four or five months, especially members of my section. I figured that I had better find something to like because I was going to spend a lot of time with these folks. Our section was very sociable, undoubtedly the most sociable of all the sections. Peter, the priest, quickly emerged as the unofficial social director of the group. Each Wednesday night members of my section got together. Peter turned out to be a connoisseur of redneck bars, and we rotated around the various watering holes in Palo Alto from week to week.

Contrary to my expectation, once I started getting to know people, I found I had even less in common with them than I thought, even some of the people I had initially befriended. Though I was older, I don't believe that my alienation derived from my age. In the past I had always had friends, including students and former students, who were younger. My friend Enrique, for example, is younger than I am. He was my student, but we did not become friends until five years after he graduated. Ethnicity and race may have had something to do with it, but again, I didn't think this was the problem. The source of my alienation appeared to be more political and class based. There were only a handful of students I could relate to politically, ideologically, or socially.

My former student Cristina Gabriel had mentioned there were a lot of progressive people at the law school. I was shocked to discover that the student body was quite conservative; the faculty as a whole were much to the left of the student body. At Berkeley, the situation was reversed. I met some

Boalt law students at a party, and they told me that the students actually boo and hiss professors who are perceived as conservative or sexist. In comparison, Stanford students seem compliant and respectful. The people I befriended at the beginning of the year were on the left in the law school, and they were moderate Democrats. Except for gender and sexual orientation, I would say that there was essentially no left at Stanford Law School. Most people were in the center or right of center.

The Federalist Society was popular. It is a conservative student organization found at most major law schools that generally invites speakers who subscribe to a literal interpretation of the Constitution. When I attended a Federalist Society reception I was surprised to find that two of the officers in the organization were members of my class.

Hispanics and Other Panics

One of the things that drew me to Stanford is its unique Lawyering for Social Change (LSC) program, which was designed by Rick Romo and other progressive faculty members. An underlying premise of the curriculum is that you cannot work effectively with subordinated communities unless you have a theoretical and practical understanding of them. The Lawyering Process class and the Subordination class are the prerequisites for taking advanced courses in the LSC curriculum. The Lawyering Process course was important because it established the foundation for other courses in the curriculum, and it was normally taken in the second semester of the first year.

The class began slowly. Professor Jimmy Rae Lee spent the first week or so having students introduce themselves and talk about their backgrounds, addressing questions such as why they came to Stanford and the reasons for enrolling in the course. Lee was Asian American but he had grown up around Mexicans and spoke Spanish. Though Lee was patient and asked a lot of questions, the time devoted to each person was uneven. I was one of the last to introduce myself, and my presentation lasted only a couple of minutes.

On the second day of class, Daisy Parken, a light-skinned Puerto Rican American, started out by saying that she was "Hispanic" and that she was from upstate New York. The previous summer she had worked for a congressman, focusing on issues relevant to the Hispanic community. During the discussion, Professor Lee commented on the fact that she had referred to herself as "Hispanic" and wondered if there were other terms that were used, such as "Latino."[6] Guillermo ("Memo") Rodríguez, a personable and talkative Puerto Rican from the island, added that he also considered himself Hispanic and that "Latino" was not used in New York. It was clear that Lee wanted some discussion on ethnic identity and the pros and cons associated with various labels and possible differences in ethnic identity between Puerto Ricans from the island and *mexicanos*.

I liked Daisy and was tempted to let it slide, but Lee had said on the first day of class that he encouraged frank and open discussion. He expected that we would often disagree with him and with one another. Discussion was a crucial component of the class. I raised my hand, and after some discussion, I finally got the floor:

> I believe that people should call themselves whatever they want. I would be the last person to tell you what you should call yourself, but I can tell you why there are some people, and I'm one of them, who prefer not to use the word *Hispanic*; who are offended by it. *Hispanic* connotes white or European. If you go to México or some other countries in Latinoamérica, you will see that we are basically an indigenous people. It's ridiculous to call Indian people "Spanish."

I went on to say that Spanish was a colonial language imposed on the Indian peoples of the Americas. Calling us Spanish would be like calling American Indians English simply because they spoke English.

I noted that I preferred "Latino" to "Hispanic." The term "Latinoaméricano," not "Latin," is used to refer to the *indio* or mestizo people who were the product of the mixing of the Indian and European races. There is a saying in Spanish, "Juntos, pero no revueltos." It means something like "United but not mixed up" or "Similar but not the same." Regardless of what we call ourselves, we were still *puertoriqueño*, *mexicano*, or whatever. "Latino" in other words, was a way of recognizing our points of commonality while acknowledging and respecting our differences.

My comments were followed by a brief, somewhat heated discussion between Memo Rodríguez and me before the period ended. It was spirited but not nasty or angry. I mentioned that in Chicago, Mexicans and Puerto Ricans who united to pursue common political interests had used the word "Latino" successfully.[7]

I liked Lee's class. It was at the beginning of my second semester of law school, and it was the first time I felt I had some specialized knowledge or training that might give me an advantage over others in the class. After all, we were talking about the stuff that I had been teaching and writing about for years. I thought I was qualified to teach these kinds of classes. In fact, Lee had taught an advanced immigration class in the first semester and an article I had written was on the required reading list.

A few days after the class discussion on the "Hispanic" label, Ricardo, a third-year Chicano student, mentioned kiddingly that he had heard through the grapevine that I had really blasted and humiliated Daisy in Lee's class. I was shocked and hurt by the comment. I responded that this was ridiculous and related what happened. I told Ricardo that Daisy and I got along well.

The next time I ran into Daisy near the first-year mailboxes, I took her aside and, without mentioning Ricardo, told her that the rumor mill had it that I had attacked and humiliated her in Lee's class. She shook her head in disbelief and asked me who told me this. Later I learned that Daisy spoke with Ricardo and Jessie about the incident.

A few days afterward, on a flight from southern California, I found a copy of *Hispanic Magazine* at the Ontario Airport terminal. I read the magazine on the plane and was about to discard it when I thought of Daisy and Memo, and decided to keep it. My intent was to use the magazine as an inside joke, an icebreaker I hoped would make light of our differences.

After class I stopped Daisy and said, "I have something to show you." When I took the magazine out of my book bag, Daisy was not amused. She said angrily, "You're ridiculing me, aren't you?" I said, "No, I was just kidding. I also thought you might be interested in the magazine." Several days later Daisy left a note in my mailbox, asking whether I might have time to go for coffee because she wanted to talk to me.

We went for coffee and had a really nice talk and worked to clear the air. Daisy told me that she respected me but that she was sensitive about her ethnic background. As an undergraduate, the Latino students had given her a hard time because they felt she was too assimilated and because she hung out with the white students. She was also sensitive because she was only half Latina, did not have a Spanish surname, and was not fluent in Spanish.

I explained that I liked and respected her and assured her that I was not trying to ridicule her. I felt that we had a joking relationship about "Hispanic" and that I had thought of her immediately when I saw the magazine.

If we could joke, it would show there were no hard feelings and that we were friends. I was surprised that she had gotten so angry. I guess I hit a raw nerve. I also told her that when I was a teacher I had encountered a lot of students like her. I felt that if she was secure in her identity, which she apparently was not, she would not have gotten upset. I certainly would not get upset if someone called me "Latino" or "Chicano." In any event, for me, it wasn't a personal thing, and I wanted to work with her to improve the relationship. I felt good. The problem was solved.

A Letter from the Stanford Jail

In Professor White's Modern Legal Theory class we read "Letter from the Birmingham Jail" by Martin Luther King, Jr., in which King articulates a natural rights view of jurisprudence. The title captured my increased sense of alienation. Each day I grew angrier and more estranged. I felt increasingly imprisoned, not physically, but mentally. The weather was perfect in Palo Alto, and I was fortunate to be attending an elite law school, but I felt trapped nonetheless. As I thought about how I was feeling, I was reminded of the lyrics of a Mexican song about a person who felt imprisoned in a relationship and exclaimed, "Although the cage may be gilded, it is still a prison."[8] I was beginning to feel mentally enclosed.

One day in Lee's class we read an article by Professor Lucie White concerning a client, "Mrs. G."[9] The article deals with a client, a welfare recipient, who has received a $600 settlement as compensation for an automobile accident. According to the welfare rules, she is required to report the money as "income" and to have it deducted from her stipend. After conferring, White, the lawyer, and Mrs. G. agreed that during the hearing, Mrs. G. would testify that she had used the money for basic necessities, things like school clothes, sanitary napkins for her teenage daughters, and groceries.

During the hearing, Mrs. G. shocked White when she inexplicably presented a very different story. She proclaimed that she had used the money to purchase "Sunday shoes" so that her girls could wear them to church. Although Mrs. G. was eloquent in her testimony and she prevailed, the attorney was upset with her.

Professor Lee started the class by asking, "Would you get upset when a client doesn't do what you agreed or expected? If so, would it matter whether the client was a paying client or not? In other words, would you get more upset with a nonpaying client?" It was an excellent question, and there was a lot of response. Most of the students acknowledged that they would get upset and that even though it should not make a difference, they probably would have gotten more upset if the client was not paying directly for the service.

I asked whether this argument could be extended to people who hold a "liberal" philosophy of lay lawyering and see themselves as "helping" subordinated communities. Would "liberals" be more apt to get upset with the client? This led to a class discussion of "good" (altruistic) and "bad" (selfish) motives for pursuing a career in public interest law.

At the center of the discussion was Lizza Goldfarb, a student who was very vocal and had taken a conservative stance on a number of issues throughout the semester. Lizza was a white student who considered herself progressive because her father was a lawyer who ran an immigration service in California. She acted as though her father's experiences gave her special insights into subordinated communities. Lizza talked a lot, and a number of students of color had grown impatient with her.

Throughout the discussion Lizza remained steadfast in her argument. She would not care whether it was a paying or nonpaying client, a wealthy or a poor person. She would be angry if the client did not show up for an appointment or do what he or she had agreed to do, and there would be consequences for the client.

As the semester progressed, racial and ethnic tensions had intensified. It wasn't that there was tension with all of the white students, just the more vocal conservatives. Lizza was especially irritating. She was loud, aggressive, and rude. On several occasions when someone was talking, she would say, "Excuse me? Would you stop interrupting me!" It was hilarious because she was the one who was always talking and interrupting. I think it would be fair to say that most of the people of color in the class resented the fact that Lizza always seemed to be the center of attention and that she considered herself an expert on the cultures of subordinated groups. Yet everyone had tolerated her. They rolled their eyes but let her talk. Lizza sat with and was friends with Daisy and a conservative African American woman.

Professor Lee indicated he respected her view, but he wanted to probe further. He asked again, "And it wouldn't matter if the person was a paying client?" Lizza was firm in her answer: "It would not matter." When asked how she would handle such a situation, she said she would ask why the client had missed the appointment or not followed through on what had been agreed on, and if the client did not give a satisfactory response, she would take appropriate action.

I bit my tongue. Finally, after about forty-five minutes of listening to Lizza's monologue and moral outrage, I got tired of listening. I didn't think about the setting or worry about what the professor or Lizza or the other students might think or say. I simply said what had to be said. I looked directly at her and said:

> You know what? I really don't care that you are upset with what the client did or did not do. You know why I don't care? I don't care because, in the end, you are not the one who's going to go to jail; you're not the one who will be affected by the outcome.
>
> In this class, we have been talking about "rebellious" or nontraditional lawyering. In traditional lawyering the lawyer is up here [gesturing with my hand], and the client is down here. What we are trying to do is to equalize the relationship, but I think the needs of the lawyer should be subordinated to those of the client.
>
> It's not equal. It's their [the client's] case; it's not your case. It's their life; it's not your life. If they screw up, they will suffer the consequences, not you.
>
> As long as you are in a position to judge whether the reasons given by the client are acceptable, you are still the one in control. You are still doing traditional lawyering.

As I spoke I realized that I had broken a sacred commandment of law school etiquette,[10] not only because I spoke with passion and commitment, but because my comments were directed at another student and were not mediated by the professor.

You could have heard a pin drop when I was talking. After a brief pause, Malcolm Watson, a vocal African American, jumped into the discussion and, surprisingly, began to argue with me, and the class ended with our heated discussion. Malcolm's position was that he was not going to let the client "jerk him around." You had to get the client to respect you. One of the Asian students, Ted, said that my position would not hold up as far as "time" was concerned because "everyone," meaning all cultures and groups, place a value on time. What was most significant during the discussion was that, for once, Lizza was silent.

After class I talked with Malcolm and some of the other students of color in the law lounge. I kidded with Malcolm and said that it had looked like we were going to come to blows. I also asked, "Whose side are you on anyway?" There was a feeling of camaraderie among the people of color. An African American student, Lamar, came up to me, shook my hand, and said, "I agree with you completely! Your comments were right on." He was very nice, quiet, low-key, and sincere. He did not talk much, but when he said something it was very good. Lamar came from a rural area with a long history of segregation. His ultimate goal was not to work for a large firm but to return to help his community.

That noon I ran into Professor Lee on the stairway going up to the library. He smiled knowingly and said, "You know Lizza was really pissed. She came storming into my office after class, saying that she had been personally attacked." I said, "I'm sorry, but I just could not take it anymore. I just got tired of listening to how she would be pissed and how she didn't care if the client was rich or poor." Lee said, "But you must have run into things like this when you were teaching." I replied, "Yeah, but as a teacher I had to be more restrained. You have a lot more freedom as a student than you have as a professor. I can tell her things that you can't." Lee smiled and said, "Good, maybe some day I'll take a class from you and do the same thing for you!" We laughed and parted company. There were no hard feelings.

The Reprimand

Then I hit a low point. After my confrontation with Lizza I had to go out of town for several days. When I returned and checked my mail at the law school on Saturday morning, I was surprised to find a memorandum in my mailbox from Professor Lee. It was dated Friday and was addressed to both Lizza and me, asking us to come to his office that afternoon at 2:30.

Since Saturday was Minority Admit day, I had a chance that morning to see most of the people of color who were in Lee's class. I learned that Lizza had gone in to complain. She told Lee that she was outraged by my conduct. I also learned, much to my dismay, that Lee had asked a number of white students to come in to talk about how they felt about the incident. He had talked to only one Chicano, Leo Gómez, and to not even one black or Asian.

I was upset and disillusioned with the way the incident was handled. I believe that if someone disagrees or is not happy with what is said, he or she has a responsibility to speak up in class and to express the disagreement. What upset me most is that it came out that Lee apparently had been meeting with the white students in his office throughout the semester.

The following Monday, Professor Lee began the class by making a comment to the effect that perhaps we might have to bring boxing gloves to class. He seemed nervous and acted very differently. It was awkward because it happened to be the regular Admit Day, and so we had a number of visitors in the class. Lee announced at the outset that we would not talk about the incident until he had a chance to meet privately with some key individuals. He did not identify us by name, but everyone knew that he was referring to Lizza and me.

There was an underlying tension in the class that day, a tension which centered on a videotape that had been done in a previous class. The script was simple and straightforward. A client, Marianne, went to see a housing attorney because she was being harassed by the manager of her apartment complex. She told the attorney that things had been all right until her husband moved out of the apartment. Then the manager began to harass her. Marianne was very nervous. The attorney was cold and efficient and did not try to put the client at ease. After some probing as to why the manager might be giving her such a hard time, Marianne said the problem started soon after her roommate moved in. When the attorney asked for his name, referring to the roommate, the client was quiet and guarded. As it turned out, the roommate was a woman and they were a gay couple. The couple also had been harrassed by other residents. Apparently they had been vandalized and verbally abused by other residents.

At the conclusion of the tape, Professor Lee asked what we would do when we had a client whose sexual orientation or lifestyle conflicts with that of other tenants. The apartment complex was predominantly Latino. If we were the attorney working with a client or a tenants' group, would we have a duty or responsibility to tell them about Marianne? To whom does the attorney owe a duty, Marianne or the tenants' group?

Despite the tension, or perhaps because of it, the class dynamics were especially interesting. There were eight white women, about a third of the class and by far the single largest ethnic and gender group, and two white men. Two of the women in the class were openly gay. The white students seemed very comfortable during the discussion, and also relieved to be talking about something other than race or ethnicity. The change in attitude was subtle but clear. It was as though homosexuality was exclusively a white issue, so now they could feel at ease. The students of color were uniformly silent.

I felt that this was an important topic to discuss but was bothered by two things. First, I was bothered by the underlying assumption that the "gay issue" is a white issue; it is not. Second, I was even more bothered by a related, unstated assumption that homophobia and gay bashing are peculiar to, or certainly more prevalent among, communities of color, specifically, among Latinos.

I tried to look attentive and listen with interest to the discussion, but I could not. Instead, I spent a good deal of time passing notes back and forth to two of the more vocal African American students, Angela Harris and Malcolm Watson. I was still bothered by being asked to talk to the teacher outside of class. It felt like I was being sent to the principal's office to be reprimanded. I did not think it was necessary to talk to Lee and Lizza, and I conveyed this in the notes. Angela and Malcolm agreed that I had not done anything wrong, but they thought that it was necessary for me to talk with them privately so that we could then open it up for a more general discussion. I disagreed. It was a very frustrating class for me because I really felt like I and the other students of color had been censored. I had been silenced for bringing up the issue, and now, indirectly, I was blamed for the silencing.

When the class ended, I went up to talk to Professor Lee but had to wait until Lizza finished talking to him. I started to tell Lee that I did not understand why I had to meet with him and Lizza. He said, "That's okay, because Lizza has decided that she does not want to pursue it any further. So we don't have to meet." I went to the law lounge immediately after class and talked to Angela, Malcolm, and Lamar. We had been jubilant last week; now we were upset that Lizza was calling all the shots and determining how Lee handled the situation. Lee may have felt that the issue was settled, but for us it was not settled. Many questions remained. Would we now talk about the issue in class? What had been resolved? Was I out of line? Had I been chastised? Did Lizza overreact?

In the end, the issue would not be discussed or resolved, and the people of color would be silenced. For me, it was as if the class ended on that day. We met for another month, and I did not miss a class during the entire semester, but we had learned a very important lesson. We learned that despite the apparent "open" atmosphere in the class, despite the fact that this was an elite law school, despite the progressive curriculum, the class was not open. We had learned that by simply complaining that her rights had been abridged, a white student could unilaterally shape the structure and direction of the class. As I reflected back on the incident, it was ironic. The class was designed to sensitize students to cultural differences. It was specifically designed to increase knowledge and awareness of subordinated communities. We, the people of color, had been encouraged, even implored, to talk and to share our experiences. We had talked. We had shared openly. But in the end, people did not want to hear what we had to say. What we had to say made them uncomfortable. They had complained, and we had been silenced. I wondered what would have happened if a student of color had complained about being intimidated by the white students? The professor would have laughed and said something like, "Welcome to law school!" Since Lee was Asian American, I also thought about the view of Asians as a middle minority between whites and blacks and Latinos. Lee was a compassionate man, but he was caught in a conflict between the white students and the students of color.[11]

Postscript

I remained troubled by the way the incident had been handled. About ten days later, I went to talk to Lee. I had gone by his office a couple of times, but he was not there or he was busy with someone else. I decided to wait this time until he finished talking to another student in the class. I was sitting outside on a small vinyl couch without a back. The door was open, and I could hear a good portion of the conversation. After about ten minutes he asked her about our class, and my ears perked up. As soon as he asked about the class, the door closed. I don't know who closed it, although I could hear some of the conversation. I was disgusted and left.

I made several attempts to see Lee after that, but we didn't connect for some time. Finally, about a week later, I found Lee alone in his office. He said he was sorry I had not come in sooner because he wanted to talk to me. A group of about six or seven students of color had come in to voice their concerns, so he was well aware of them and assumed that I shared them. He said he knew that we felt we were being silenced, but he wanted me and the other students to know that he had no intention of silencing us and that he wanted us to continue to speak up. I think what Lee might not have understood is that it was too late.

I told Lee that I knew the students had gone to see him. I had thought about going with them. I decided against it, since I was a central figure in the whole thing. Lee said that the prevailing feeling among the white students was that it would be better not to talk about it in class because it might get out of hand.

When I said the rest of us were aware that he had been meeting with the white students all along, he denied it but acknowledged that several white students had come in early in the semester to express the concern that they did not feel free to discuss their views. I was incredulous.

Professor Lee smiled and said, "Alfredo, I don't know if you are aware of this, but you can be very intimidating to people. They think it's unfair because you are older and because you have a Ph.D. They just feel intimidated by you." I responded, "Well I don't want to sound presumptuous, but we are talking about things that I know something about. I think that often the problem is that we are talking on very different levels. They are giving their personal opinions, and I am talking about theories and general issues." After thinking about what Lee had said, I added, "This is really strange. A lot of times people question the qualifications of minorities. So are they saying that I am too competent? Why don't they speak up? No one is stopping them."

CHAPTER FIVE

Making the Grade

Libertad (Freedom)

I am standing at the *reja, or* front gate, of the neighborhood school. It is my first day of school. My young mother has left me at the entrance to the Catholic school, crying and screaming. As I look down the street, I can see her peering around the corner of the *barda* (wall) that borders the school, looking forlornly at me. Her hands gesture in the air, first blessing me, and then gently blowing a kiss from the palm of her open hand. As I turn to walk into the schoolyard, she slowly moves the cupped fingers of her upturned hand and waves goodbye.

As a young child, I hated school. School was boring. I spent much of my time in kindergarten talking or with my head on top of the desk, resting or sleeping, as the children recited the alphabet or chanted their numbers in unison, counting on tiny abacuses. As the days passed, I would wave at my mother, waiting until she disappeared from sight. I would then turn around and spend the day *en la pinta* (cutting school), playing near my neighborhood or walking on the railroad tracks. When it was time for school to end, I returned home with the other children.

It is the last day of kindergarten. I have just attended a graduation ceremony where the children sing and dance. I run home excitedly to show *mamá* the medal that I have earned. I proudly hand her my *medalla de plomo* (lead medal). I don't understand why she is angry and upset. I later learn it is because I didn't get a real medal like the other children in my class. I received *una medalla de consolación* (consolation medal). My medal was "special," but it wasn't a good kind of special. It was given to the children who were deemed not ready to advance to the next grade.

I still have fond memories of the time before kindergarten, when I was free of the restrictions of school, *cuando estaba libre*. We lived on a little *privada* in *Tacuba*, a *colonia* in the northern part of *la capital*, México/Tenochtitlan. Our *vecindad* (neighborhood) was a little cul-de-sac called *Colegio Militar*, because the historic México City military school was nearby. While my older brothers were in school I spent endless hours playing in the yard, climbing the *tinaco* (water tank) or exploring the mysterious jungle of *carrisos* (bamboo) that separated our side yard from the neighboring houses. The little neighborhood was my self-contained universe, and I was known by all of the neighbors. One of my friends was a lady named *Doña Chucha*. She had a wonderful yard with plants and dozens of exotic *pájaros y pericos* (birds and parrots) housed in a wide assortment of metal and wooden cages. I came daily to visit and see her exotic *pájaros*. One morning she emerged from the house and was devastated when she discovered that all of the cages were open and empty. Her birds were nowhere in sight. She found me at the edge of the patio, along with my makeshift wooden sword and cape, pointing proudly toward the sky and dramatically proclaiming, *"Están libres!"* (They are free!). My mother was understandably shocked and embarrassed that I had released all of *Doña Chucha's* birds. She apologized and even offered to pay for the birds. I was severely reprimanded. But later, the old lady relished the story and said she would never forget *el muchachito*, Bebo, who had "liberated" *sus pájaros*.

Staying on the Treadmill

Law school had its perverse side. The final examination schedule in my first semester is an example. Classes ended on December 11, and the first day of finals was January 2. This ensured that the serious student would spend the holidays studying and reviewing. The professors, writing instructors, and Two Ls and Three Ls advised the One Ls to take some time off, but it was very difficult to do. I took a couple of days' vacation, but I was never able to really put finals out of my mind.

Another interesting practice, as I subsequently learned, is that in the second or third year, the policy in the writing classes, which required a paper rather than a final examination, was that papers were generally not due until approximately two months after the end of the semester. The paper deadline for the fall semester, in other words, was around April 6, and the deadline for spring semester papers was August 10.

Just before the paper deadlines, second- and third-year students would emerge out of nowhere. You would see them working feverishly, almost around the clock, on papers that should have been completed, or at least started, months before. They were everywhere—in the computer room working on Lexus and Westlaw; on the couches on the third floor of the law school library taking naps; in the lounge consuming massive quantities of coffee, sodas, and junk food. Though the official explanation was that the policy gave students extra time, it struck me as a form of intellectual serfdom or indentured servitude, designed so that students were always under the control of the professor and the law school. The practice meant that you were destined to never catch up, so that during any given semester you were working on stuff that was past due and neglecting the current semester's assignments. It was an ingenious method that enabled professors to get more work out of students and to extend the semester. Even in the summer when students were working for a firm or a public interest organization, most were still busy completing papers. No wonder there was no summer school at Stanford Law School. Who would have had time for summer school?

I wondered why people did not finish the papers in the same semester that they took the course. You were permitted to complete papers before the deadline, after all. I asked Jessie, one of the Chicano third-years, why people didn't finish the papers earlier. He said, "That would be the smart thing to do, but I've never done it, and I know few people who have."

Law school culture is filled with lore. Professors and older students say that one of the reasons reading and writing assignments in law school are so demanding is to prepare students for life after law school. Whether working for a firm, a public defender, a public interest group, a judge, or in private practice, you would always feel overwhelmed. Carlos Romero, my Contracts teacher and a visiting professor from UCLA, told me that the feeling of not being caught up would never go away, so I should get used to it. He also said that being able to pick out what was significant from a mass of material was an important skill that you had to develop as a lawyer. In the more advanced classes there was an unofficial competition to see which professor had the thickest reading packet at the copy center.

A few days after finals, I went to the registrar's office to inquire when grades for the fall semester would be available. The two women in the office looked at each other and smiled knowingly. The registrar, a stately white-haired woman, said, "Oh, it takes several weeks for the professors to finish the grading. It will be late February or March before the grades are ready." Her tone implied that I should understand that professors needed that much time to finish the grading. I felt foolish but smiled and left.

About seven weeks later, on Thursday, March 5, the word spread like a California brush fire: grades for the first semester were out. There was electricity in the air, as students stood anxiously in line awaiting the verdict. I sat quietly eating a burrito on a bench by the *Falcon,* a modern French statue in front of the law school that did not look much like a falcon, and watched as people walked by with smiles or looks of disappointment or despair on their faces. Many seemed disappointed and depressed, but there were a few beaming faces. I thought about Cristina Marín, my former student, who had said that grades were not important at Stanford because you competed with yourself and not with other folks.

The line at the registrar's office was long and growing longer, so I decided to wait until after Modern Legal Theory, which ended at 3:05, to pick up my grades. Professor White started the class with a big smile and said that he knew today was the "big day," but he implored us to relax and not take the grades too seriously. He would do his best to move forward with the material, although he realized it would be difficult for us to concentrate. When class let out, the line at the registrar's office had grown even longer. I decided to wait until the next day. Friday was a busy day because the first draft of our moot court brief was due. We were assigned to work in pairs, and I had teamed up with my friend Aqueil, a Pakistani American. I was busy putting the finishing touches on the brief and did not think about grades until I was ready to go home in the early afternoon. I had already unlocked the lock on my bike when I remembered. I was feeling quite content and decided that I did not want to deal with grades at this point. There was no particular rush. It would wait until Monday. When I got home that afternoon there was a message on my recorder from a prospective summer employer. I scheduled an interview to clerk for a U.S. district court judge in San Francisco for the following Monday and left for the interview immediately after Constitutional Law ended at 12:05. As it turned out, I got back from the city late and did not pick up my grades.

As the days passed, grades became less and less important to me. Immediately after final examinations ended, I was frankly curious to see how I had done. I felt good about my performance, except for Contracts. Contracts had been the first exam. Before finals, everyone, including my Contracts teacher, Carlos Romero, had advised us to read the question two or three times before we began writing. At the beginning of the exam, I felt like I was frozen. I could not begin writing. It was awful. I waited and waited, but I couldn't get started. Perhaps I was nervous because I had not taken an exam since my Ph.D. qualifying exams several decades earlier. Because I waited so long before I began answering the first essay, I was forced to rush through the rest of the exam.

The day after grades came out on Friday, I attended a meeting of the Chicano Graduate Student Association at El Centro, the Chicano Cultural Center on campus. At the meeting I ran into Leo Gómez, a One L who was one of only a handful of politically conscious Chicano students at the law school. Leo's grandfather had been one of the founders and organizers of the Unión de los Trabajadores Mexicanos at the Portland Cement Plant in Colton in the late 1910s and early 1920s. As an undergraduate at the University of California, Santa Barbara, Leo had been involved in campus politics and was chair of the Chicano student group, MEChA (Movimiento Estudiantil Chicano de Aztlán). Leo was modest but admitted he had been one of the leaders in a campus hunger strike, protesting cuts in the Chicano Studies Department. He was usually an easygoing person and not very competitive, but now he looked very upset, and I asked what was wrong. He said, "It's the grades, man. I can't get over it. I did a lot worse than expected, and there was no relationship between how much I studied or how I felt about the class, the professor, or the exam, and my grade in the course. In fact, it seemed like I did even worse in the classes that I felt good about. Even in Contracts, I did terrible. Man, Romero didn't give me a break. He gave me a B-."

I tried to console Leo by saying things like "It will get better as you go on," "What matters, in the end, is that you will have a degree from Stanford," "Grades don't matter." Though I said these things, I knew he didn't believe me. I could always go back to teaching if I did not like law or law school, but for Leo, grades mattered a great deal, especially in a depressed job market. They say that you are what you eat, but at Stanford I was beginning to think that you were your GPA or LSAT score. I thought about what Cristina had said about Stanford not being that competitive and started to wonder.

I wanted to talk to Leo, but when I asked if he wanted to go for a drink, he said that he had been drinking since he picked up his grades the previous afternoon. After drinking in his room for a while, he had run into Ricardo and Jessie, the two Chicano third-year students, at Crothers. Talking to these two *veteranos* (veterans) had helped him a great deal and allowed him to put grades into perspective. Both had done very poorly their first semester. In fact, they boasted that in Torts, they had gotten the two lowest grades in the class. Jessie said they were bored and stopped going to class after the second week and started reading Gilberts instead.

I had run into Ricardo earlier that afternoon by the *Falcon* and he had invited me to go to a Happy Hour with them later. Although I went to the wrong restaurant, I ran into Jessie, another Chicano third-year named Alejandro, and a white friend of theirs at the restaurant. The friend, Jim, was an Italian American from New York. He apparently was very smart but rebellious. I figured that if he hung out with these crazy guys, he must be okay. In fact, when they introduced him, Jessie went out of his way to say that Jim was a "friend." This was a code word that meant that although the person was not Chicano, he was cool and you could speak freely.

We talked about a number of topics but mostly about grades and our families. I told them that I had seen Leo and that he was very depressed. Jessie said, "It doesn't matter. Look at us. We all have jobs with good firms. Of course, the market is getting tighter now, so it will be harder for you guys." They wanted to know how I had done. I told them I had not picked up my grades because I did not want to ruin my weekend. Jessie looked concerned. "But you're going to pick up your grades, aren't you?" I said I would, sooner or later. They laughed and said that in their first semester Jim held the record for being the last person to pick up his grades. Jim had apparently done very well, but he felt that the focus on grades "was a lot of bullshit that was promoted by the big firms."

We talked about our backgrounds and how we wound up at Stanford Law School. Both Jessie and Alejandro mentioned that the support of their families, especially their mothers, had been very important to their success. Jessie was from the Mission District in San Francisco. He was born in Mexico and came to the United States when he was fourteen. His family was working class, but they had a small store in the barrio. The family was close-knit, and they encouraged him to continue his education. Jessie had done very well on the entrance examinations and received a scholarship to attend St. Ignatius, a very good private Catholic school in the city. His younger brother was enrolling at Harvard the coming year, but his sister had not gone to college even though she was very smart. She was twenty-two and had recently started taking classes at a local community college. Their parents were reluctant to let her go away to school. Jessie said that it upset him a great deal because his parents did not put as much emphasis on educating their daughter as they did their sons. He was trying to convince his parents to let her go away to school because it was just as important that she get a good education.

Ricardo was a third-generation Chicano from New Mexico who was not that fluent in Spanish, but I admired his effort to speak it. Jessie and Ricardo had met and become good friends as undergraduates at Yale. They were what Rodríguez terms the "New Scholarship Boys," and yet it was refreshing that neither one seemed to fit the label.

Alejandro was *muy mexicano* but more oriented toward business, somewhat politically conservative, and married to a white woman. They had two beautiful children. He would often bring his family to SLLSA functions, and everybody liked him and his family. Alejandro's political orientation was not uncommon. He was from Los Angeles, and his parents were Mexican immigrants. He had grown up poor, spoke Spanish, and was as Mexican as the *nopal* (a type of cactus that is cooked by Mexicans). He was very much opposed to gangs and blamed a lot of the problems encountered by Mexicans on Mexicans themselves, especially "the culture," which he felt kept us down. He had made it by hard work and perseverance and did not understand why other *mexicanos* could not do the same. He believed that you could speak good English, do well in school, work for a large firm, and even marry a white, and still not lose your cultural identity and heritage. Doing the things that white people do did not make you white. You could be smart and successful, have nice things, and still be Mexican. You could literally have the best of both worlds. I respected and liked Alejandro a great deal, but in our discussions, I tried to point out that Mexicans lacked opportunities and were discriminated against. Most of our people were not as fortunate as we had been, and it was unfair to blame them for their lack of economic or educational success. It was like blaming the victim.

Resisting the Hierarchies

I had been curious about grades at the beginning of the semester, but by the time they came out I was engrossed in second semester classes. The first-semester grades seemed passé, anticlimactic. I am not sure when I consciously decided not to pick them up at all. I noticed that not knowing my grades seemed to make me more interesting at parties and receptions because grades were often the main topic of conversation, particularly soon after they came out. Throughout the second semester my friend Aqueil and I often had lunch together or talked on the phone, and every couple of days he would ask, "Have you really not picked up your grades yet?" I would say, matter-of-factly, "No I haven't. I don't want to deal with it now. I'm too much into this semester. I'll probably wait and pick up the fall and spring grades at the same time during the summer." Aqueil had a Ph.D. in mathematics and had been a university professor for a couple of years before law school. His parents were born in Pakistan, and apparently he came from a highly educated family that put a lot of emphasis on education. His father was a physicist and a professor at the California Institute of Technology. He felt pressure to excel. My friend was very competitive, and I don't think he believed me.

Although I had an explanation, or explanations, for my decision, the truth is that I was not really sure why I had not picked up the grades, just as I didn't know exactly what drove me to go to law school when I had a very satisfying and successful career as an academic. I think the core of the decision about the grades was based on a need to rebel against the feeling that I was totally under the control of the law school. It bothered me that people were so dependent on grades to form their self-conceptions and their conceptions of others. I wanted to do what I could, in my own small way, to break this dependence.

Looking back on the experience, I have to add that anyone who thinks that law school is like undergraduate college or even graduate school just doesn't know much about law school. I had been an undergraduate and a graduate student and had taught at major state universities in five states, and there is no comparison. The hierarchies in the law school classroom and the deference to professors make one feel like one is in the nineteenth century. The systematic attempts to change the student's identity are unmistakable.[1]

There were many things that I could not control in law school. I couldn't control which classes I took in the first year, who my professors were, the examinations, or even the grades I received. But picking up my grades was something I could, and would, control. It was a way to retain a sense of autonomy in the fact of pervasive controls. I didn't need law school to legitimate me or to tell me who I am. I knew that the grades would not make me any smarter or more deserving or any dumber and more undeserving than I had been before law school. I was still the same person. It was just that life wasn't as much fun.

The Scarlet Letter

Grades were due out for the spring semester more than two months after classes had ended. My friend Aqueil had a 4.0 average, and he was still fixated on grades. He had been calling the registrar almost daily, and the office kept giving him different dates when grades would be out. Our Modern Legal Theory teacher was apparently holding up the grades.

It was well after 11:00 p.m. when the telephone rang. It was Aqueil. We chatted for a few minutes about miscellaneous topics. We should get together for tennis; his father is visiting the area for a few days. After a pause he asked abruptly, "By any chance, have you picked up your grades?" I told him I had not. Aqueil responded,

> Well, I picked up my grades today. They all came out the way I expected, except White's class. He gave me a 3.2! I couldn't believe it. I am definitely going to meet with him to find out what happened. I was really upset. I wanted to wring his neck. Unless it's a mistake. Do you think it could be a mistake? No, it's unlikely to be a mistake. I called because I knew that you would have some reassuring words.

He was wrong. I didn't know what to say. Aqueil was such a good student and so consistent that it was hard to believe that he could have gotten anything other than an A. Since the end of the semester we had talked about White's take-home final. I knew he felt good about his exam, as I did about mine. He talked glowingly about his answers and then said jokingly, "Yeah, I probably blew it!" Then, in a sarcastic tone, as if trying to convince himself, he added, "Who cares. Grades don't matter anyway."

He became very serious and uncharacteristically vulnerable on the telephone that night. I had never seen his vulnerable side before. He said, "What concerns me is that maybe I can't do this type of open, creative work. What if I try to get a Supreme Court clerkship or a teaching job in a law school, and someone says, 'Look he got a B in this class, he can't write or do the creative, scholarly stuff'?" In the next breath, like a good lawyer, he would counter his own statement: "Most employers aren't going to care about one grade. One grade doesn't really mean anything. You know, it really does not make that much difference in the overall grade point average. I still have a 3.9 overall."

I said jokingly, "Do you think maybe we were too complicated or abstract? It seemed like the class was taught on a very superficial level. White probably didn't like my exam either. He probably gave good grades to all of the folks who are real shallow." The truth is that many people did not seem to take the Modern Legal Theory class seriously. It was one of those soft courses that were not part of the hard-core curriculum.

The shock of learning that my friend had not done well in this class made me wonder about my own grades. I figured I had done well in Constitutional Law, and I had taken Property pass/fail because I had a hard time following the professor. I would have been disappointed if I did not get an A in Modern Legal Theory and shocked if I did not do well in Lawyering Process, with Lee. Yet White and Lee had a reputation for being what the students' call "bunchers" rather than "spreaders." Stanford imposed a mandatory mean, or average, on all classes, to which faculty had to conform. Bunchers were the professors who gave most people an average grade so there was not much variation among students. Spreaders achieved the same result with a much larger variation among grades. I preferred spreaders because the other system seemed to favor mediocre students.

In the next few days I thought a lot about the class. I took out my exam and reread it several times. It was even better than I remembered. Yet I was obviously too close to be an objective judge of the quality of my exam. Usually when I write something and I reread it later, it sounds even better than it did when I first wrote it. I have heard that many people have the opposite experience. I wondered whether this meant that I underestimated myself or whether I had a lower self-concept than I should; or perhaps it meant the opposite.

White's final was handed out on May 8, the last day of classes, and was due in the registrar's office by 4:00 p.m. on May 22, the last day of finals. Of course, we were preparing for other exams and writing other papers at the same time. The questions were broad and open-ended, unlike any law school exam I had taken. I liked the exam and enjoyed preparing my answers. It asked us to comment on whether the following two statements were reconcilable: "Holmes [Oliver Wendell] maintained that 'the life of the law has not been logic; it has been experience.' He also wrote, '[P]ractical men generally prefer to leave their major premises inarticulate, yet even for practical purposes theory generally turns out the most important thing in the end.'" The answer could not exceed twelve double-spaced typed pages.

Although the class of seventy students was large for an elective and there was not a lot of class discussion, I enjoyed the class, the professor, and the exam. Regardless of the grade, I had learned a lot. Professor White had a no-nonsense, irreverent approach to legal theory. He laid out various schools of legal thought, traced their evolution and development, and then let the students figure out the rest. He generally refrained from imposing his biases and preferences, but sometimes he told us what he saw as a problem or issue with a particular school or theory. This is what I had expected law school to be like—challenging, creative, and relatively open. I had expected law school to be like graduate school, but it was not. I understood that law school was supposed to be a professional school, where you are expected to acquire a body of knowledge, but it seemed more like a trade school. Perhaps what distinguished law from other professions is that you were not directly exposed to the body of knowledge. Some first-year teachers liked to "hide the ball," that is, present the material as though it were open so you had to first figure out the body of knowledge before you could acquire it. Other professors were said not to have a ball to hide.

One concern that I had is that despite the apparent openness of the class, it was a survey course taught at a somewhat superficial level. One day, for example, we discussed the role of myth in the work of Thurman Arnold, a major figure in the Legal Realist school. Arnold wrote:

> The fundamental principles of law do not represent what we do, but what we ought to do. The science of the law is not the method which judges actually use, but the method which they ought to use. It is a sort of Heaven which man has created for himself on earth. It is a characteristic of all paradise that they should be different from what we actually experience in everyday affairs. Otherwise there would be no object in creating them.[2]

White was critical of Arnold and the Realists' conception of myths, remarking that if these are mere "myths," they are not real. "How do we determine what is real?" he asked. Though this was a rhetorical question, the way White talked about myths made me wonder whether he really understood the sociological and anthropological conception of myth. He seemed to be treating myth in a commonsense way, as something untrue or unreal. Although I and a few other students entered into a class discussion and tried to correct him, he did not seem to grasp the notion that myths are real, not in an ultimate sense but in a socially created sense. Once things are defined as being socially real they are in fact real in their consequences, I argued. Religion, our conception of the Constitution, liberty, and so on were all mythical, but they are very real, powerful myths nonetheless.

I began at this late date to seriously reevaluate the course. Was it as open as it seemed? Was the openness an illusion that masked a superficial treatment of the topic? Was it a facade, a myth? Was White, one of my favorite teachers, also guilty of hiding the ball? I knew some things for sure. I knew Aqueil was incredibly smart. I knew he was not superficial. I knew he had put a lot of time and effort into the class. But mostly I knew that he had gotten an average grade and that there was nothing average about this guy. I also knew that a lot of other people did not take the class seriously and had done well.

There were two possible solutions to the puzzle. One was that Aqueil had not presented his ideas clearly or effectively. I had read some articles written by White, and they were well written. He also said in the instructions for the final that clarity of writing would be an important factor in evaluating the exams. I had not seen much of Aqueil's writing, except when we worked together on the brief for moot court. I had done a lot of editing on his drafts. We had both downplayed it. The other possibility, which I did not want to face, was that the class was shallow and those whose thinking had more depth and was more abstract had not done very well. I was led to worry about my own grade. I was very curious about how I had done, but I now felt that not picking up my grades had become a principle, and I was not going to violate it. It was inevitable. Someday I would probably learn my grades, but it would be nice to wait until I had finished law school. Then I could laugh and say, "The hell with it all."

I recall that a few days after we had gotten the take-home exam and before I started working on it, I asked Aqueil if he had any idea how he might approach the exam. He laughed and said, "We have an honor code here at Stanford which I can't violate." I didn't know whether he was kidding, but his response turned me off. It was as though he did not want to share his great ideas with me, fearing that I might incorporate them into my answer. A few days later he called excitedly to tell me that he had used Holmes in answering one of the questions. I had started working on the exam and begged him not to tell me because it would spoil my own creativity. I actually got mildly upset and said, "See, once you tell me you did this or that, I will feel intimidated answering. Even if I had thought about it independently, I will feel like I am copying your ideas." We didn't talk about the exam again until after we turned our papers into the registrar.

Ironically, in the instructions, Professor White had encouraged us to talk about the questions with each other. I did not understand how you could do that. Two students in the class, Kim Chang and Bob Steward, asked us if we wanted to get together to discuss the questions. They were both very nice people, and we had played tennis with them. Kim and I had become friends during the first semester. Bob was a white transfer student, quiet and unpretentious. These were rare qualities at Stanford Law School. When Bob called, he said he did not think Aqueil was interested in getting together because he was acting like someone who had all kinds of information that he did not want to share with anyone. I thanked Bob and told him that on this type of test I would rather work on my own. I wondered how Kim and Bob had done. It would be ironic even if they had done better than Aqueil. Though I never found out Kim's grade, Bob and I continued to play tennis with Aqueil, and he later indicated that he had gotten an A- (3.5).

In the midst of preparing for the exam, Lisa Fong, an older Asian woman in the class, called and asked if she could borrow my notes. Apparently she had been out of town and missed a lot of classes. I did not know her well, but I recognized her voice. She told me that Bob and other people in the class had told her that I took excellent, detailed notes. I told her that my handwriting was very difficult to read, and she said, "That's okay, let me try to decipher it." It was awkward, but I told her I did not feel comfortable doing this. What I wanted to tell her but did not is that I felt it was exploitative to miss a lot of classes and then expect someone to hand you their class notes on a silver platter, especially someone you did not know very well. It would have been different if a friend had to miss a particular class and to borrow your notes for that day.

I turned in my exam at around 1:00 in the afternoon, Thursday, June 21, one day before it was due. As I was standing in the registrar's office, waiting to hand in the exam, a first-year student whom I knew only by sight, and who seldom came to class, asked me if that was White's exam in my hand.

When I said that it was, he asked me when White had handed out the exam. He was shocked when I told him that we were supposed to pick up our exams from the registrar on the last day of classes. He looked panicked and told me he thought it was a one-day exam that we were to pick up on Friday morning. He asked the registrar, and she gave him his exam. He took off with a look of fear and desperation on his face, apparently to begin working on the exam. At the time I felt sorry for this fellow. Now I also wondered how he had done in the class.

In early August I received a mysterious unmarked letter from the registrar's office. It was in a small innocuous envelope, with the return address, "Office of the Registrar, Stanford Law School," in bold red letters. I was tempted to open the envelope. After all, the summer was over and the registrar had apparently decided to do me the favor of sending me the fall and spring grades, which I had neglected to pick up. The envelope lay on the coffee table for several days. I finally decided that I would not open it and went running above the Stanford campus. It was a magnificent day. I was overwhelmed by the view of the ocean and the surrounding countryside and filled with a sense of calm and euphoria.

TWO L

CHAPTER SIX

"Walk Like a Man": Law Review

"The Devil Dogs"

I was never in the military. In fact, the closest I came to boot camp was when I was sixteen years old and a couple of my close friends and I attended a ten-day mini-camp at the Great Lakes Naval Station outside of Chicago. The program was called the Cook County Sheriff's Devil Dog Teens. It was sponsored by the Cook County Sheriff's Office and sought to divert poor and minority kids from gangs. My friends and I were not gang members, but we were what many people today would call "at risk." But a majority of the juveniles in the program were in gangs and had been in trouble with the criminal justice system. We soon learned that the gang members were not really that tough once you got them alone and stripped them of their identity and support group. The program, run by the Marines, was essentially a mini–boot camp designed to weed out the men from the boys. The philosophy and ideology was to work you like hell, harangue you, and break down your self-esteem. In the end you were supposed to feel dependent on the drill instructors and learn that you really weren't that tough. We got neat white T-shirts with a bright red-and-black logo of a devil that said, "The Sheriff's Devil Dog Teens," fatigues, and a Marine cap.

Most of the day was spent marching and barking out the cadence, "One, two, three, for your left. Left, left, right, left." We also had to do push-ups, run laps, and conquer obstacle courses, as we were berated by the drill instructors. We even got to see a drill instructor beat up a couple of recalcitrant Marines. We had one advantage over the gang members, I found. We were athletes. We had played football, baseball, and wrestled. My friends and I were in excellent physical condition, we could more than keep up with the Marines, and, most important, we knew how to take punishment.

My middle brother, Héctor, was forced to join the Marines by my dad when he was only seventeen. It was either the Marines or jail, according to my dad, Judge Ray Hall, and his probation officer, William Pierce.[1] Although Héctor talked about his experiences, I don't pretend to know what Marine boot camp is like. I am sure that what we got here was a very mild version. It was a "scared straight" program for delinquent or at-risk youth. No one died or was hospitalized. In fact, we ate very well and came out of it feeling *chingón,* or bad-ass. At the same time that the program was designed to show us that we weren't as tough as we thought we were, we came out feeling good about ourselves. The Devil Dog experience actually improved our self-esteem.

Law Review Workshop

August 24.

The Law Review Workshop began promptly at 10:00 a.m. with a welcome continental breakfast and introductory remarks by the president, Carl Williams, and other high-ranking Review staff. This was followed by the main speaker, Robert Bloom. Bloom had been president of the Stanford Law Review (SLR, referring to the organization) some fifteen years earlier and was now a professor at the law school. He was witty, and never seemed to take himself, or anyone else, seriously. Watching Bloom made for an interesting contrast with the young staff members who, with the exception of Williams, were aloof, uptight, and took themselves very seriously. It made me wonder whether it was Bloom or the SLR that had changed so much over the years.

The decision to participate in the Review workshop had been a difficult one for me during the summer. Everyone said how awful the law review process was, everyone hated it, but a lot of people ended up participating in it. Why? I didn't understand the mystique surrounding the SLR.

At most law schools, law review is competitive and restrictive. It is sometimes based on grades, so that only the elite can participate. At other schools one has to "write on" to law review, that is, write and submit a publishable article. At the first workshop, Williams, the president of SLR, told us that Stanford was different. Stanford took pride in the fact that the Review was "open." Theoretically, anyone and everyone could be on law review. I was shocked to learn there were no criteria for trying out, other than being a regularly enrolled student in the law school, agreeing to participate in the fall workshop, and successfully completing all assignments. I was amazed. It seemed you didn't even have to show that you could walk a straight line and chew gum at the same time to make law review.[2] It didn't take long to learn that there was an additional, unstated requirement—being able to endure pain and degradation. I soon discovered that just as in lifting weights, so with the SLR, the prevailing motto was "no pain, no gain." The SLR was also supposedly "receptive" to people of color. This was not discussed openly, but everyone knew the past three presidents had been African American.

We learned the fall workshop would begin in the third week of August and last until October 17. At the conclusion of the workshop, candidates would be evaluated and either admitted or rejected from membership on the SLR. The official criteria for admission were that one meet what was euphemistically termed a minimum "quality standard." Candidates would be assigned an anonymous number, which was ostensibly known only to the ombudsman. Evaluations would be anonymous, and two members of the editorial board would review each candidate. A final requirement was to complete and submit a student law review note, or article, that was described as being of "publishable quality" by early February.

I had received mixed advice on whether to do law review. After talking with various people, I concluded there were at least two schools of thought on the subject. One school of thought, represented by my mentor, Rick Romo, was that grades were important in vying for a law teaching position but that law review was not that important, especially in my case because I had so much writing experience. Romo had not been on the SLR, and it didn't affect his ability to get a teaching job. He thought it more important that I publish some law-related articles. Others also cautioned against doing it simply because it looks good on the résumé. At the end of my first year, I had clerked for an U.S. district court judge in San Francisco, the Honorable Jane Carter. On the train ride to San Francisco, one of the third-year students who had been on law review told me she did not think it was crucial at all, at least not for getting her job in a law firm. Her advice was to do law review if you enjoy doing a lot of mindless, tedious work, but don't do it just because you think you have to. The firm that hired her had not even asked whether she was on law review, although it was listed on her résumé.

The second, more prevalent school of thought was that being on law review was essential to getting a teaching job or a prestigious clerkship and that it helped a great deal in getting a good firm job. The other Chicano professor at the law school, Martínez, held this view. Martínez was one of the few professors who had been a trial lawyer, and he was a very good one. He was supportive of students and willing to counsel and advise them. When we had lunch in the spring of my first year, he told me three things were important in preparing for a teaching position in a law school: hands-on experience during law school, grades, and SLR membership. "If you were president of the law review," he said, "it would open up a lot of opportunities for you. It would be wonderful, and we've never, as far as I know, had a Latino president." I told him that I would enjoy doing that and believed I was qualified because of my background and experience. Martínez agreed.

My summer clerkship played a critical role in leading me to decide to participate in the law review. Judge Carter's permanent law clerks, Nacho and Judy, had attended Harvard and Yale law schools, respectively, and each was on the law review. They said it was a drag and that their colleagues were mostly neurotic, anal-retentive nerds, but they advised me to participate nonetheless. Nacho told me that perhaps as many as 80 percent of judges considering applicants for clerkships would automatically exclude from consideration those who did not list law review on their résumés. He also said that being a clerk at the Supreme Court or the U.S. Court of Appeals was almost a prerequisite for a teaching position at a top law school.

A Trial Run: Spring Edit

Near the end of the first year I decided to participate in the spring Editing Exercise for First Years. The editing exercise was ostensibly designed to give us a trial run of what law review was about. We were assured that how we did in the spring workshop would not affect our candidacy in the fall, positively or negatively. At the end of March, all first-year students received the following memorandum from Carl Williams and the managing editor of the SLR, Herb Price, inviting us to participate in the spring editing exercise. The memorandum stressed:

> This Exercise is voluntary and your participation will not affect your ability to participate in the fall. However, it will be your main opportunity for meaningful feedback before a majority of the fall workshop has taken place. Also, especially good edits may benefit you in the fall selection process. We strongly encourage all those interested in being on the Review to take part in the spring Exercise.

It was clear that would-be lawyers had written the memo. In one sentence the letter said both that participation was "voluntary and would not affect your ability to participate in the fall" and that "especially good" edits may be beneficial in the fall selection process. Did this mean that participation would not count against you but that it could count for you? I soon learned that the spring edit did affect participation in the fall. Those individuals who began but did not complete the voluntary spring exercise discovered that they had been disqualified from further consideration for SLR membership. One of the One Ls, Rick Díaz, wrote a letter to the editor of the *Stanford Law Journal* indicating that he was shocked when he received a letter from the president of law review informing him that he was not eligible to participate in the fall workshop because he had failed to complete the spring edit. Williams's letter stated, "As was explained, failure to compete the editing exercise disqualifies you from becoming a candidate for membership [on the SLR] in the fall."[3]

Later I learned that the prevailing view was that the "free exercise" was actually part of a sinister plot concocted by the senior law review staff to get hundreds of hours of free, cheap labor out of the first-year class. It was the best of all worlds for the law review staff because you got the people to do all the work and did not have to decide whether to admit them to the Review. You also got a preview of who the compulsive people were. Rick Díaz summed it up well when he noted that through the spring edit,

> Review killed three birds with one stone. A substantial amount of editing was completed, they had a good idea of who was the "better"

and more committed Review candidates, and several potential members were eliminated from consideration. I have no illusions as to our
anonymity, since my pink slip came straight from the President of
Review and not from the Ombudsman, who was supposedly the only
editor who would know our name during the entire process.[4]

The senior editors of the Review wrote a response to Diaz's editorial, noting that making completion of the spring edit mandatory was imperative
because they could not afford to reassign unfinished edits due to a "very tight
production deadline."[5] (This rationale supports the view that the SLR was
using the One Ls as free labor.) The decision to exclude members who did
not complete the edit was ultimately justified not as an editorial judgment
but as a business decision, so that even if the Review staff had been unclear
about the consequences of not completing the edit, they were not unclear
that the assignment was mandatory once it was accepted because "as a
student-run publication, the Review cannot function unless members and
those interested in being members, accept their responsibilities. After all,
not only is the Review a student organization, it is also a business."[6]

In the end, then, the free edit was not free at all. For students like Díaz
who failed to complete the edit, it meant elimination from further consideration as SLR candidates. The free edit was a windfall for Review staff. They
had dozens of the best and the brightest young people as research assistants,
running all over the law library and other campus libraries checking on references and citations in articles that were going to be published by the
SLR. Although I had not enjoyed the spring workshop, I assumed they were
trying to scare people away and that the fall workshop would be a more positive experience.

Academic Boot Camp

Being in the Law Review Workshop reminded me of my days as a Devil Dog
Teen, because this was like being in an academic boot camp. We didn't run
laps or do pushups in law review, but it was physically demanding. More important, I sensed that it was motivated by the same kind of ethic as boot
camp or hazing. The ethic was one that went something like this: We know
you all think you're smart. [We're all smart!]. We know that you're all very
busy. [We're all busy!]. We know we can't use grades or other traditional criteria to exclude you [We are an "open" Review!]. We know we can't do these

things, but what we can do is to work the hell out of you and see if you can take it. We are going to give you lots of mindless, tedious assignments. We are going to do this for a couple of months. We are going to do it until it hurts, until you drop, and, in the end, we're going to see whether you still want to be on Review. Okay?

The schedule during the fall workshop made the Devil Dog Camp seem like a picnic. It started in August, one week before classes, and continued nonstop until almost the end of October. After the Welcome Breakfast we were provided with workshops on the editorial process, the production process, cite checking, Bluebooking, and "copy dress" editing. Then our first editing, or Bluebooking, assignment was distributed and was due in the managing editor's box by 7:30 p.m. Our first copy dress assignment would be in our mailboxes by 2:00 p.m. on Monday and was due by noon on Thursday. The following day, Tuesday, we received the first Source Pull assignment in our mailboxes, and it was due by 7:00 p.m. Wednesday. In our spare time we were expected to take law library refresher tours and mandatory Lexis training.[7] We were expected to work from roughly 9:00 a.m. until 10:00 p.m. Our only break was when we were provided with daily pizza or cookie breaks.

It was hard to understand how an organization that touted itself as being open and egalitarian could be so hierarchical and elitist. At the top of the hierarchy were the president and managing editor, followed by the senior editors, the associate editors, and the rank-and-file members. At the very bottom were candidates for SLR, all of whom were One Ls. The air of superiority among the Review staff was evident to all of us who attended the two orientation meetings for the spring edit. At the first meeting on April 8, several of the editors joked that the president, Carl Williams, was being too nice and that he should toughen up. Williams was trying to give a more positive spin on the Review by saying that it was not as bad as its reputation. He was wrong. At this meeting at least, it was clear that the anal-retentive mentality prevailed. At the second meeting, on April 15, one of the senior staff announced that because he knew we would be going out for Review en masse in the fall, he would not bother to learn our names; it would not be cost effective.

Bluebooking

One cannot understand the Review workshop without first understanding the Bluebook. The Bluebook is to the Review staff what the Bible is to fundamentalist preachers, *Das Kapital* to Marxists, the Little Red Book to followers of Mao, and the *White Man's Bible* to white supremacists. It is the final word on all editing decisions.[8] Officially, the Bluebook is described as a uniform system of citation compiled by the editors of the *Columbia Law Review*, the *Harvard Law Review*, the *University of Pennsylvania Law Review*, and the *Yale Law Journal*. It is essentially a compendium of rules and sub-rules for citations in legal writing and is aimed at producing stylistic uniformity for court documents, legal memoranda, and SLR articles.

In the first and subsequent workshops we were told by the Review staff that we should each have a copy of the Bluebook and become very familiar with it. We were also given a copy of the Redbook, the *Stanford Law Review Guide* for citations that listed areas where Stanford conventions deviated from the Bluebook. In other words, this was a book of rules that were exceptions or modifications to the general rules.

It was clear from the first meeting that this was serious stuff for the Review staff. Carl Williams raised a hypothetical question to show that there were gray areas that were ambiguous or unresolved. I don't remember the specific question, but I do remember that the managing editor and Corina Presley, an associate editor, got into a heated argument about it. Presley had an Anglo surname and was married to a white student, but she was Latina. She knew the Bluebook inside and out, and her ability to cite from it, the way people cite passages, chapter and verse, from the Bible, was astonishing. I could understand why people might be fanatical about religion or politics, but I could not understand this type of fanaticism. It seemed to me to be a waste of mind and talent. It was scary. Would I be doing this in a few months? Could I learn to become passionate about such things?

There were two basic components to editing, we learned, substantive editing and Bluebooking, and two types of assignments, substantive and copy dress. Both substantive editing and Bluebooking would be considered in our evaluations. In most editing assignments an article was divided into sections. Each student was assigned eight to ten passages of text. The first task was to read the manuscript so that you had a context for editing. Then you had to read your section with a fine-tooth comb, do a substantive edit, and Bluebook and cite-check the piece. Though we were told that both components counted, substantive editing and Bluebooking, I learned by experience that the evaluation was based almost exclusively on your use and application of the Bluebook.

My first assignment was a Review Note authored by one of the senior editors, Ron McDonald. Notes are shorter articles written by students and placed at the back of the issue. Turow describes these notes as "sort of a junior version of a faculty article," so that law review students are like junior professors and help the faculty with their articles.[9] One of the criticisms leveled at the Review staff was that a disproportionate number of notes were coming from the senior editorial staff, so they were essentially publishing their own work.

I had met Ron when I visited the campus on Admit Day and sat in on a Constitutional Law class taught by Professor Kahn, a man who would become Ron's mentor. I noticed that during the class, which was about *Bakke* and affirmative action,[10] Kahn talked about reverse discrimination and juxtaposed it to "benign" government actions. I remember remarking to Ron and a few other students who were on the welcoming committee that "benign" did not seem to me properly opposed to "reverse discrimination"; benign seemed like a middle point of action, between reverse and remedial action, and I wondered why this issue wasn't addressed by Kahn or the Court. I wanted to ask the question during class, but it did not seem appropriate because visitors were supposed to be observing, not participating. Ron said to me in jest, "Yeah, that's a great point, you should write a Review Note on it." He was mocking me.

McDonald's note was only mildly interesting. The style was dry, uninspiring, and plodding. I spent a lot of time editing and rewriting the piece, and I think it was much improved. I rewrote not only my section but also the entire note. I also caught a few minor Bluebooking errors, but the note seemed fairly clean on that score. One of the comments that I made may have been sensitive. I noticed that he cited Kahn's casebook as an authority throughout the note. My question was whether it is a better practice to cite the original case source rather than a casebook.

The Review editorial staff promised to give us consistent feedback on our editing. About a week after I turned in the editing of Ron's note, I had a meeting with one of the senior editors, Lucy Spears. She had been on the welcoming committee and was one of the students I met on my visit. Unlike Ron, she seemed to be genuinely impressed with my comment about "benign" categories and had asked me whether I had a background in law. The meeting was structured so that Lucy's role was to summarize the comments made by other Review staff about my editing. She was not one of the people who had actually evaluated my work. Although each edit would be evaluated by three staff members, the feedback we received was based only on the first reading so that we could get feedback as soon as possible.

Lucy began by telling me that she hated Bluebooking but that it was a necessary evil. There were a lot of good things about my edit. My substantive edit was very good and thorough, although my handwriting was sloppy and difficult to read. "It was clear that you write well," she said. But I made some common Bluebooking errors consistently throughout the piece. One of the things I "missed" was underlining the punctuation. For example, if you underline something like the title of an SLR article, you have to make sure that the comma at the end of the title is also underlined. Another error that I made, and I apparently did this consistently, was to not leave a space between "F." and "S" in the citation for the *Federal Supplement*. It is supposed to read "F. Supp.," not "F.Supp." But "F.2d" does not have a space between "F." and "2d."[11]

I did a number of edits over the next few months. The pattern was always the same. I did substantial editing, revising, and reorganization of the assignments, all of which was largely ignored. Though I began to catch on to Bluebooking, new rules were constantly devised that I did not know. I got better, but the standard got higher. "You shouldn't be making these kinds of mistakes at this stage," I was told.

Despite my distaste for Bluebooking, I thought that my substantive editing would make up for my deficiencies, and I remained confident that I would make law review. I had only two feedback sessions, and both of the people were cool. One session was with Lucy Spears; the other, with Jim Peters, a progressive, older guy who was raised in Appalachia and had previously worked as a community organizer. Both of them had given me positive evaluations. But Jim warned, "You have to be leery of the people who are really anal compulsive about Bluebooking. They might shoot you down."

The feedback sessions were difficult to interpret because they were oral and you didn't get a concrete score. I was told verbally that I clearly exceeded the quality standard in my first edit and that my second edit was "marginal" and could go either way. Ironically, the only written evaluations I received were during the spring workshop. They were not very encouraging, although we were warned that the scores might seem a bit harsh because no allowance was made for the fact that this was our first edit. If our scores were low, we should expect some natural improvement. One reader rated my edit a 2 on a five-point scale, which meant that I was "marginal," and provided no comments. A rating of 3 was good but "uninspired." The second reader marked it a 2+ and actually had some positive things to say.

> Not bad for a first time edit, but you really need to ratchet up your level of intense scrutiny—you have NO IDEA how obsessive you have to be to be a truly wondrous Bluebooker. At least when you're starting out, it's best to look up virtually every single thing in the Bluebook and Redbook. BE PETTY!!
> . . . BE MORE INTRUSIVE. You're obviously a good writer, so unleash yourself. Take more of a global approach to the piece, rather than a word-by-word, line-by-line piecemeal approach. . . . Don't get discouraged. With one edit under your belt, you should be in great shape in the fall—I hope you come to Workshop. (Though I have no way of knowing—you're just a number at this point.) Have a nice summer!

On October 24, at the conclusion of the fall workshop, I received a letter from Carl Williams stating that the membership committee appreciated my interest but was "unable to offer you membership on The Review at this time." However, "the selection process does not necessarily end here, and you may remain a candidate and continue working toward Review membership." Williams added that the membership committee would reevaluate my membership file at the conclusion of two additional edits. "If you would like to remain a candidate," he concluded, "please inform Max Sumner [the ombudsman] by Thursday October 29, at 5:00 p.m." And if I wished to discuss my workshop file, I was to schedule an appointment by calling the Review office.

I immediately contacted Sumner and told him that I was interested in remaining a candidate for the Review. I sent the following response to Williams:

Dear Carl:

Thank you for your letter of October 24, informing me that you are unable to offer me membership on the Review at this time. This letter is to inform you that I would like to remain a candidate for the Review and to continue to work toward Review membership.

I am interested in being on the Review not because it looks good on the résumé or because I need to take on additional responsibilities but because I enjoy editorial work and because I believe that I may be able to contribute something of value. As you may know, I have writing and editorial experience. I have published four books (two with the University of Notre Dame Press, one with Harper & Row, and one with the University of Chicago Press) and more than fifty journal articles.

I will be available to meet with you at any time on Wednesday, October 28. Please let me know the specific time that you are available. In addition to the oral feedback, I would appreciate written comments so that I can work to improve my edits. Over the years, I have had a number of successes, and setbacks, but failure to make the Review may be the most unusual and perplexing.

Atentamente,
Alfredo Mirandé

The feedback session was unsatisfactory. Williams asked Corina Presley to sit in on the meeting and provide an oral summary of my file. When I entered the room I noticed that Williams seemed very different. This wasn't the affable young man I had known in the past but an uptight guy who looked irritated and upset. He was annoyed that he had to explain to me, or justify to anyone, why I was not accepted for membership, and really nervous about the whole thing.

Williams began with a brief overview of the process. We did three edits, and each edit was evaluated by three people. They dropped the high and low scores. My first edit on the McDonald note was the best; the last one was the worst. I guess this meant that I had steadily declined. Using this method, some people are "in" and others "out." My file had not been looked at by the entire editorial committee, however. There were three categories, he explained. Those who clearly met the quality standard and were automatically offered membership, those who were borderline and whose outcome had to be decided by the entire committee, and those who fell below the quality standard and did not go to the entire committee for discussion. Unfortunately, I was in the third group.

Corina then gave me specific feedback, but it was not systematic feedback, and there were no written comments as I had requested. She also seemed nervous and unprepared. I sensed she was uncomfortable in her role as enforcer of the quality standard. She fumbled through the file like she was looking at it for the first time, grabbing things out of the air as they caught her eye. She went over some Bluebooking errors in McDonald, my "best" edit. There were "order of authority" problems, which refers to a hierarchy for citing citations so that, for example, in a footnote, federal Supreme Court decisions are listed before Courts of Appeals decisions, which in turn are listed before district court decisions, and so on. Also, when you delete a signal, such as a comma, you should explain why. I should be aware of the proper order for signals such as *See also* and *See generally*. She whipped out the Bluebook and opened it to rule 1.3:

> When more than one signal is used, the signals (together with the authorities they introduce) should appear in the order in which they are listed in rule 1.2. Signals of the same basic type—supportive, comparative, contradictory, or background (rule 1.2)—must be strung together with a single citation sentence. Signals of different types, however, must be grouped in different citation sentences.

I was embarrassed. How could I not remember something that simple?

Corina reluctantly admitted that the strength of my last two edits was in the substantive area but said little beyond that. In the second edit, I had not caught some problems in the headings. She told me to learn the rules for headings on page 79 of the Redbook. I had also left two extra spaces and had not underlined commas. This was a common but apparently fatal error. In the final edit, I had done some good things, but when I commented on bad transitions, I should have suggested better ones. Finally, in one instance, I had failed to italicize *see also*.

I realized I had made some blundering Bluebooking mistakes, but I had spent a lot of time editing and rewriting. Good writing skills were rare qualities among the SLR students and among many of the faculty members who published in the Review. In the case of the final edit, I completely rewrote the introduction and condensed twelve pages into a page and a half. It appeared that my efforts did not make any difference.

Williams tried to downplay the importance of substantive editing. One of the last things he said was that it was impossible to evaluate the quality of people's writing. He said, "You might write a certain way, while I write another way, and Corina a third way. It's just a personal, subjective, stylistic thing. You can't evaluate writing." I disagreed. I could write like a sociologist and use the appropriate jargon, or I could write like a lawyer. I could write like a community activist or a journalist, and when I worked for a judge, I wrote like a judge. As I left the meeting, I reflected on Williams's comment. I couldn't believe that the editor of the *Stanford Law Review*, one of the premier law journals in the country, believed that writing was so subjective that it could not be evaluated.

"*Sí, Mi Presidente!*": Law Review Presidency

I completed two additional edits and eventually made law review. In the final edits I got smart. I spent less time on substantive editing, and I had some friends check my Bluebooking. One person who checked my edit was Buzz Johnson, who dated and eventually married Maya Sullivan. They were Three Ls and a very nice couple. Maya was half-Mexican. Buzz was a good student but different. He was a burly, muscular guy and had a working-class, practical, unpretentious charm. He had been on SLR and had quit because, as he put it, "I couldn't take the bullshit." He felt it was like "a fucking, close-knit, elite club" and that the president was elected not because he was very smart or qualified but because he was innocuous and well liked. He said, "Shit, it's a popularity contest, man!" Nonetheless, early on in my first year both he and Maya had encouraged me to run for an office. After I had problems making the law review, Buzz revealed that members of the editorial board would generally hold it against you if you did extensive substantive editing because it created more work for them. It was only then that I realized that my careful substantive editing might actually have worked against me.

After completing the two additional edits, I finally made law review but I remained alienated. I thought about quitting but decided against it. It was a no-win situation. If I had been rejected, I would have been very upset, and if I made it, I would still be upset. Having made the Review, I now had to make an important decision. Would I join the ranks of students, particularly Three Ls, who are members in name only, or would I get more involved? Buzz related an incident in which Williams harassed the rank-and-file members for not putting forth enough effort. At one meeting he offered them a sort of unconditional amnesty, saying there would be no hard feelings if they quit. Buzz said, "I got pissed off and said, 'Okay, here I quit,' and I walked out of the room."

The sad truth is that I loved writing and editing, and I hated the way the Review emphasized Bluebooking at the expense of writing and editing skills. I did not hold myself up as the model when it came to writing, but I also knew that all people were not equally gifted writers and felt I could distinguish good writing and bad writing. Ironically, Corina was an English major and knew a lot about writing and grammar. Professor White was widely recognized as an excellent writer, and he was. White had read my exam in Legal Theory and one of the papers I wrote when I took a directed research class from him, and he had told me that I wrote well. I also thought writing and editorial skills were important and that they were devalued by the Review. I couldn't stand the ethic that prevailed.

I finally decided that if I was going to be on the Review, I would get involved and run for an office. Despite my alienation, the idea of being an officer and trying to bring about change was appealing. I spent several weeks asking people about the various positions. I was reluctant to run for president because I feared it would be too time-consuming. I considered other positions such as senior articles editor but learned it too would be time-consuming. This position was appealing because I would be involved in selecting and editing articles for publication. After talking to a number of folks, I decided to run for president.

The decision reminded me of an incident that occurred several years before when my son was about seven years old. At the time I was president of the Casa Blanca Home of Neighborly Service, a nonprofit multiservice agency in the Riverside barrio. We were on our way to attend the Installation of Officers Reception at the Mayor's Patio at city hall and had stopped at McDonalds to get something to eat for the kids. We were in separate cars, and as we were leaving, Alejandro had to decide which car he would ride in. As we walked to the parking lot, he said, "I'm going with the president!" These are the kinds of things that parents tend to take for granted, but for a young child, that his dad was president of anything was important. It had a nice sound: "the President" or, better yet, "Mi Presidente."

The electoral process entailed writing a Candidate Statement, which was due at the Review on February 14. The Candidates' Statements for all offices for the past two years were available for inspection in the Review library. Each class essentially elected its own set of officers so that only Two Ls who were members of the Review were eligible to vote in the elections. My statement was a lengthy two-page, single-spaced document.

I outlined my plan for the Review in my statement, but I also tried to include some humor. A number of people stopped me in the hallway and on the stairs to the library and told me they enjoyed my statement and the humor. After saying something about my background and mentioning that I had written four books and dozens of articles, I asked the membership to support my candidacy. I said I loved a good challenge and pledged to "work to engender an environment that defines Review as a more positive experience and reduces the gap between the editorial staff and the membership." Review was serious business, but it should also be "fun and enjoyable." I pledged to put more emphasis on writing and editorial skills, to "dispel the idea that Review is anal drudgery, and to promote a more positive image of the enterprise," so that you could be cool and on the Review at the same time. Finally, I implored my young colleagues, "Vote for Alfredo, the guy with the mustache."

A Question of Privilege

I was not elected president of the Review. On the day of the election, we were told that the results would be posted by 6:00 p.m. outside the Review office. I went about my normal routine and did not check the results that evening. The next morning I was on my way to Rick Romo's class when I ran into Becky Thatcher, my principal opponent in the election. I was parking the Alfredomobile behind the law school when Becky ran up to me. She was smiling, telling me that she had tried to call me but that my number was not listed. She had wondered whether I might want to run for another office because she thought I would be great.[12] I said, "Does this mean that you won the election?" She nodded. I said, "No, I ran for the position that I felt I was best qualified for."

One of the things that enabled me to survive the Review experience is that during my second year of law school I was able to take advanced classes in the Lawyering for Social Change curriculum. Romo's classes were a refuge from the Review and the law school at large. During a discussion in one of Romo's classes, a white student, Karen, commented that all of us were privileged by virtue of the fact that we were at Stanford.[13] One of the things that concerned me about this comment, and the class as a whole, is that it reflected a lack of sensitivity to gender, race, and class dynamics and tended to homogenize the law school experience. I felt that being Stanford law students might have provided us with a common experience, but it did not make us the same. Everyone in the class, even Romo, agreed that we were "privileged." As usual, I disagreed, because I didn't feel privileged. I thought it important to recognize class and the advantages that educated people of color gain, but being educated did not make us the same, or equal. When the police on the street stop me or when I walk into a restaurant, I am still a

Mexican. I remembered Malcolm X would sometimes ask audiences rhetorically, "What do we call a black man with a Ph.D?" The audience would respond in unison, "A nigger!"

The issue of privilege came home to me as I reflected on my unsuccessful campaign for president of the Review. I noticed that the candidates for the various offices started doing strange things in the weeks before the election. My opponent, Becky Thatcher, exhibited the most bizarre behavior. A number of people, including my friend Jim, commented that they noticed she had started talking to and smiling at people she had previously ignored. She was even said to have invited most of the members of the Review to lunch to talk about the issues. One of the Latino students, Eddie Meraz, told me that he and his roommates hung up on her when she called them to invite them to lunch.

It turned out that a couple of the officers on law review came from wealthy families. One was a successful attorney with a large corporate firm in Washington, D.C., a powerful man, a corporate Rainmaker. Jim and a couple of my other friends said that when this influential attorney visited the campus, the dean would have breakfast with him and cater to him because he was a major fund-raiser. Kahn, one of the most eminent professors at the law school, was also very close friends with the benefactor. I thought about my father, about Leo's father, about all of those parents who have never been near a law school, and began to wonder just exactly how privileged I was. If we were, we were not all equally privileged.

Stanford is like a good taco stand. When I was in Mexico City a couple of years ago, a good friend took me to a special taco place. It was literally a hole in the wall, but the tacos were delicious. My friend pointed out that the taco stand was the great equalizer in Mexico. The place was nameless, and they didn't have valet parking, take reservations, or accept American Express. The food was cheap and delicious. It didn't matter how much education you had, whether you were a businessman or street peddler, rich or poor. They did not accept tips, so if you wanted a good taco, you had to stand in line like everyone else, desperately trying to make eye contact with the guy who took the orders. There were no chairs or tables, so you had to eat standing. But the taco stand was only a temporary equalizer. After the meal all of us would assume our previous places in society. But some of us would continue in the struggle to bring about equality and a more permanent transformation.

CHAPTER SEVEN

Pan y Chocolate: Lawyering for Social Change

I hear an old woman's voice, "Niño, niño? Despierte, aquí está su té" (Child, child? Wake up, here is your tea). I sit up in bed, take the clay cup by the handle, and slowly ingest the warm liquid. I take a couple of slow, soothing sips, as Anita, the hunchbacked old lady, waits patiently over me. I curl up. I am back asleep. My body is filled with a warm rush.

When I think back, it's hard to describe the experience. It tasted good, smelled good, and felt good. I loved the feeling. You could "have your cake and eat it too." It was morning, but night had not ended. You didn't have to get up, but you were up. As I went back to sleep, I felt warm and secure. Life was good.

It was a ritual that continued for decades. Anita was *tuerta,* a one-eyed old woman who lived with my paternal grandmother Ana María, grandfather Alfredo's wife and *Tía* Tere's younger sister. For me, Anita was one of those people who had always been old and stoop-shouldered, had always been blind in one eye, had always been arthritic, and had always served tea in the mornings. She brought me *el té* from age 5 to age 25, and even when I was an adult with a Ph.D. she called me *niño*.

It was a ritual. Every night before going to bed, Anita would ask if we wanted *el té de la mañana.* In the morning she would be up before dawn, getting ready for work and preparing the morning tea for everyone in the household. This was not "Lipton," "Good Earth," or "Sleepy Time." These were wondrous, exotic flavors made from natural, mysterious herbs. To this day the teas remain a mystery to me, unlike anything I have ever smelled or tasted. The mystery and the tradition died with Anita.

I learned more about Anita as I grew older. She was not always old and hunched over, and she wasn't always *tuerta.* She was once a little girl, an orphan taken in by my great-grandmother, Carmela, or Mamá Mela, as we knew her. She and my grandmother, Ana María, grew up together, and they remained together. Anita continued to live with my grandmother for the rest of her life.

Anita worked as a *lavandera,* or washerwoman. She got up early every morning and went to people's homes to wash their clothes. In those days people didn't have Maytags or Frigidaires. They washed clothes by hand outdoors in large *fregaderos* or *lavaderos.*[1] Clothes were scrubbed and beaten by hand over a large cement washbasin until they were clean. As a teenager she had accidentally rinsed her eye out with sulfuric acid and had been blinded as a result. I also learned that her hands were not always arthritic. Over the years she had grown stoop-shouldered and arthritic from washing all those clothes.

———

Today I am sitting in Rick Romo's Lay Lawyering class. The first week of classes has just ended, and we are having an all-day Saturday workshop. It is being videotaped. Romo has asked each of us to bring something to eat or drink and share with the class. I made gourmet coffee. Others brought juices, cheeses, bagels, fruit, and pastries. Romo was a tall, rangy Mexican with a great metabolism. He seemed to eat like crazy, but he didn't gain weight. Romo arranged the menu meticulously. At the end of class he asked each student what he or she would be bringing to ensure that we had enough food and a balanced menu.

When we got started, Romo went over some simple but important ground rules for the class. First, we should not be self-conscious about the camera. Second, he wanted to encourage a positive and supportive atmosphere in class. He wouldn't tolerate someone, for example, being "more Chicano" or a "better Chicano" than someone else. We shouldn't bring political rhetoric or any excess baggage into the class. Third, this class was about "us," and anything that was said or anything that happened was not to be discussed with anyone outside the class.[2] In addition to reading articles on lawyering and subordinated communities, theoretical readings on subordination, and a few case studies written by students in previous classes, we would be doing in-class simulation exercises, which would be videotaped and in which we would have an opportunity to practice and critique our field placement presentations. In field placements, we worked on a project involving particular types of legal problems, under the supervision of an attorney, usually an attorney in the Stanford Law Project. (The Law Project was a student-run and student-administered law clinic, which provided free legal services to poor people in East Palo Alto.)

As I sit drinking my gourmet coffee and munching on a pastry, my mind began to wander. I thought about Mamá Mela, a stately brown woman with large hands and high cheekbones. I envisioned Mamá Mela holding a small bell in her right hand and ringing it. Like Anita's morning tea, I have incredibly fond memories of *el pan de las cinco*. Every day my great-grandmother would ring the bell at exactly 5:00 p.m. and yell out, "Niños! El pan de las cinco!" (Children! The five o'clock bread!). This was the snack that would hold us until *la sena* (supper) late in the evening. No matter what I was doing, climbing the large tree, playing soccer with my brothers, feeding the chickens, I would come running into my great-grandmother's room for the 5:00 p.m. snack, which was essentially a chocolate sandwich. It was a *bolillo*, or Mexican French roll, with a bar of chocolate inside. Romo would have loved it, I think. It was reassuring to know that no matter what happened, we had our daily bread and chocolate.

A Rose Blooms in Winter: Lawyering for Social Change

It would be an understatement to say that law review was a low point in my law school experience. I resigned from the Review even though I loved writing and editing. I found that the hierarchies continued after I was offered membership. What a strange form of hazing, I thought. It was endless. I had naively thought that once you made law review you would be accepted as a member of the club. I was not accepted. The hierarchies and the split between the officers and the membership would continue as the new slate of officers assumed their new posts and positions of power. Basically, if you weren't an officer, you were expected to do all of the shit work. Law school problems and issues have a way of cloning themselves, I guess. They are recurrent, endemic, unresolved, and, seemingly, irresolvable.

I did not realize it at the time, but Romo and the Lawyering for Social Change curriculum would be the high point of my law school career. Though my initial experience and the experience of most of the people of color in the Introductory Lawyering Process class had been negative, LSC would prove the beacon that would guide me during this dark period of my life. And though some of us felt silenced in Lawyering Process, in retrospect, we knew it was the only class in which we had been given an opportunity to speak, not simply to talk, but to actually "speak." Ironically, we could not have been silenced unless we were first permitted to speak. I had good classes and good teachers outside of LSC, and students in these classes didn't always agree, but the LSC curriculum was different. We could think and challenge the things that were taken for granted in the rest of the law school. The LSC, specifically Romo's classes, were an oasis for people who were alienated or disaffected from law, law school, and traditional notions of lawyering.

One cannot really understand the LSC without first understanding the traditional law school curriculum. There is a common perception among students and a good number of faculty that law school is prolonged. The perception is that you essentially learn most of what you need to know about law in the first year. There are important courses such as Evidence and Advanced Civil Procedure, but surely these could be fit into a two-year curriculum or learned in the bar review courses after graduation. Is a three-year curriculum necessary? The answer is, of course, yes—not because there is more to learn, but because of money and status. You keep people around for a third year so that you can collect a third year of tuition. There is also the fear that making it a two-year program would lower the status of the profession.

The point is that, unlike graduate school or even undergraduate school, students do not typically have an area of concentration or specialization in law school. After the required core courses in the first year, students take a broad assortment of disparate courses with little rhyme or reason. At

Stanford there were ostensibly a number of specialized curricula. In addition to the LSC, there was Business Law, Environmental and Natural Resource Law, Comparative and International Law, and Health Law and Policy. Though some 82 percent of my classmates would go on to law firm jobs, the truth is that most students were in suspended animation after the first year and took a smattering of unrelated courses.

After the core courses in the first year, one was required to take a "perspectives course" that examined the American legal system from an interdisciplinary perspective and three courses in which a paper was required. I preferred the writing courses, and all but one of my classes after the first term were courses in which I wrote a paper or had a take-home essay examination. But most students preferred courses in which they had an exam.

The LSC was different in that it had two courses, Lawyering Process and Subordination, which were prerequisites to more advanced courses in the curriculum. After the first semester, I took as many LSC courses as I could until graduation. I complemented LSC courses with those that were of interest to me: Advanced Criminal Procedure, Child Abuse, Modern Legal Theory, and Directed Research.

Because I had such a broad and varied experience and a number of field placements in the LSC, it isn't possible to discuss each one. Instead, I will focus on selected aspects of two of these experiences in this and the next chapter. One of the things that I really liked about Romo's classes is that he required students in a field placement to prepare weekly field reports.[3] This allowed me to reflect not only on the placements and the class but on the law school experience as a whole.

Journal Entry, Year Two L

January 15.
My New Year's Resolution is to do my journal entries dutifully each night, or shortly thereafter. I've noted before how difficult it is to keep up the journal on a day-to-day-basis and how, the more that is going on, the harder it is to keep up. Rick has really developed into a full-fledged mentor. This past semester had been terrible, the worst one yet. He has been the only bright spot in the whole thing. I think he is really smart, and a great, caring person. I don't think I've ever I respected anyone the way I respect him. He has been

able to be both friend and mentor at the same time. Perhaps his greatest strength is that when you meet with him, he focuses completely on your agenda and your needs, not his needs. This is a very important quality for a teacher, or a lawyer. I have known a lot of teachers who use their time with students as an opportunity to tell "war stories" and complain to the students about their own problems and issues.

The worst part of the semester was law review. The second major setback was the interviewing season in the fall. I interviewed with a number of firms, got three "callbacks" (second interviews), but did not get any offers, although I eventually landed a job with a small, progressive firm in Oakland. What is ironic is that I think I interviewed well. What then was the reason for the rejection? Age discrimination was a real possibility, but I couldn't prove it because there was no one like me who was younger. When I raised the issue indirectly, the firms all said that being older and mature was a plus, a definite advantage. I didn't believe them. Perhaps the firms did not see me as a firm type. I had a very hard time convincing them that I really was serious about working at a large law firm after graduation. With a tight economy, firms only want to make offers to people they think are pretty certain to accept a permanent offer after they graduate. An attorney at one of the firms jokingly remarked that I had probably written more books than most of the lawyers in the firm had read. A more typical comment during interviews was, "Oh, you have a very interesting background, it's really fascinating, but you look like someone who would probably be interested in teaching." They were right, of course. On the other hand, I think I came up with a pretty good rap, a rap I came to believe. I wanted to teach, but I felt it was important to practice first if you are going to be a good teacher.

At the same time, there were some high points in the first semester of my second year. One high point was Romo's Community Law Practice, where I had a field placement in Education and did a full-scale simulated trial. I felt like I did very well in the class, both in class discussions and in the simulation. I was able to use my experience and skills in teaching and public speaking effectively and to develop a courtroom style. The second positive point was that I wrote two terrific papers and that I got them in early. I took three paper classes this semester. Papers are not due until April 5, but I was able to turn in my paper for Subordination before the Christmas break and my directed research paper yesterday. I have one more paper for Romo's Community Law Practice.[4]

El Diablo es Más Sabio por Ser Viejo que por Ser Diablo
(The Devil Is Wiser Because He's Older, Not Because He's the Devil)

The topic for discussion in class today was a chapter in a book about rebellious lawyering that describes the experiences of a progressive gay Jewish lawyer, Dan, who goes into a low-income community to work with a black lesbian lay advocate named Etta.[5] Because the chapter focuses primarily on Dan's journal entries, we see the world through Dan's eyes. Dan is initially very impressed with Etta and marvels at the way she focuses on details and is able to be effective even though she is understated. Dan, on the other hand, has what Romo termed the "white man's disease": If it isn't big, it's not important.

Romo started out by asking how Dan's experience relates to our placement. I'm not sure that we ever addressed the question, but we had a great discussion. What was Dan up to? Why did he decide to go into the community? Juliet, one of the white students, thought he was bored with his practice. A couple of other people agreed. I thought that it wasn't that he was bored but that he was lost. I believe he went into the low-income community looking for direction and meaning in his law practice. Dan was from Chicago and had attended law school at Boalt Hall. When he went back to Berkeley, he found it was no longer the 1960s Berkeley that he once knew. His family background was also activist. His grandparents were Jewish immigrants and heavily involved in the labor movement.

As time went by Etta started screwing up. There was supposed to be a phone tree, for example, that she never followed up on. Romo asked a critical question: "Does Dan set up Etta for a fall?" Does she really "fall," or is it that she is not meeting his unrealistic "expectations"? I felt that Dan had set the bar so unrealistically high that Etta was destined to fail. I also thought that this example had broad implications, since white liberals often set unrealistically high standards for people of color. We got into a long discussion of what it means to be good at something. Most of the class thought it was related to self-satisfaction, so that it was a subjective standard. I listened but did not buy the idea that if you felt good about what you did, you were good. There was also quite a bit of discussion about internal, "subjective" assessments and external, "objective" assessments.

As you grew older and more experienced, you were bound to get better at what you did. But as you became "good" from an objective perspective, at some point it was bound to get subjectively less satisfying or less challenging.

I related my own experience. I felt that I usually peaked in my teaching around the third or fourth time I taught a class. The first time, I didn't know what I was doing. But after the fifth or sixth time, it started getting stale. I guess what I was saying is not that you don't get better, because I know that you do, but that at some point you start getting diminishing returns on satisfaction. Another thing that happened to me is that I started wondering whether there were other things that you could be good at, or whether you were destined to be good only at one thing and keep getting better at it. I went to law school, I think, because I knew that I could teach, that I could write academic stuff, that I could talk and do the things that I did well as a professor, but I wondered whether I could also be a good lawyer.

Romo's response indicated that he didn't understand what I was trying to say. I sensed that he thought I meant that older people somehow saw the world "more clearly," which was not what I meant at all. Rather than compare older people with younger people, I was making an "internal" comparison of individuals at different points in their life cycles. This is silly to have to say, but older people are different from younger people because they have been young whereas young people have not been older. As a result, the older you are, the more complete your perspective is, at least potentially.

"*Queso*: Smile and Look into the Camera"

The Saturday workshop was good, however. Everyone seemed to get really comfortable with everyone else. It was a more relaxed atmosphere than the fall workshop. Each of us took turns role-playing: you play the role of someone you are likely to encounter in your placement, and another student plays your role as the student in the placement. The ostensible purpose of the exercise was to get you to identify with the people in your placement and to anticipate how they might respond to you. But I thought that perhaps the unstated purpose was to break the ice and get you used to performing in front of the camera with your classmates, since all of our role-plays and skits were videotaped. I think Romo was too smart to not realize that this is the real function of these sessions.

The students in the class are in various placements: Housing, Redevelopment, Education, and Day Laborers. My group deals broadly with immigration and immigrants' rights, focusing on Central Americans and on issues that are especially relevant for women. The sketches were good, sometimes elaborate. A few of the scenarios centered on tenant-landlord disputes.

Since we were not able to finish all of the presentations on Saturday, we continued on the following Tuesday. The first skit, on the education placement, involved a parent who is concerned about his child's progress in school, with Betty playing the parent and Miriam, a Puerto Rican student from New York, playing the teacher. The skit was good. Miriam reminded me of many teachers I have encountered over the years. Although they appear to be concerned, supportive, and interested in the "welfare" of the child, regardless of what happens, the parent or child is always at fault. Miriam said afterward that a lot of children are labeled "behavioral problems." The teacher tells the mother that she should "talk" to the child more about fighting with other kids and disrupting class.

Miguel, one of the Chicano students, talked about a little Mexican boy who was disruptive during a class he visited. He noticed that when the teacher involved the class in a discussion the kid became excited but that the teacher never called on him. He wondered whether the boy was just looking for attention and whether his behavior would have improved if she had gotten him more involved.

I mentioned that this had happened to me at Stanford. Without identifying the person by name, I said I had a professor who would not call on me. I once kept my hand up to see how long she would ignore me, and she went on for what seemed like an eternity. Also, when I made comments, she responded very negatively. She once told me in front of the class, "Well Alfredo, in this country, we do things this way." Everyone wanted to know who the professor was. They couldn't believe that something like that could happen at Stanford. I had the sense that some people wanted to minimize the racial elements in my example. Juliet said, "Oh, that happens to women too." Another white woman, Marge, said, "It's hard to call on everyone." I pointed out research conducted by the U.S. Civil Rights Commission concluded that teachers are more likely to call on white students than Chicanos and more likely to compliment whites for their contributions. Of course, Juliet was right that silencing of women exists in the classroom.[6]

Leo was working with the Day Laborer group, under the supervision of Jessie, one of the two third-year students I got to know during my first year. Jessie was no longer a Three L. He had graduated the previous year and was awarded a fellowship to organize day laborers in the Bay Area. The other students in the placement, in addition to Leo, were Patricia (Patti), the Chicana from Texas, and Berta, who was from Puerto Rico. Jessie and Berta were bilingual and were good friends. Leo and Patti did not speak much

Spanish. Miriam, the *nuyorican* in the education placement, also did not speak Spanish. Because Leo was self-conscious about his Spanish, his skit focused on the problems faced by Latinos who have limited Spanish-speaking ability. Leo did a dry run of his presentation in Spanish with Miguel, who was playing Jessie as field supervisor for the day laborer group. The skit was very funny. Leo was really trying to speak in Spanish, and Miguel kept correcting him and ridiculing his Spanish. Miguel was very insensitive in the role of supervisor. He was great.

Berta had taken the class the previous year with Jessie. She had a dominant, outspoken personality. During the discussion, she mentioned that she is irritated when she sees mistakes, especially in written Spanish. Romo brought up Jessie's buddy, Ricardo, who had also been in the class the previous year in the Housing placement and had endeared himself to the people at the Mead Apartments because he plowed along in his Spanish.

I mentioned that we should see language ability as a continuum. Some are better than others, but no one is perfect, and each of us was trying to improve. When I go to Mexico, people correct me in a very matter-of-fact way, without ridicule. Romo agreed and said, "Even in English people make mistakes, so why not in Spanish?"

The last part of the class was a discussion of "spontaneity" and "planning." Romo said that no matter how spontaneous you want to appear, if you are going to be good at what you do, you have to plan and practice. He used the example of a jazz musician, but Miguel, who is a musician, disagreed. However, Romo made a good point. If it's all spontaneity, why do you have to learn to play an instrument before you can be spontaneous? Miguel didn't have an answer. I felt they were both right but did not have a chance to comment.[7]

Reflections on the Lay Lawyering Class

Two weeks into the second semester I was not feeling good about the Lay Lawyering class.[8] It started with the class discussion on January 28. Romo began by noting that it was important to do the reading and come prepared to discuss. For each class period one of us would lead the discussion. But leading the class did not mean criticizing the presenter.

The Housing group (Juliet, Marge) was to work with the housing attorney, Virginia, and present a series of workshops on landlord/tenant problems. The goal of the project was to prepare tenants to file a petition with the EPA Rent

Control Board. Juliet pointed out that there was room for refining our skills, since workshops demonstrate how to deal with groups with common problems and to develop lay advocates. Marge mentioned there would be an advantage to doing workshops at the Law Project, as opposed to the previous year, when the group worked with a single apartment complex.

The previous year I had served as the interpreter for Ricardo and the other students in the placement who worked at the Mead Apartments. I asked, doesn't the answer as to whether one way or the other of doing it was "better" depend on your goals? If your goal is simply to transmit information, what you are doing is better, but if your goal is to train community leaders to deal with a broad range of problems that might arise in the future, working in the apartment complex might be better. Evading the question, members of the Housing group went on to talk about the goals of the project: to give information and to create a group of people who can spread the word to improve awareness. They were targeting all tenants. Rudy, an Indian student, mentioned that his Education group was doing something parallel to the Housing group.

I asked whether both groups weren't inadvertently defining what's important for people. This was like raising a red flag. Many hands were raised. As the discussion unfolded, all of the focus turned toward me rather than Romo. People were asking me to call on them, even though I was not the teacher or the designated discussion leader that day. I felt like a teacher again. There was excitement in the air. Betty in particular seemed very emotional. It seemed as though the class was divided—me versus the students in Education and Housing, defending their placement and supervisors.

Romo talked about the value of the knowledge that you have as an attorney or a law student. How do you value what you know without overvaluing it or undervaluing the knowledge that clients have? Romo reinforced the point that over time lawyers develop a sense of the needs that people have. Thus it might appear that they are imposing their views when they are not.

I sensed that everyone had gotten very defensive as a result of my questions and felt compelled to comment, even though they went on to another subject. After the break I asked Romo whether I could editorialize for a minute, and he nodded his head. I said, somewhat apologetically:

This is not directed at you, Rick, but at the class as a whole. When I ask questions, I am trying to do what you said we should try to do. I remember that the first day of class you told us that you wanted us to come in here prepared and that you wanted us to question and to challenge ideas. I did that. I'm looking at issues, but I felt that people responded as though I was attacking them personally. If they are going to respond that way, then I'm probably not going to say anything.

I was upset and there was tension in the air. It was like the encounter with Lizza in the Lawyering Process class a year earlier. I spoke with passion and with conviction, not worrying about the response. Several people were put on the defensive and had to justify their placement. Rudy and Miriam mentioned that in the Education group, Bob had already decided that he was going to have a group that would center on special education. So they did not have a choice on the matter.

I don't know whether he was referring to my comment, but Romo returned to the earlier discussion and asked, "How much are you willing to go off the track?" It's a general problem of teaching. It depends on what your goal is. Is the goal to transmit information or to get people involved in the process? This is always a problem in teaching a doctrinal course in law. What do you do with questions that are out of line or with a strong comment? During my first year, I felt that my questions were almost always off line, or were they really on line? What is a strong comment? I wasn't sure.

Though we went on to talk about other issues after I made my comments, the tension remained. I didn't know how other people felt, but I was no longer comfortable speaking up. I had done what Romo had asked, and people couldn't handle it. I also felt badly because there was a point when all of the comments were being directed at me and Romo was no longer mediating.

I saw Rick later and told him that I was disappointed with the class response. I also apologized and told him to tell me if I was overstepping my limits as a student. He smiled, shook his head, and told me not to worry. He welcomed my comments and liked the discussion.

Non-Regnant Hierarchies

Despite the inevitable conflicts, the LSC classes were a welcome and essential escape from the rest of the law school. The classes were the way I had expected law school to be—exciting, challenging, creative, and intellectually stimulating. Classes were limited to about twelve students. The LSC drew not only some of the best students in the law school but also those who were generally disaffected with the traditional curriculum and traditional lawyer-ing. For me, and probably for most of us, the LSC made the Stanford experi-ence tolerable if not enjoyable. In fact, in my second and third years, as I got involved in various placements, in writing field reports, and in preparing papers, I began to feel largely disconnected from the rest of the law school.

At the same time, though I genuinely liked and enjoyed the people in the class, I realized that if it weren't for law school I would have had little in common with them. We bonded not because we were similar but because we were different. What brought us together was our disaffection with the law school. Because we had so little in common in other respects, I could not communicate with the students in the LSC. I mean really talk, like I talked to my brothers or my close friends. In the end, I didn't have much in com-mon with the Anglo woman whose father was a lawyer and who would prob-ably be working for a large firm some day; the *puertoriqueña* from the elite family in Puerto Rico; the assimilated Latina who did not speak Spanish and seemed alienated from what she termed "Mexican culture." Her discussion of "Mexicans" reminded me of *Tía* Tere because it sounded like she wasn't one even though she looked like one.

As the semester progressed I also came to the realization that there were hierarchies even in the LSC. They were not institutionalized as they were in the law review. In the LSC they revolved around things like who had taken more classes in the curriculum or who had worked on more projects at the Law Project or who was in charge of more clinics. Some of the people in the class were in charge of student-run clinics; others served on the board of directors at the Law Project.

In the fall semester I had noticed that during Romo's Community Law Practice class, which was held at the Law Project, Berta would make an-nouncements or chastise us about one thing or another. Once she told us not to schedule our office hours on Mondays because that was a very busy day at the Law Project. I didn't say anything, but I resented her assumption of this role. My response was something like, "Wait a minute, she may be a third-year, but she's a student just like me. Where does she get off giving us orders? I'll make my office hours when it's convenient for me and my super-visor." Berta continued to lecture us, especially the Latino men in the class (there were four of us), and I continued to ignore her. As an aside, I should note that for some unknown reason, Berta and I conflicted from the start. Miguel commented on this several times. He liked both of us and did not understand why there was so much friction between us. I remember that I got off to a bad start. On the first day of the Subordination class in the fall, I had inadvertently called her "Bertha." She immediately scolded me: "The name *en español* is B-E-R-T-A, *not* Bertha!"

One of the things that really bothered me about the class was what I call, for lack of a better term the "*chingón*"[9] or, in Berta's case, the "*chingona* syndrome." This was a disease peculiar to third-year law students in the LSC curriculum. These students were LSC junkies. They took every class and clinic that was offered, worked in every possible capacity at the Law Project, were officers in the Stanford Public Interest Law Foundation, and even took the Lay Lawyering placement a second time. Jane was the exception, I thought. She didn't have the disease, but Berta and Jessie had a bad case of it. Berta was taking the class for the second time, and although Jessie was now a supervisor, this would be his third time around. That people wanted to take the class again was a tribute to Romo, but it created problems. One problem that I have already alluded to is that there was discontinuity of experience. The "repeating" students attended only the field placement segment of the class and did not do the readings or participate in the more theoretical discussions. A more serious problem was that because the repeaters had dealt with the issues in the past, there was a tendency for them to think that they had already resolved the questions. I found it interesting that much of the conflict in the class was with the Day Laborer group, specifically, with Jessie and Berta. This surprised me because before the class, I hardly knew Berta and I liked and respected Jessie.

Another form of competition among the students was their relationship with Romo. I learned that some students had a key to his office, but I assumed it was because they were working on research projects with him. But I remember having a conversation with Leo, who did not have a key, in which he mentioned that having a key to the office was a sign that you had really arrived. I guess it was like having a key to the executive bathroom in corporate firms.

I felt that there was a lot of resentment toward me, which I could not understand at first, especially since I didn't have a key. One possibility was that the resentment was generated by my outspokenness and strong opinions. Another possibility is that people resented the fact that I was older, that I had a Ph.D., and that I had been a professor. Perhaps they felt that I had an unfair advantage in the competition. I think the resentment may have had something to do with my relationship with Romo. My view is that Rick treated people fairly and that he treated them according to who they were.

He didn't treat me like a twenty-five-year-old because I wasn't twenty-five. I think he treated me like he would have treated anyone else with my background and experience, as he treated others according to their background and experience, but no one had my background and experience. I noticed that he also treated Peter with deference and respect. He treated me differently but not necessarily better.

From the minute I arrived at the law school, I experienced what sociologists have termed status incongruence. During the first year, the students in Lee's class, including Berta and Jessie, were reading a piece I had written. This caused some interest and commotion when Lee announced that one of the authors of the readings was a One L. Jessie and Ricardo were ostensibly my mentors but they were much younger than I was. On a couple of occasions Jessie commented that it felt strange to be my mentor or give me advice. During Lawyering Process, Lee also recognized my background and would sometimes draw on my specialized knowledge of sociology or race and ethnic theory.

What I am saying is that in part, the resentment may have come from my breaking or inadvertently challenging the hierarchies. In Romo's class, I was a Two L who was treated with considerable deference and respect, as much or more than most of the Three Ls. I wouldn't say that I was closer to Romo than the other students. In fact, I always had a difficult time catching him or getting an appointment. But in class he always treated me with respect and sometimes drew on my expertise. Despite the conflicts and tension, as I look back on the experience, I have fond memories of the LSC, Romo, and my fellow students, particularly Jane, Miguel, Jessie, and Berta. Romo's class was a genuine learning and growing experience. We did important group work and had stimulating discussions.

But something had changed fundamentally. In the field reports Romo required, I was now "Alfredo," a character in a complicated play about life, death, identity, and law school. He was an old, angry Mexican who drove an old Chevy Caprice called the Alfredomobile. He was alienated from almost everything and everyone and occasionally blew up in class. He was no longer the vibrant, affable, charming man who started law school with anticipation, excitement, and enthusiasm. Alfredo's eyesight was failing from reading and working on the computer. He had gotten heavier, grayer, more wrinkled, and was even becoming stoop-shouldered. Like Anita, *la Tuerta*, he was hunched over all the time and appeared to be getting shorter with each day. *Pobrecito!* And there was no *té en la mañana* to invigorate him.

CHAPTER EIGHT

Sex, Flies, and Videotapes

La Noche Buena

I have fond childhood memories of Christmas Eve, *la Noche Buena* (the Good Night), but what I remember most vividly is not the presents, snow, sleighs, or reindeer. What I remember most is the food. In my family, as in other Mexican families, the tradition was to have a huge feast or dinner on Christmas Eve. My great-grandmother Mamá Mela and my grandmother Ana María were excellent cooks. My mother, Rosa María, was also a fine cook, and as I learned, her *suegra* (mother-in-law), Ana María, had taught her to cook. They cooked wonderful food every day. But this evening was special. For Christmas Eve they prepared a meal to end all meals, things that we did not normally eat. There was Mamá Mela's *salpicón*, shredded meat and avocado prepared in a delicious marinated sauce; crisp, golden *tacos de picadillo* made with minced meat and raisins; *chiles adobados*; *tortas de elote*; and the main dish, *mole poblano*. Yet what I remember most are the traditional *tamales* with *atole*. There was a wide assortment of *tamales*: red meat, green meat, and sweet raisin. The *atole* is a thick drink, like chocolate, that comes in various flavors and is made from corn meal. The desserts included *arroz de leche* and flan.

Now it is early in December of my second year at law school, and my daughter Lucía and I are attending Rick Romo's traditional end-of-the-semester party in San Francisco. It is not *la Noche Buena,* but it is the beginning of the holiday season, and the food and good company bring back childhood memories. It's like a *posada,* except for the *piñata.*

Everyone attended Romo's Christmas party, it seemed. He was careful to schedule the party on a day when we were all available—students and attorneys at the Law Project, as well as family and friends. Cristina, my ex-student, had told me that Romo held great parties at the end of each class and that he was the only law professor to invite students to his home.

The Placement

Jane Carter and I were assigned to work under the supervision of Cathy Bates, a Stanford Law School graduate who worked at the Auxilio Immigration Clinic in San Francisco. We would also work closely with the Mujeres group. Rick felt that Jane and I would make a good team. She was thorough and had good organizational skills but was reluctant to be in the placement because she did not speak Spanish. I spoke Spanish and had experience working with the Latino community. Jane was a single mother and did not want to spend a lot of time commuting into the city, where the project would be implemented. We would commute at least once a week and would alternate driving.

The major goal of the project was to "sensitize" legal service providers to the unique needs of Latino immigrants and to the importance of coordinating with other services and making referrals. We would focus on Latino immigrants who have been in the United States for less than five years, emphasizing issues of particular concern to women such as domestic violence, children, and child care.[1] We would first consult with local grassroots organizations, service providers that deal with new immigrants, and recent immigrants themselves. We would then talk to target organizations about the services they provide, current systems of referral, and their views on improving services to recent immigrants. Finally, we would conduct interactive workshops to share our ideas.

As I look back on the experience, perhaps what is most surprising is not that conflict occurred but that we were unprepared to deal with it.

In the Lawyering for Social Change curriculum we read student papers from previous classes. I benefited most from those that openly addressed internal conflicts, problems, frustrations, and failures.[2] Here I choose to focus on the conflicts that arose among us in the field placement; conflict is an important and necessary aspect of group work, and the differences cannot be dismissed as individual, idiosyncratic, or personality quirks. The three of us in the group genuinely liked each other as individuals. But our differences were structural and extended well beyond the confines of this particular placement. My intent here is to focus on the larger issues and questions that are suggested by our differences.

In our planning sessions, we decided to develop a role-play to use as an example of a service provider who was insensitive to the unique needs of a recent Latina immigrant and to present it to the class.[3] Cathy would play a *salvadoreña*, María, who comes to the Milagro Refugee Center seeking information on asylum. "María" is a single parent, undocumented, and unemployed. I played the polite but insensitive Latino legal service provider, Rodrigo Crenshaw Gil. In the role-play, we asked the class to be the staff at Latino Legal Services, an agency that we would be working with. We explained that we would go through the role-play once. Then, without commentary, we would start again and stop at key intervals to ask for comments and for volunteers to show us how they would change my part. We went into class with a lot of enthusiasm, having written out the script and practiced it several times. I was beginning to ponder the possibility of a career as a playwright. Cathy was clearly a frustrated actress waiting to be discovered. Jane would direct, of course. Our dreams were shattered by the class response.

As we debriefed, we agreed that the class discussion had been very negative. If this were Broadway and our classmates critics, the curtain would not have risen the next day. The Day Laborers group, particularly Berta and Jessie, were especially vocal in their criticism. The thrust of their criticism was that my legal service intake worker was too much of a caricature. No one could be that insensitive. Leo felt that Latino service providers might be insulted at being depicted that way.

As the three of us walked toward the Student Union Cafeteria, we wondered what had gone wrong. There seemed to be three possible answers: (1) Our skit stunk, and we did a poor job of framing the issues; (2) the class focused on the substance of the presentation and missed the key critical issues, which were implicit in the skit; and (3) some of the class members responded negatively toward us rather than to the substance of the skit.

Jane and Cathy agreed that the class response was one-sided, harsh, and perhaps unfair, but that it was done in good faith. They also thought the discussion would be useful for revising our presentation. I was less positive. I came away from the class with a bad taste in my mouth and with the feeling that some people were not playing with a full deck. What bothered me most is that the other groups were not asking themselves the same hard questions that they were asking us. I wondered whether the people who were most vocal in their criticism, the Day Laborer group, really understood the purpose of the skit and the placement. When Berta got up to role-play she focused largely on being nicer and providing more information about amnesty. This was good. But our skit was not about amnesty. It was about cultural and gender insensitivity.

Part of the problem was that our project was unique. The other groups in the class were focusing on "know your rights" workshops.[4] This was certainly true of the Day Laborers, Housing, and Education groups. Our focus was on improving the quality of legal services for recent Latino immigrants. In our discussion we commented that many of the class members did not seem to understand the project. We could understand that, but we could not understand why they were so negative. Was it that people were negative toward things they didn't understand? Was it that they didn't think it was important? Was it fluff? Did they see it as too far removed from clients and client services? There was something in the class dynamics that we did not understand, and that I, at least, did not like.

Jane confided, "Perhaps because Alfredo was a professor or because he has strong opinions on a lot of things, that this is part of the reason that he is being targeted." There might be something to this theory, but it broke down when you considered that there were other people in the class who were vocal and who had strong opinions and the same kind of negative energy did not seem to be directed at them. We came away thinking that we needed time to let everything sink in before we made any decisions.

A Crack in the Armor

On Tuesday, March 16, our group met to fine-tune our presentation, not realizing that this would prove the most significant meeting of the semester. It was only after this meeting that we put aside the veneer of consensus and began to speak with our own voices. Jane fired the first volley in her field report. She said we had developed a good working relationship. Although we had "developed a high degree of respect for each other" and "considered each other friends," she became uncomfortable during one of the meetings when I suggested that she do the introduction to the role-play. She stated in her field report:

> In the meeting Alfredo first suggested that Cathy could do the intro-
> duction, then he said that no, maybe I should because even though I
> was nervous it would be a challenge. Because I respect Alfredo, I took
> both comments very seriously. I also was seriously offended, first be-
> cause I thought that there was an implied criticism and second be-
> cause I didn't want him to decide what was good for me. If I didn't like
> him, I think I would have perhaps had the same feelings, but would
> have quickly thought, "Well, fuck you," and dismissed the thing. In-
> stead I couldn't get a handle on what I thought about it and being
> angry was very uncomfortable. I think Alfredo had similar feelings
> about changing the role-play, but of course, I can't be sure.[5]
>
> At the time, there seemed to be no way to resolve the situation
> then. Instead we decided to take some time to cool off and think about
> it. After just being pissed off, and then getting some space, Alfredo
> and I were able to talk about the interaction that night. I explained
> what my reaction was, and that it may not even have been entirely re-
> lated to our group work because the class had raised questions about
> people being uncomfortable talking in groups. He assured me that
> there was not an implied criticism and that he did not share my con-
> cerns about my presentation. In addition, we talked about how his
> disagreements about the class criticisms of the role-play left him unen-
> thusiastic about changing the role-play. So in the end, we were able to
> get back on track relatively quickly, but not painlessly.

I was initially surprised and disappointed by Jane's response. But after I recovered, I actually felt relieved—like a weight had been lifted from my shoulders. I welcomed the opportunity not only to respond but also to vent my own frustration. My response came in the next field report.[6] It is summa-rized here. For me, the important issue was not whether I criticized her but her response to the perceived criticism. Let's assume that I did criticize her.

Why, then, did she respond so negatively? Surely I am not the first person to criticize her, nor am I the first person to criticize her whom she liked. A troubling implication of her position is that people who like and respect one another typically are not, or should not be, critical of each other. Cathy's response to my not so implied criticism of the placement was similar to Jane's, and more intense.

I noted in the field report that my cultural and familial experience was different. I expect, welcome, and sometimes even demand criticism from people whom I like and respect. What matters is not that we disagree but that they have my best interests at heart. Although I was careful to emphasize that my comments were not intended as a personal criticism of Jane and Cathy but as a self-criticism for not standing up for my principles, Cathy's response was both negative and direct.

I don't know how we learn to cope with criticism, but I suspect that, like many things, it begins in the family and is linked to culture, class, and gender. I know very little about Jane's family, except that she is from Arizona and her father is a minister, and even less about Cathy's. But in my family, conflict was and continues to be a way of life. During my childhood, there was a lot of overt conflict. As I've noted, my dad was the prototypical, authoritarian father figure and a strong disciplinarian.

I have also noted that my father was violent with his sons. He beat us with his belt or open hand, rather than his fists, and he hit us in the back or buttocks. He drew blood and left scars. But I do not hate my father, harbor resentment toward him, or feel that we were abused, although we were probably neglected. I think he believed that using corporal punishment was the right way to discipline one's sons.

My father never hit my mother, and he taught us that hitting a woman was one of the lowest things a man could do. If he had had a daughter, I am certain that he would never have hit her, but he would have scolded and punished her. He probably would have made her write "I promise not to misbehave" twenty thousand times, instead of ten thousand, as we had to. What is interesting is that he liked and was drawn to strong women, like my mother.[7]

I took a child abuse class in law school. There were twelve women and six men in the class. During a number of class discussions, some of the Asian and Latino students revealed that they had experiences that were similar to mine. It seems clear that there were class and cultural differences in the conceptions and perceptions of abuse. A Korean woman said her family had a "hitting stick" made of bamboo and that she and her siblings had to get the stick from the corner so that they could be beaten when they misbehaved. The white students were appalled and felt that parents who physically abused children should be put in jail. However, during discussions later in the semester, these same students would be much more tolerant of sexual abuse. This seemed very strange to me. I could understand corporal punishment, though I did not approve of it. But I neither understood nor tolerated sexual abuse of children. For me, it was the worst thing that a parent could do.

Despite his violent temper, my dad wasn't all bad. He had a lot of self-respect and dignity and was proud to be a Mirandé. There were very few of us, so it wasn't like being a García, González, or Martínez. My brothers and I were taught, essentially, that we had a special advantage over folks who were not Mirandés. *Los tres mosqueteros* lived by the slogan, "Uno para todos, y todos para uno" (One for all, and all for one). Most significantly, he taught us to have dignity, self-respect, and to stand up for our beliefs. My father was not very successful, however, and had difficulty implementing his ideals. Because of a bad temper and a lack of education and discipline, he was always quitting or getting fired from jobs. He lost a lot of jobs, but he never lost his self-respect.

The point of this digression is that I have always been around conflict and violence. My older brothers were very close, but they fought like crazy. I don't understand how one could think that we shouldn't criticize or be criticized by people we like or love. Alex, the eldest, always won and would usually inflict a black eye or bloody nose on Héctor. What was interesting is that Héctor would protect him from my dad and make up a story: he fell down the stairs or got hit by a baseball. Alex used to discipline me and sometimes hit me on the top of the head with the tip of his knuckles (it hurt like hell). Even as adults we got into violent arguments and sometimes seemed on the verge of coming to blows. Beyond the violence, there is a lot of intensity and passion in my family. We would argue, fight, criticize, get *sentido* (hurt). But we would ultimately apologize and give an *abrazo* (hug), and we always knew that we were hard on one another precisely because we cared.

I can't generalize about other cultures, but I think age is important in Mexican culture. In our *cultura*, age has its privileges, and in my family, regardless of my educational or professional accomplishments, I was always the kid brother. Because they were older, my brothers did not hesitate to guide, advise, or reprimand me. They saw this as a responsibility. They believed they would always have to look after me.[8]

Underestimating Clients

One of the recurrent themes in the Lay Lawyering class, and the placement, was concern with over- or underestimating clients. Although we sometimes idealize clients and assume that they can do more than they are equipped to do, or that they can do no wrong, underestimating appears to be a more common problem. Leo mentioned several times in class that he found himself being surprised by what the day laborers were able to do for themselves. He was concerned because he assumed that the fact that he was surprised meant he was underestimating them.[9] I commented that I was always surprising myself and underestimating my own abilities. I asked, "If we don't have a good sense of our own capabilities, why should we expect to have a good sense of the capabilities of others?" There was no response.

Overall, I felt that all of the groups in the class tended to underestimate clients and to focus more on transferring information than on empowerment. Greg, for example, was self-consciously critical of his group and said that they had a preconceived plan to bring a bank to East Palo Alto, and though they pretended they were only providing technical services to the community, they did things to legitimate those community members who agreed with their views.[10] Rudy felt that in the Education group, because the "parents were always ahead of them," they were able to compress four or five workshops into one.[11]

But the Day Laborer group may have been the worst offender. They appeared to have a predetermined agenda to do "Wage and Hour" workshops and had a difficult time incorporating the emergent day laborer organization into the placement. They were unprepared to deal with the steering committee that emerged and did not know what to do when the issue of picketing a chiropractor near the work site came up. I think the chiropractor may have called INS and complained about the workers hanging around the parking lot. The group did not know whether to try to "organize" the day laborers. When I asked what the goal of the group was, Jessie smiled, looked at Berta, and said, "Oops, wrong question," and then, avoiding the question, responded, "Have you read our curricular plan [laughter]? We are not really sure!"[12] This flippant response made me feel that Jessie was underestimating the people in our class, or at least underestimating me. Instead of giving me a straight answer, like Professor Morton did, he tried to put me on the defensive. I had read their curricular plan. And I reread it after class. The goals of the group were not in the plan and remained unclear.

The issue surfaced at one of our workshops, although in different forms. There were several blatant examples of underestimating clients. One occurred at the workshop at the Bay Area Immigration Center with a staff person, Beverly, who looked white but presented herself as a strong advocate for *la gente* (the people). Beverly saw clients as essentially incapable of doing much of anything for themselves. Her clients "could not be expected to do things on their own because they couldn't read, write, or speak English and because they were unfamiliar with U.S. institutions."[13] When another staff person, Sharon, pointed out that she had worked with a Redwood City man who was able to do things for himself, Beverly responded, "Sure there were some, but not many who could gather this type of information."[14]

At San Francisco Legal Aid (SFLA), we encountered an Asian paralegal, Jackson Wong, who felt that because of his "special training" he had very specific questions and information that had to be "extracted" from clients. It did not seem that he expected clients to do much for themselves. In contrast to the Immigration Center or SFLA, one of the richest and most extensive discussions of client empowerment occurred at Latino Legal Services. When we asked how we could determine how much a client should do, Marisela, the director, said it depended on the client and the confidence you had in the client's abilities. She emphasized that it was important for clients to tell their stories in court in a clear, simple, convincing way. Another staff member, Mercedes, agreed but added, "Some people are illiterate. You have to make a judgment on what they can do. For some people, you know they're going to get eaten up."[15] But Rosario, a young paralegal, cautioned against underestimating clients: "I know when I was working, referring people to Small Claims Court, people expected you to do everything. When they went to court and were on their own, they were really empowered. Every single one of them. They weren't aware of their capabilities."[16]

In the Watsonville farmworker project described in a paper written by students in a previous class, Vanessa, a working-class Chicana who had been able to attain upward mobility and to attend Stanford, found it difficult to accept the idea that Chicano parents and students should set more "realistic" goals and expectations, that is, that they should not have high aspirations. The other students in the placement, Jay and Bob, and the supervisor in particular, cautioned against having the parents and the students aim too high lest they be disappointed and disillusioned. When they discussed taking the students on a field trip, Jay and Bob favored visiting a state college, a community college, or a technical school rather than a prestigious school such as Stanford.

The issue of underestimating clients was more covert in our placement and more difficult to unpack. Though the primary objective was to sensitize legal service providers to the needs of recent immigrants, I think there is a sense in which we underestimated the latter. We started the semester with a client focus and with the idea of working very closely with the Mujeres grassroots organization. However, as the project unfolded, we became more oriented to serving the legal service providers. Our mission initially was to consult with grassroots community groups and assess the needs of recent immigrants, but we only talked to two members of Mujeres, a nonlegal service provider, Dora Ramírez, and a client, Hilda Muñoz. And when I suggested using one of the Mujeres or Hilda in the role-play, the response was that it wouldn't be a good idea because it would "change the dynamics of the group."[17] That we were so uncritically positive in our evaluation of the Immigrant Legal Resource Center (ILRC) Workshop, I believe, also reflects a legal service provider bias. There is a sense in which ILRC is a legal service provider for legal service providers.

We underestimate clients when we preclude the possibility of direct dialogue between the clients and providers out of fear of offending providers. We underestimate clients when we choose to speak on their behalf rather than allow them to speak for themselves. We underestimate clients when we devalue their language and culture. We underestimate clients when we are unwilling to subordinate our needs to theirs. It was ridiculous that our meeting at Latino Legal Services was conducted primarily in English; they deal almost exclusively with Spanish-speaking clients, and their daily work is conducted in Spanish.[18]

Dynamics of Race and Gender

I agree with law professor Gerald López who argues that we should focus less on ethnicity and talk more openly about race.[19] We seldom talked about race or gender and the impact each might have on the dynamics in the placement. From the beginning, I think, Jane and perhaps to a lesser extent

Cathy were aware of the racial dynamics in the group, but they never talked about them. Jane knew that if the issue arose she would be an outsider not only because she did not speak or understand Spanish but because she was not Latina. Cathy's Spanish is quite good, but she too is not Latina. Any non-Latina working in a Latina organization has to be somewhat aware of her outsider status. Cathy confided that she has had conflicts with some of the Latino men at Auxilio who were sexist. What is interesting is that she presented this as an issue of gender rather than race.

Because Cathy works in the Latino community and is accepted and re-spected, she is what sociologists term an "outsider-insider."[20] As a Latino from Stanford, I, on the other hand, could be characterized as an insider-outsider. It is also worth noting that all Latinos are not the same. For exam-ple, I was very conscious of the fact that I am not Central American and have had no experience working with Central Americans.

The interpersonal dynamics in the placement were further complicated by the intersection of race, class, and gender. I think what Jane and Cathy failed to consider is that they are women and that in the placement we es-sentially worked with women. Not only the Mujeres, but the majority of the legal service providers we worked with were women. From the start, I was aware of my outsider status as a man. I knew that the Mujeres started out with a focus on domestic violence and that many of the problems experi-enced by recent Latina immigrants are directly and indirectly linked to *machismo* and male dominance. I also knew that there was a sense in which I symbolized the problem. Unlike "Rodrigo," I was very much aware of my "masculine privilege." After the workshop at SFLA, one of the young women took me aside and told me that my contemptuousness in the role was ex-tremely convincing. She smiled and said she "hated me," the way you despise a classic villain in a movie. I twisted the end of my mustache, smiled cyni-cally, and told her I was a natural for the part.

On the micro level, gender dynamics played an important part in our group. There was some hint of it in our initial meetings with Cathy, but I first became fully conscious of it in our session with one of the legal service providers, Kim Karnes. I was amazed by the rapport Kim and Jane estab-lished, and I commented on it to Jane. In retrospect, however, it is clear that Jane and Cathy shared a similar rapport. I know that they talked indepen-dently of our meetings, whereas I never talked to Cathy outside of our regular meetings. Sometimes they stayed after the meeting to talk, or Jane would confide that she had talked to Cathy the night before. Cathy never called me or talked to me unless I initiated it. I am not suggesting that there was anything wrong or sinister in this. What I am suggesting is that the gender bonding had direct and indirect effects on the placement. More often than not, Cathy and Jane agreed. Thus, although our meetings were open and democratic, I was often literally odd man out, and was generally outvoted. After a while, I stopped making suggestions or disagreeing because I felt that they would do what they would do, regardless of what I might have said. We were able to maintain an air of civility to the end, and Cathy even suggested that we all go bowling with one of the attorneys at the Law Project and a good friend of Cathy's on the last day of class. I could be polite and cordial at lunch after the last class, but I could not muster up much enthusiasm for bowling. I declined and said I had to begin work on the paper for the class.

Although important, gender bonding may not transcend race. I bonded well with Rudy Torrez, the head of SFLA and the only Latino man we had contact with, except for Steve, a paralegal at Latino Legal Services, but Rudy also related well to Jane and to Cathy and did not ignore them in the same way that I felt Kim ignored me. I submit that the gender bonding that occurred was racially specific: white on white, brown on brown. I related well to Rudy but also felt a lot of warmth from the Mujeres group and the *mujeres* at Latino Legal Services. I certainly felt no special bond with the other men we had contact with—the Anglo at SFLA, Jackson Wong, or the director of the Immigration Center. Jane similarly did not seem to establish any special rapport with Latinas or with Asian women in our placement the way that she did with Cathy, Kim, and other white women. She essentially bonded with white women, whereas I bonded with Latino men and women.[21] A number of Latina and African American feminist scholars have noted that there is a closer bond between men and women of color than there is between white men and white women.[22]

On one of our trips to San Francisco, Jane commented that it was interesting to observe Latino men interacting with one another. She said there was an incredible amount of warmth and affection that was shared. When she saw Rudy and me bonding, it reminded her of the way I had related to her friend Roberto, a graduate student at Berkeley who occasionally joined us on the drive to San Francisco.

There is a great deal of empathy and a storytelling mode in interactions among Latinos. We bond through language, and code switching (going back and forth from English to Spanish) and by reference to people and common experiences. Significantly, the bonding with Rudy was not about law or enhancing services but about people we both knew. We tried to "translate" these experiences for Jane, an outsider, through storytelling. The point is that there is often a lot of warmth among Latino men, and Jane felt she did not see the same warmth among white men. (It should be noted that she is referring to Latino men who have just met, not close friends.)

Although we did not set up a formal mechanism for evaluating the workshops, we ranked them informally. Jane's and Cathy's evaluations of each of our workshops were remarkably consistent. Neither was impressed with Latino Legal Services, which was our only predominantly Latina group, whereas I felt it was our best workshop. Both were impressed with ILRC; I thought it was our worst workshop. And both were much more impressed with the Immigration Center, a predominantly white female group, than I was. I had to wonder whether racial and gender dynamics might have played a part in our evaluations.

I am not sure when we decided to videotape some of the sessions. I know that at our first meeting, when Cathy said it would be good to have a "product" from the placement, I suggested doing a videotape. It would have two functions. We could share it with legal service providers, and it might be useful for future lay lawyering classes. I also believed that the videotape would be a way of incorporating the Mujeres into the placement. The idea surfaced again during our meeting with Kim Karnes, when Jane and I joked about setting up a consulting firm after law school. We thought we might be able to make a living at it and even had a name, J and A Associates. As the workshops approached, I again suggested videotaping them. Cathy thought we might be able to videotape one workshop, and she suggested we check with Roger to see if he could schedule it. Roger was available for the dates of the Latino Legal Services or the Immigration Center workshop. We decided on Latino Legal Services because we had not gotten much cooperation from the Immigration Center and were apprehensive about that workshop. It would also enable Cathy to see how we had done, since she would not be able to attend the session. I independently arranged to tape the last workshop at SFLA.

As it turned out, I did the field reports for the two sessions that were videotaped. Both were lengthy direct transcriptions. What impressed me most is that there was very little relationship between my initial impression and the videotape. I felt good about the session at Latino Legal Services, but I also thought there were some very slow and awkward moments. I expected that Jane and I would participate equally in conducting the workshop and did not anticipate having to assume the role of facilitator. During the workshop, I had to think on my feet about the next step, so I could not analyze what was going on at the moment or take notes. By doing the transcriptions, watching the video, stopping and rewinding, I was able to appreciate the depth and nuance of the discussion.[23] The session had much more coherence and direction than I had realized.

We had gotten off to a bad start at SFLA and were running late. Traffic was heavy, and we had a hard time finding parking. The setting did not help. It was not conducive for a workshop. People were crowded into a small rectangular room with a table that was too large for the room. One of the attorneys commented that there was a lot of wasted space because the table was much larger than necessary. Lots of people were standing against the window, sitting on the floor, and squeezed together. Videotaping the event also proved awkward. We had a simple camera, and it was not possible to pan over the room. As a result, the camera focused on the end of the table where the three of us sat and the role-play took place. Finally, it was extremely hot and the office is located right above the cable cars. It was a circus down on the street, and there was a lot of noise because the windows were open. Several flies were buzzing around the room. I felt very uncomfortable. Faced with the choice of closing the windows and being very warm or being disturbed by the noise from outside and the flies, we opted for the noise and flies.

Because Jane had gone ahead while I parked the car, everyone was waiting for me when I finally arrived. I came into the room running and was very hot and sweating for the first ten or fifteen minutes. The sweat seemed to draw the flies as I kept wiping my brow and swatting them away. I had also made the mistake of wearing a dress shirt and black sports jacket. It was unusually hot for San Francisco, so hot that I wore shorts on the drive to the city and changed in the bathroom at SFLA. Rudy was wearing jeans, and most people were dressed casually. I don't know if it's my body chemistry or my cologne, but flies seemed to be especially drawn to me.

In any event, when I saw the tape my response to the workshop was much more positive than I had expected. There would always be the Jackson Wongs of the world, but there was also an excellent exchange of ideas and experiences. I felt the workshop was especially effective in raising issues of racial and cultural differences, translation, and letting clients know which services we can provide and which services we cannot.

An additional benefit of videotaping the sessions was noted by Rosario of Latino Legal Services. She said that being on camera made you examine what you do "externally" and think about how others see what you are doing. This made her realize that she should look more carefully at what she does and how the client might respond to it. I also sensed that videotaping made the participants feel that what they had to say was important and worth recording so that others might benefit from their experiences.

As I studied the videotapes, I began to wonder, how it is that we come to know the things that we think we know? We do a ninety-minute workshop, come back to law school, and return with a limited, condensed summary of what transpired. We conclude that we bombed or that we were incredible. Whether depressed or ecstatic, we repeat these initial impressions, embellish them, and reinforce our views. But how much faith do we have in these judgments? To what extent do we reinforce or reify our preconceptions? How do gender, culture, and race influence what we see or, more significantly, what we don't see? When Jane and Cathy talked about Latino Legal Services, I wondered whether we had attended the same meeting. I felt exhilarated when I left the workshop, and Roger and Jane also said it had gone well, but Jane changed her mind over the weekend. When she said the staff at Latino Legal Services were good at raising issues but not at "unpacking" them, I wondered whether this might be a case of underestimating subordinated communities. Cathy's assessment was more negative toward the workshop, even though she was not present and had fast-forwarded through most of the videotape after the session.

In the class I felt we often lacked sensitivity to gender, race, and class dynamics and tended to homogenize the Stanford experience. We seldom talked about how our race, gender, or class backgrounds might influence not only how clients saw us but how we saw ourselves and the things that we experienced. Being law students provided us with a common experience, but it did not make us the same. In the discussion of the Watsonville project, one of the students dismissed the conflict between Vanessa and her colleagues by stating that "all of us were privileged by virtue of the fact that we were at Stanford."[24] Everyone but me agreed. It reminded me of the dean's welcome address in orientation week. I was uncomfortable with the term "privilege" because it made me feel that I was getting more than I deserved. A privilege implied being granted a special right or favor. It bothered me because I thought it was a way of trying to get us to identify with other privileged folks, to separate us from our communities and our families by making us feel like we were different, smarter, or somehow better than the people we had left behind. It was ultimately a way of affirming the hierarchies as meritocratic.

THREE L

CHAPTER NINE

Guerrillas in the Mist: Reflections on the Immigration Law Clinic

Meeting My Client

The first meeting with my client took place at the Law Project at 1:00 p.m. on September 20. I had a class that ended at 12:35 and was therefore about three minutes late. I was concerned because Mark Levin,[1] the attorney supervising the case, had admonished us not to be late; it was important that we not keep the client waiting.[2] Because Mark said my client was educated and middle class and that Nicaraguans were thought to be fairly demanding, I had a definite expectation of what my client would look like. I expected a well-dressed, sophisticated, polished person. As I rushed into the waiting room at the law clinic, trying to look composed, I was met by a man dressed casually in tight jeans, a short-sleeved knit shirt, and tennis shoes. He had short hair, long sideburns, and a beard. What most impressed me was that he was sporting aviator sunglasses indoors. The net effect was that he looked very macho and quite ominous. It was not hard for me to imagine him in army fatigues, as an outcast general leading the Contra rebels, or as an underworld figure, a Mafia hit man, a Colombian drug dealer, a crooked small-town Mexican cop or politician, or one of the bad guys in the film *El Mariachi*. My client's appearance was quickly offset by his demeanor, however. He smiled, stuck out his hand, and introduced himself, Ricardo Falcón Guerra, *para servirle* (at your service).

I recalled sitting in Mark's office at our first meeting, when he had called to confirm the appointment with Mr. Falcón. As usual, Mark was jovial and quite loud, joking extensively with the client on the telephone. One of the other students commented that Mark seems to get louder when he speaks Spanish, especially when he is talking on the telephone. As I listened, I realized that it was true. He speaks with a distinct American accent but has a good command of the vocabulary necessary for communicating about a case and has great rapport with clients. Later Mark mentioned that "Ricardo" has a very good sense of humor and likes to joke around. Mark had not met with Mr. Falcón but had talked with him on the telephone several times. I did not see Mr. Falcón's sense of humor initially. He appeared serious, sincere, and pleasant. His intensity and intelligence were obvious immediately. He was not at all what I had expected.

————

In law school lore, to become a third-year law student is to achieve a state of Nirvana, a state in which you know everything and care about nothing. Three Ls are largely invisible to other students. They party a lot, drink heavily, sleep late, do not attend or are late for class, are universally cynical, and always wait until the last minute to write papers or prepare for exams.

I was not a very good Three L. I always went to class and got my papers in before the deadline and never slept in. I used the third year to take classes that seemed important, interesting, or useful and to fill gaps in my training. Immigration law was a natural area of interest for me. I had taken a number of clinical courses, but most of the work was simulated or involved helping clients with problems with their landlords or finding placements in private schools at school district expense for East Palo Alto African American and Latino students with learning disabilities. It wasn't direct trial experience and I wanted to be a trial lawyer. The immigration clinic gave a student the opportunity to represent a real client in an immigration hearing. I looked forward to the class and to the experience because I felt it would fill an important void.

Professor Lee taught the class. I still had painful memories of feeling silenced in Lawyering Process, but I did not have negative feelings toward the professor. I took the Immigration Clinic and Immigration Policy class because I felt that Lee was an expert in this area and I could learn something of value. I tried to put the negative experience in Lawyering Process behind me.

During the first class meeting, Mark Levin gave a brief summary of my case. He mentioned that Nicaraguans in general, my client in particular, seem to have higher expectations of legal service providers. I wasn't sure what he meant by this but wondered if it was a class more than nationality thing. I feared that he would want to develop a traditional attorney-client relationship. Although we had not discussed this in the clinic, I took it as a given that we would be attempting to implement a progressive model of lawyering, the foundation of the clinical curriculum at the law school.

Progressive lawyering generally focuses on breaking down the barriers that lawyers establish between themselves and clients, yet clients also buy into the hierarchy. I recall that in the Lawyering Process class we talked about black or Mexican clients who sometimes preferred a white lawyer because they assumed that she was a "regular" lawyer and more competent. The professor related his experience as a young legal service attorney in a Chinatown clinic. Much to his dismay, the little old Chinese ladies "loved" the Anglo lawyer even though he was unkempt, wore sandals, and put his feet on the desk, and was certainly not more qualified than Lee.

The next area of concern was my client's politics. I worried that I might have a conflict of interest if I were placed in the situation of having to represent a client who had a political cause that was different from, or worse, at odds with my own. Professor Lee brought up this topic at the start of our second meeting of the Immigration Clinic. He mentioned that he had represented Christopher McFarland, an IRA member accused of terrorist activities. He had also represented Carlos Muñoz, a Salvadoran rebel suspected of torturing government soldiers, a case decided on fairly narrow grounds.[3] If you believe that the Nicaraguan military is committing atrocities, he asked, are you going to be more skeptical of a client who himself may have persecuted others?

I could not see myself representing a counterrevolutionary, nor did I envision a progressive clinic representing such a client. I fancied myself a progressive lawyer, or would-be lawyer. During the Nicaraguan revolution, my sympathies were with the Sandinistas, and after the revolution I supported the presidency of Daniel Ortega. During the 1980s, it became fashionable for "progressive" people to visit Nicaragua after the Sandinista revolution. Though I did not make the pilgrimage, I had a number of friends and students who did. Was my client a Somoza supporter? Was he a Contra? Worse yet, had he persecuted others? What had he done to be targeted for persecution by the Sandinistas? Was he lying about being persecuted and needing political asylum? As an attorney, I knew that my ultimate responsibility was to my client, but I wondered whether I would be capable of being a zealous advocate for a client whose political ideology and activities were antithetical to mine. Would I have to compromise my political beliefs? Could I be a strong advocate?

Finally, and this was really important, it seemed that my client did not have a compelling case for political asylum. The case would be difficult because there was a common perception that persecution by the Sandinistas had ceased once Chamorro, the leader of the *Unión Nacional Opositora* (UNO; National Opposition Union), a coalition of eleven political parties, took power. The case would be difficult because during the Sandinista era, the United States actively supported the Contras and was therefore predisposed to be sympathetic to their asylum claims.

Mark and I met at the Milagro Immigration Clinic on Friday, September 10, in preparation for our first meeting with the client. Mark gave me a brief orientation, showed me my mailbox, the files containing briefs prepared by students who worked in the clinic in the past, and various resource materials. One resource that proved invaluable was the Immigrant Legal Resource Center Manual. Mark also introduced me to Lisa, the University of San Francisco law school student who was working as an extern with Mark and would be helping us in the clinic. Lisa was pleasant and enthusiastic, and I was grateful for the help. Mark said that Lisa could help specifically with getting information and documentation on the current political situation in Nicaragua. This information was important to support our argument that the Sandinistas retained control of the army and the police and that our client has a genuine fear that if forced to return to Nicaragua, he would surely be persecuted and probably killed.

As I read through the file, several problems became apparent. First, the client's declaration was not detailed or persuasive. Second, and more significantly, there appeared to be significant contradictions in Mr. Falcón's declaration. Finally, there were questions about his marital status. In her declaration, his wife referred to him as "my common-law husband." The client listed four children of varying ages on his application, whereas his wife identified only one child, and we knew that his nine-year-old son was living with him. Two of the children were born in the same year and were only four months apart. I could not help but wonder about the inconsistencies.

I also had some general concerns in approaching my first client. The first was that I lacked experience working with Central Americans. During my placement the previous semester in Teaching Self-Help and Lay Lawyering, I had the opportunity to work with Central Americans at the Auxilio Refuge Center in San Jose. I attended a meeting of Mujeres Activas, a Latinas self-help group, and met two of the leaders, Maria Ochoa and Blanca Rosa Pineda. It didn't take long for me to begin to question the notion of a "universal" Latino ethnic consciousness. Latinos, although they share a common name, are diverse and do not automatically feel an immediate bond with one another. I realized that although being Mexican and speaking Spanish may provide some basis for relating to Central Americans, it would not guarantee instant rapport or automatic acceptance. Being Latino and Spanish-speaking was not a substitute for gaining knowledge and understanding of the unique history, problems, and culture of each group. I realized that despite the internal diversity among Mexicans and Chicanos, we are also culturally, linguistically, and phenotypically different from Central Americans and other Latinos.

The second area of concern, surprisingly, was my client's educational and social class level. I seem to have less trouble establishing rapport with people who do not have a lot of education or a high class standing. Perhaps it is because I am "educated,"[4] in the sense that I have been in school for a long time, that I sometimes find the Latino upper-middle and upper classes both pretentious and condescending toward those who have less education.

These fears were allayed somewhat by the knowledge that in this cultural context I had two inherent advantages over and above my ability to speak Spanish. The first advantage was gender; the second, age. One point of commonality across Latino groups is a hierarchical ordering of the society along age and gender lines.[5] As a middle-aged man, I knew that I would automatically be accorded a certain amount of deference and respect and that this would be a definite advantage in relating to the client—unless I acted in a way that indicated I was undeserving of such treatment. Thus, unless I blew it somehow, I would be treated respectfully because of my age and gender.

———

When Mr. Falcón joined us on September 20, Mark always referred to him as "Ricardo." This is not something that we talked or even thought about, but I felt more comfortable addressing him as Señor Falcón. I dropped his second name, "Guerra," for convenience. I think there may be a cultural difference here. Americans tend to equate informality with intimacy so that you feel close to people by calling them Bill, Mark, or Rick. Latinos do not make this equation, so that one can be formal, respectful, and intimate. When we did the mock presentation in Moot Court later in the semester, the Puerto Rican student interpreter, Memo Rodríguez, called our client "don Ricardo." This struck me as a nice way to blend informality and respect. It is important to note that both Mark and Memo were younger than Mr. Falcón, and it would have been considered especially rude and condescending for a younger person to address someone who is older by their first name, or to address them as *tú* (informal *you*) rather than *ústed* (formal *you*).

After outlining our respective roles in the clinic, Mark explained what would be expected of Mr. Falcón, as the client. Because this was "Ricardo's story," it was very important that he be comfortable with it. I would take notes as Ricardo told his story and would subsequently prepare "Una Declaración" based on what he had told us that would be submitted to the court. The declaration would be the official version of Mr. Falcón's story and would be closely scrutinized by the judge and the government attorney.

Mark asked Mr. Falcón about his children and how many of them were living with him.[6] He also asked whether he was legally married to his wife. Mr. Falcón acknowledged that he was not legally married because his first wife would not give him a divorce. Mark said he did not want to pry into his private affairs, but it would be better for them to marry legally in a civil ceremony before the hearing, if this was at all possible. This would give him and his common-law wife "two bites at the apple" rather than just one.[7] If either one of them won their asylum claim, the other would qualify as a spouse. Mark told him, "In this country, you can't get married if you are not divorced from your first wife." He mentioned that you could get a "quickie" divorce and did not need the other party's consent. Mark smiled and said, "They have to get that ring on the finger!"

Mark next went over the relevant law—the two requirements for political asylum. First, we had to show that Falcón's fear of political persecution was well founded.[8] Second, the fear has to be both personal or subjective and objective. We had to show not only that Ricardo himself had this fear but that a reasonable person in a similar situation would fear persecution. And we had to prove that the persecution was because of political opinions or membership in a social group.

Based on his reading of the file, Mark felt that our client had essentially three possible arguments based on what had happened to his father-in-law, what happened to his wife, and what happened directly to Ricardo. He also stressed that under the law, if the applicant had persecuted anyone because of religion, race, nationality, or political opinion, he or she was automatically disqualified, unless he or she had been engaged in a war. Mr. Falcón seemed disgusted with the suggestion that he might have persecuted someone. He nodded his head and said indignantly, "I have never done this." Mark said that he needed to know if Mr. Falcón was ever a Contra, but he did not want to know whether he ever persecuted anyone. Finally, he asked, "Tiene una pregunta, sobre la oficina, o alguna otra cosa?" (Do you have any questions about the office, or anything else?)

Presenting a Credible Story

During class Mark had given us an overview of how one should conduct a meeting with a client and prepare a declaration. Once you had explained how the clinic functions and the law, Mark liked to ask open-ended questions and let the client ramble. Mark said it was very important for us to write up our notes right away, while the information was still fresh.

Ricardo Falcón Guerra was initiated into Nicaraguan politics as a child because his father was a landowner but was on the side of the campesinos and active in the Conservative Party, which opposed Somoza. At fifteen, he distributed leaflets in support of Fernando Aguero Rocha, a popular opposition leader. Falcón and others were disillusioned with Rocha because he apparently made a secret pact with Somoza. Falcón recounted the infamous "January 22 Massacre" in which hundreds of supporters were killed and many more injured when the Somoza police turned on the crowd as they listened to Rocha speak. After this incident he was not involved with politics until many years later, when he became active in UNO. He also recounted that he began to be persecuted by the Sandinistas immediately after they lost the elections. He was singled out because he was the local UNO representative and because he served as an election observer and was viewed as having taken a political stance in opposition to the Sandinistas. He was very visible and was even in the newspapers. After being forcefully evicted from his home, he and his wife went to the press and denounced the Sandinistas.

Mark started our second meeting by mentioning again that lots of judges think that because the Sandinistas are not in power, there is no reason to fear them. It was, therefore, very important that we mention at the beginning of the declaration that fear of the Sandinistas still exists. He next asked, "Ricardo, quién recibió las amenazas de muerte?" (Who received the death threats?). Falcón responded that they were anonymous but were clearly directed at him. They were put under the front door of the house, picked up by his wife, and given to him.

We talked about taking pictures of the scars on the client's face that resulted from a motorcycle accident after the Sandinistas pursued him. Mark said, "A mi esposa le encanta tomar fotos, y ella puede venir a tomar fotos de sus cicatrizes para la corte los lunes o viernes" (My wife loves to take pictures, and she could take pictures of your scars for the Court on Mondays or Fridays).

Mr. Falcón's appearance concerned me from the start. He had short hair like a convict, and a beard (no moustache) and very long sideburns that joined with his beard. I asked Mark whether it would be appropriate to suggest that he shave before the hearing. It finally dawned on me that the obvious reason for the beard and long sideburns was to hide the scars from his motorcycle accident. I felt badly for not recognizing this immediately.

On the day we were scheduled to take the pictures, I was pleasantly surprised to see that my client had gotten a haircut, trimmed his beard, and cut his sideburns. He looked much better and younger.[9] Unfortunately, by the time of the hearing his beard and sideburns had grown considerably. I did not have the nerve to ask him to shave because I sensed that he was sensitive about the scars. Mark's wife came and was very gracious in taking the pictures. It turned out to be a family affair. They went outside and took close-ups of the scars. Afterwards, she took pictures of the entire family, Ricardo, Lupe, and their son, Ricardo Jr. They looked very proud. This scene, watching my client and his family, and the thought that I might be able to help them remain in the United States were probably the highlight of the semester for me. It made me feel that this kind of work was important. This might be a class for me and yet another client for Mark, but for Ricardo Falcón Guerra, his life and the future of his family were at stake.

Something else happened earlier that I felt was significant. Mr. Falcón brought his wife and son with him to one of our meetings and introduced me to them. I met them in the reception area of the law clinic, took them upstairs, and escorted them into the interview room. Just before entering the interview room, he smiled and asked whether Mark was in. I told him that he was but that he was busy. As we sat down, I suddenly realized that something was wrong. Mr. Falcón was obviously disappointed. He wanted to introduce his wife to Mark. I excused myself, interrupted Mark, and told him that Mr. Falcón had brought his wife, and it would be "nice" if he just popped into the room so that he could meet her. Mark graciously complied. This may seem like a minor detail, but it was extremely important to the client. I think it reflects the value on *personalismo* in relationships among Latinos.

One of the major problems that we faced was resolving contradictions in the story. Some of the discrepancies were minor; others were not. There were minor discrepancies in dates. In his declaration Mr. Falcón said that his wife and father-in-law were forcibly evicted from their home and that her finger was almost severed as she held on to an army cot. But an earlier declaration indicated that his wife's finger was almost cut off by a machete. Mr. Falcón responded by smiling, shaking his head in disbelief, and reassuring me that it was not a machete. She was holding on with all of her strength to a metal army cot as she was dragged from the house.

There was no reason to question his account. In fact, if one were going to lie, saying that her hand was cut by a knife or a machete would have been more dramatic and believable. What was more difficult to reconcile were discrepancies in the date of his father-in-law's death. I did not understand the discrepancy and found it difficult to believe that one could not recall the date of the death of one's father or father-in-law. What I learned from all of this is that there can be honest discrepancies in the client's story and that there is danger in trying to "stretch" one's case. It seems to me that you develop a more compelling case by using more limited but clear and consistent grounds than by using grounds that, though dramatic, are inconsistent and implausible.

Preparing for the Hearing

The preparation for the hearing was intense. Less than five weeks elapsed between the date that I first met my client, September 20, and the hearing, October 27. I had a little over a month to review the record, interview the client, prepare the declaration, do library research and Shepardize the cases,[10] write the brief, practice the direct examination, prepare an opening and closing, and gather supporting materials on political conditions in Nicaragua. During this period, the work seemed endless, and my other classes suffered. It was taking about 80 percent of my time.

The work was nonstop. We went into the home stretch during the week of October 11, practicing the direct examination at least four times between October 11 and October 21, our Moot Court date. I did the direct examination and Mark interpreted. The last two sessions we also practiced cross-examination, with Mark playing the role of the government attorney.

I felt we were well prepared going into the practice hearing. Each day I became more impressed with my client. He was a strong person, spoke with confidence and conviction, and was actually better under fire. Overall, we felt he was very credible, but Mark suggested he should look at the judge more when answering questions.

The practice hearing was realistic. Mark played the judge, and Professor Lee was the government attorney. We were fortunate to have Memo, a Puerto Rican student, as interpreter. What I liked most is that he translated with the same tone and conviction as Señor Falcón. It was awkward at first because our client spoke too fast and did not pause for the translation.[11] Memo asked for a brief time out and explained to Mr. Falcón that it was important to pause after he spoke one or two lines. My client caught on very quickly. Soon they were in sync, and you forgot that there was a translation. After the hearing, we thanked Memo and complimented him on doing a great job.

Working with an interpreter is doubly difficult for a bilingual person. You tend to not wait for the translation, since you understood both your question and the answer. It is also very strange to force yourself to ask your questions in English when you speak Spanish. I wondered, why am I talking to Mr. Falcón in English?[12] I learned, however, that it is a two-way street. There are definite advantages to being a bilingual advocate. First, I heard both the question and the answer twice, which gave more time to think and reflect. Also, if the client understands any English at all, he too can reflect on the answer during the translation. We had practiced this so many times and he was so sharp that I doubt Mr. Falcón did not know what was coming. The downside is that it may be more difficult for a Spanish-speaking client to establish rapport with the judge because the relationship is mediated by the interpreter.

This is not a problem when you have a skilled interpreter like Memo, but it can be a problem if you do not. An even more significant downside is that the proceedings are slowed considerably. Presumably, a monolingual hearing would take almost half as long as a bilingual hearing, which is a problem if you have an impatient and insensitive judge. Mark and Professor Lee had warned me repeatedly about the judge assigned to my case. He was old, unpredictable, and had a heart problem. He was also very impatient and expected deference from everyone. I think Lee said it best: "He's a real SOB, and you have to kiss his ass."

The feedback was interesting. A concern that I had before the practice was that Mr. Falcón was a very strong person with a hard edge, which could make him less sympathetic. He was macho, in the best sense of the word. There is a saying in Spanish that captures it: "Feo, fuerte, y formal." It is the Mexican counterpart to "tall, dark, and handsome." What it means literally is "ugly, strong, and responsible." Such a person is viewed positively as a man not because he is handsome but because he is strong, physically and spiritually, and especially because he is dependable. In other words, he keeps his word and can be counted on, especially in a pinch. But I wished that Falcón would show more emotion and vulnerability. When he recounted the harrowing experience of having to cross the swirling Río Bravo with his little boy on his back and being washed downstream by the heavy current, Mr. Falcón remained calm and controlled. As we prepared for the practice and the hearing, I finally got up the nerve to mention it to him:

> Señor, I know that talking about these things is very difficult for you. I can talk about them and imagine what it might have been like. I know that you are a very strong person, and I admire and respect that, but I don't think it would hurt if you showed a little bit more emotion. You don't have to break down altogether, but it is okay to show your feelings.

I felt that when he testified, he demonstrated more anger and disdain toward the Sandinistas than fear. I reminded him that we had to convince the judge that he actually feared the Sandinistas. During the direct examination, I would pause and say, "I know this is very difficult for you, but . . ." I could see by the look in his eye that he understood. Mark and I may deserve a bit of credit for the preparation, but the bulk of the credit goes to the client.

In the debriefing after the practice session, there was consensus that my client was very convincing and credible. He slowed down at critical points, and it was very effective. The *consejos* (advice) had paid off.

However, some minor questions were raised. Mark suggested that Falcón still needed to look at the judge more often. Some people thought the the motorcycle accident story was not convincing. During the cross-examination, Lee had tried to trip him up about just exactly how far he was from the Sandinistas when they chased him. Why did Falcón fear them if he was on his motorcycle and they were on foot? If you were on a hit list, why would you ride your motorcycle from your home to downtown in the midst of a Sandinista riot? Did this seem like a person who feared persecution? The client did a great job under the pressure, but one point came out that had never come out before: he was on foot when the Sandinistas came after him. He responded that he was on foot at first and got on the motorcycle after the Sandinistas started to chase him. I don't know if he made this up but it was a great answer.

Because Peter is from Texas he did not find the story about crossing the Río Bravo very believable. He said that anyone who was familiar with the area would know that it was generally "shallow and bone dry" and that you could just walk across. What came out in the discussion is that there are parts that are shallow and parts that are not. It also depends on the time of year and the amount of rain. In any event, I found this one of the most powerful parts of Falcón's story.

As I reflected on the practice hearing, I wondered whether we as advocates are generally hardest on our clients. I did not question Mr. Falcón's credibility or his effectiveness in telling a compelling story. But I always felt that he could be better—by showing emotion at critical points, for example, when he talked about crossing the river with his son on his back, when he received the death threats, or when his wife and father-in-law were evicted from their home and his wife's finger was nearly severed. The fact is that he did show more emotion during the practice hearing, and he *was* better. I felt it was a question of fine-tuning our performance.

Professor Lee was surprised that I was a bit understated in my performance. He felt that I could have been more animated and picked up the pace. I agreed but responded that that was my intention. It was an unconscious way of drawing attention away from me toward my client and his story. I saw my role as being like a straight man for my client so that the spotlight would be on him and not on me. Also, what was perceived as being understated was my attempt to be deferential toward the judge. Finally, I was trying to show empathy for my client.

Mark, on the other hand, thought that I did a good job and that I was not understated, but he admonished me not to argue with the judge. He said there were a couple of instances, one in particular, when I had done so. I honestly did not remember arguing with the judge. I think what happens is that you get so carried away with the moment, so wrapped up in what you are doing, that you don't realize you are arguing.[13]

I came away from the class satisfied with my client's performance and with our preparation but dissatisfied with my performance. I guess it would be in my nature to be more flamboyant, theatrical, and assertive, but I felt inhibited. Professor Lee and Mark had emphasized that the bottom line is that you had to kiss the judge's ass. I was not a person who normally did such a thing, nor was my client, and I found this extremely difficult. I guess I felt it was unfair to ask me to be docile and compliant and then criticize me for being understated. I had to figure out a way to kiss the judge's ass and pick up the pace.

Ricardo Falcón Guerra's Day in Court

The day of the practice hearing was the longest day of the term. I had gotten up early to go over the direct one more time. After the practice exercise, there was much to do. Mark had brought collated packets of supporting materials on conditions in Nicaragua that Lisa had prepared and his suggested revisions in the brief. Professor Lee also brought his comments and suggestions on the brief. Mark said that because Peter had his hearing the next morning, if I could get two copies of the brief to Peter, Mark would file the brief with the court. The class ended at about 1:00 p.m. After class I first rushed to the law library and Shepardized the cases and then went home to incorporate the comments into the brief. My hands were full: books and notebooks, several copies of the brief, mail from the law school, and seven or eight copies of the supporting materials. What happened next was a law clerk's worst nightmare. As I got out of my car and closed the door, all of the packets slipped out of my hands. I picked everything up, went inside, and started going through the tedious and painstaking task of trying to put everything back in order. A difficult job was made more difficult by the fact that the articles were marked like A-7, C-2, and so on, but the identifying letter and number were sometimes illegible. Sometimes I had to read the summaries of the articles to make sure they corresponded with the content. Finally, some items were missing and others repeated. It was a mess. In addition to collating the materials, revising the brief, and photocopying everything, I had to make a cover page, finalize the table of authorities, and do a table of contents. It did not take long to realize that I would not finish by 4:00 p.m. I called Mark and told him that Peter had agreed to take the materials in for me when he went to his hearing the following day. To make a long story less long, I think I got to Peter's place after 11:00 p.m.

On Monday, October 25, we met with the client for the last time before the hearing. We practiced the direct and the cross-examination and asked Señor Falcón whether he had any final questions. We reminded him once again not to be afraid to show his feelings and to look at the judge. We had no way of knowing how good our interpreter would be, but we reminded him to ask that a question be repeated if it was not clear. I would be paying close attention to make sure that the translation was on target and would ask to have the question or answer reread if there seemed to be a problem with the translation. We also reminded him that we had to be especially humble, respectful, and contrite in the judge's courtroom. Though I had worked hard during the semester, I found myself with last-minute things to do as the hearing approached. Mark had told me early on that I had to prepare a five- to ten-minute closing, but I did not realize until the end that I also had to prepare an opening. Technically we were not supposed to deliver an opening, but the judge might allow us to give a very brief overview of our case. He also told me to make a separate list of points that absolutely had to be covered so that I could check them off. Another last-minute task was to prepare a list of key Spanish terms and words, with translations, that we would hand to the court interpreter before the hearing. Finally, I prepared a list of corrections and typographical errors that I would hand to the judge at the beginning.

We went into the immigration hearing feeling confident and well prepared. I would try not to be understated without being aggressive or alienating the judge. This would not be the brash, aggressive, cocky, self-assured Alfredo but the mellow, sophisticated, mature, tolerant, charming Alfredo.

I had a mental image of myself appearing before the judge in a fancy tuxedo and shiny shoes, like Ricardo Montalbán, with a noticeable but inoffensive Hispanic accent. Instead of selling a Chrysler Cordoba with Corinthian leather, I would be talking about Nicaragua, political asylum, and how any decent and discriminating person could see that this asylum claim had merit. I actually have a very positive image of someday blossoming into a sophisticated and charming Hispanic gentleman: don Alfredo.

My father was a handsome man who had worked as an extra in a number of Mexican movies and some Hollywood films that were made in Mexico. He was one of Hernán Cortés' right-hand men and appeared riding on horseback in *Captain from Castille* with Tyrone Power and César Romero. My dad was better looking than these guys, but he apparently could not act or never disciplined himself to learn to act. I was also thinking of the Mexican writer Carlos Fuentes. Fuentes reminded me of my father and was incredibly smart and articulate. This was the kind of image that I wanted to invoke in court: Alfredo as a composite of Ricardo Montalbán, César Romero, Carlos Fuentes, Xavier Mirandé (my father's stage name, Xavier Glass, was very classy), and, of course, my ultimate hero, Pedro Infante.[14] I wanted to be a Hispanic gentleman who could charm the pants off anyone, even an old, impatient, crotchety judge. I knew that I could be charming if I worked at it.

Lisa and I drove into the city together. The hearing was scheduled from 1:00 to 2:30 p.m. When we arrived at the federal court at 12:35, my client and Professor Lee were talking in the hallway outside the courtroom. I introduced Lisa to Professor Lee and to my client, his wife, and little Ricardo and told them that she helped to prepare the brief by getting information on current conditions in Nicaragua. They thanked Lisa and shook her hand.

My client looked surprisingly cool and relaxed. He was not dressed up, as I would have liked. He was wearing the mandatory macho, tight-fitting denim stretch jeans and a sport shirt but, luckily, no sunglasses.[15] And he had not shaved his sideburns. It was ironic, given my initial concerns, that I wanted him to dress up more and to look more middle class. What mattered more than his appearance was that he looked comfortable and relaxed, yet serious and intense. The man had come to do business, and he was understandably anxious to get started, but he did not appear nervous. We are supposed to try to engender confidence in the client, and I don't know whether I did or not, but he certainly engendered confidence in me. I was proud to have him as a client.

We went into the courtroom a few minutes before the hour, and waited. We waited, and we waited. We took turns looking at our watches. And we waited. Finally, at approximately 1:15, Judge Farnsworth came out of his chambers. He was exactly as I had pictured him: old, white, bald, and very crotchety. Mark introduced himself and the client. Looking over the top of his glasses, the judge asked brusquely, "And who are you? Are you an attorney?" "No, your honor, I am Alfredo Mirandé, a third-year law student working under the supervision of Mr. Mark Levin and Professor Lee." Professor Lee and Judge Farnsworth were friends. Lee had told us that he was going to try to have lunch with the judge to see if he could soften him up a bit.[16] Apparently the judge had forgotten that they would be getting together for lunch and had already eaten, so they had coffee. What was strange is that the judge proceeded to have a private conversation with Lee that was obviously a continuation of an earlier chat. The judge said something like, "See, I told you they were going to do that. You'll see, take a look at this," referring to a manila envelope. He motioned for Lee to come to the bench to get the envelope. Lee seemed somewhat embarrassed and awkward, but he complied. He got the envelope, sat down, opened it, started to read the materials, and shook his head in disbelief but so as to agree with Farnsworth and humor him. The judge and the professor had a good chuckle over this, but the rest of us had no idea what they were talking about. Lee later whispered to me that this was about a matter that was totally unrelated. It was obviously an inside joke.

I began, as Mark suggested, by informing His Honor that I had a list of very minor corrections in the brief and some clarifications of minor discrepancies between his initial declaration and the declaration that was attached to the brief.[17] Though the list contained minor typographical errors and corrections, Mark said it was better for us to acknowledge them at the outset than to have the judge or the government point them out. I expected the judge to note them and proceed. Instead he said, "Okay, why don't you meet with the government attorney and go over the changes. We will take a short recess." We were not off to a good start. The judge returned after about fifteen minutes, but the court interpreter did not. We had to wait another five minutes or so for her. When Judge Farnsworth asked if we wished to make an opening statement to explain what was at issue, I began my opening. I thought it was good, short and to the point, and I felt my delivery was just right. Yet there was something strange about the way the judge was staring at me that is difficult to explain, and I felt it each time I looked up from my outline to look at him. Again, looking over his glasses, his glance was one of disbelief. The communication occurred at a very primitive level. The look I got from the judge was the kind of look an older dominant gorilla might give younger gorillas who had invaded his turf. He wanted to intimidate me, and my client. What I really found strange is that though I was trying to act compliant and to kiss his ass, he knew I was not intimidated, and he did not like it one bit. He knew that I was confident. He knew not only that I was not intimidated but also that I was unimpressed. He knew. I wondered where Ricardo Montalbán was when you really needed him.

Returning to the hearing, we proceeded with the direct examination. Everything was going smoothly. We had an excellent interpreter, and Mr. Falcón was better than ever. His voice was clear. He was articulate and very credible. Not only did my client look directly at the judge, he never once looked away from him throughout the testimony. Mr. Falcón seemed to be glaring at the judge, confidently and defiantly. The judge, on the other hand, ignored Mr. Falcón.

I sensed that the judge was getting impatient. He seemed to get especially irritated when I would call the court's attention to specific items in the packet that corroborated Mr. Falcón's testimony.[10] At one point he said, "I'm quite familiar with the situation in Nicaragua. I have handled many, many Nicaraguan asylum cases." The message was clear: "Don't try to educate me, boy. I know all of this stuff." At one point, I think I said something like, "I beg your pardon, Your Honor, it is hard to anticipate what is obvious and what is not obvious to the Court. We did not realize that this was evident to the Court." At another point I said, "Your Honor, may I call your attention to . . . " He interrupted me: "Of course you can, you can do whatever you want to do." Once again, I was being respectful, and he made me look like a fool.

Ten minutes into the direct examination, at 1:43, the judge interrupted, looked at me, and said, "You know that we have to be out of here by 2:00 p.m. because we have another case and there is a shortage of interpreters and she has to be at another hearing, don't you?" I said, "No, Your Honor, I understood we had until 2:30." The judge let me continue for about four minutes and then stopped me, waved his arms in the air, and said, "It's clear we are not going to finish. Why don't we stop, check the calendar, and pick another time so we can continue. I will set off a whole morning." I was disappointed but felt it would be better to postpone than to rush the testimony. I would not mind coming back in a few weeks, although I realized that it might not be until January. We were shocked when the interpreter, who was also the appointments' clerk, reported that the earliest possible date was August 13.

Professor Lee made a final plea: "Your Honor, isn't there some way that you could possibly schedule this sooner?" He mentioned that this was a clinic to train students and that the clinic was held during the fall semester, so Mark Levin would not be able to find another student to take over the case until October.[19] He also said that I would be graduating and would probably not be available to continue on the case. The Judge was unwavering. He got up, adjourned, and walked into his chambers. The date for the hearing was eventually set for October the following year. I don't think I have ever been more frustrated. Mr. Falcón was confused, and we had to explain to him what had happened. His wife was in the hallway because we had hoped to have her testify, and she had no hint at what had just transpired. It took a while before we remembered she was in the hallway and went out to explain what had happened.

Mark instructed us to wait until we got out of the court before we said much more. We went down the elevator and debriefed. I felt frustrated and impotent. I did not know how to explain, let alone justify, what had occurred. How do you explain something to the client that you don't understand? I could only agree when Mrs. Falcón said in disgust, "Parecía que el viejo no tenía ganas de trabajar" (It looked like the old man did not feel like working today). She wondered how they could permit someone like that to be in such an important position. He should be fired.

I drove home, wondering what I should have done differently. I thought that perhaps it was my fault, that I should have rushed through the case when I saw the judge was impatient. But this would have meant a poor record on which to base an appeal. Peter later pointed out that even if we had prevailed we would have had a poor record, should the government decide to appeal. I thought about all of the wasted preparation. I could have done better if I had just walked in off the street and presented the case. I thought about the irony of it. We had told the client to look at the judge, which he did, but the judge never looked at the client.

I thought about another irony. In preparing for the hearing, we had stressed the importance, or necessity, of learning about American culture and American values in order to survive and succeed in the United States.[20] We told the client, in effect, that this country is based on the rule of law. It is a country of laws and rules, not of individuals. We stressed that the master rule was to always keep a paper trail and to learn the rules. In the United

States you had to keep records, be punctual, and follow the rules. The irony is that we had learned the law, kept a paper trail, and followed the rules, but we had not prevailed. I thought about the feeling of ecstasy in the court-room after Peter's hearing. I thought about how happy Nicole and her client, Patty, were when Patty was granted Suspension of Deportation.[21] It was an emotional scene with the two young women, Nicole and Patty, embracing and crying tears of joy.

I recalled the first day of class when Professor Lee was emphatic in saying he did not like to lose cases and that he seldom did. We don't often lose, he said, "because we really prepare well." I had prepared. I knew that no one had prepared more. I was very well prepared, perhaps too prepared. It's true that I did not lose, but I had not won. A thousand thoughts rushed through my mind; mostly I wondered what had gone wrong and what I could have done differently. I thought about the judge and the way he had looked at me. I thought about our ritualistic encounter.[22]

I shall never forget my first encounter with gorillas. Sound preceded sight. Odor preceded sound in the form of an overwhelming musky-barnyard, humanlike scent. The air was suddenly rent by a high-pitched series of screams followed by the rhythmic rondo of sharp *pok-pok* chestbeats from a great silverback male obscured behind what seemed an impenetrable wall of vegetation. . . . Occasionally the domi-nant male would rise to chest beat in an attempt to intimidate us. . . . As if competing for attention, some animals went through a series of actions that included yawning, symbolic-feeding, branch-breaking, or chestbeating. After each display, the gorillas would look at us quizzi-cally as if trying to determine the effect of their show. . . . I left Kabara with reluctance but with never a doubt that I would, somehow, return to learn more about the gorillas of the misted mountains.[23]

CHAPTER TEN

"Remains of the Day": The Law Firm Chronicles

Metamorphosis

Something strange happens around four weeks into the first year of law school. I had read about the keen competition over jobs and clerkships at Harvard Law School in *One L*,[1] but you cannot fully understand the interview season until you have experienced it. On arriving in Palo Alto, one is immediately struck by the casual dress style of law school students and faculty. The students almost inevitably wear shorts or jeans and T-shirts or polo shirts. The male faculty usually wear cotton dress pants or Dockers and sport shirts, and the female faculty, slacks or skirts and blouses. But sometime in October at every law school in the country there is a remarkable metamorphosis, when almost all second- and third-year students show up in fancy pin-striped suits, white oxford shirts, and striped silk ties. The men wear wingtip shoes and the women wear heels. During the first few weeks of the semester, second- and third-year students receive a notice in their mailboxes announcing that a tailor will be at the law school to measure people and take orders for business suits. The suits are described as high-quality worsted wool and offered at discount prices. The transformation is dramatic. I recall doing a double take when I first witnessed this phenomenon, but it was not until the second year of law school that my classmates and I would undergo this metamorphosis.

It is hard to describe how I felt about the interview season. My first response was that it seemed like a charade, or if not a charade, at least like the students were "playing lawyer." Here we were, like little kids, barely wet behind the ears, most of us not knowing much about law and less about working in the corporate world, and not even close to graduation, and yet to the uninitiated we looked like real lawyers, or at least like caricatures or imitations of lawyers. It was a remarkable transformation as students took their dress clothes from their lockers, entered the restroom, and emerged as lawyers. I began to wonder for the first time in my life whether it is true, as some people claim, that the clothes make the person.[2] I also wondered whether we even needed to go to law school, since we already looked like lawyers. When I finally had the opportunity to interview, I have to admit that it was fun. I welcomed the break from the daily routine of classes and lectures.

The summer after the first year was our first opportunity to play at being lawyer in the real world. The recruitment season is a major event at most law schools. Employers come to the law school to conduct twenty- to thirty minute-interviews with prospective candidates. The law school placement office coordinates the interview process. The placement office has a list of employers, job listings and descriptions, and available interview slots. It conducts workshops for students on recruitment and résumé writing and collects student résumés and distributes them to employers. Finally, the placement office has lists of jobs with firms that do not conduct on-campus interviews, public interest jobs, and judicial clerkships. At the various forums, the office told students that the job market was tight. Although having a degree from an elite school helped, it wouldn't guarantee a job. We were told it wouldn't be easy for first-years to get summer jobs with firms, although many of my classmates did. Other first-years worked for public interest organizations such as the American Civil Liberties Union or MALDEF (Mexican American Legal Defense and Education Fund), although most of these did not provide salaries or else paid minimum wage. A few students, especially those interested in law teaching, obtained judicial clerkships in the summer.

There were a number of reasons people liked to work for firms in the summer. First, one could earn $1,500 to $2,000 per week.[3] Second, if the firm

was satisfied with your work, you would have a job waiting for you after finishing law school. Third, you received perks such as tickets to major sporting
events, plays, and, of course, loads of free lunches.

The last semester of law school is difficult because students want to get on
with their lives. They look forward to clerking, working for a large firm, or
doing whatever it is that they plan after graduation. They look for classes
that are of interest to them and not very demanding. Why, then, did Alfredo
decide to take a class on the large law firm in the last semester of law school?
Why would I pass up Civil Rights, Domestic Violence, and Constitutional
Law II for a class like this? Had I finally sold out? Was I turned off to the
Lawyering for Social Change curriculum? I started worrying about Alfredo.

Actually, I was not crazy and was not turned off by the LSC. In fact, in
the last semester I also enrolled in Rick Romo's Lay Lawyering for a second
time. I approached the last semester the way I approached every other semester, making up my class schedule by conferring with Romo and asking,
Does this sound like an interesting class? Does it fill gaps in my training?
Will I learn something of value? Will I be able to write a worthwhile, perhaps publishable paper?[4]

At the end of the second year of law school, I had worked for a small civil
rights firm. I neither wanted nor expected to work for a large firm, but
after consulting with Romo, I decided to take the Large Law Firm class, precisely because I did not intend to work in such a firm and I felt that this
would afford me a rare opportunity to enter and gain insight into a world I
would not otherwise know. It seemed like an ideal opportunity to learn
something about the large firm without having to work for one. There was
something nice about the whole thing. Instead of going to the firm, the
firm would come to me. Another thing that was appealing was that the
course description stated that students would be expected to keep a journal
and write a paper.

At the first session, the coordinator for the project, Professor Roger Gold,
suggested that the participants work on a collective project such as a joint
monograph that presented different views on the large law firm. Though the
collective effort would never materialize, I kept a weekly journal and eventually wrote an individual paper that was essentially an ethnographic study of
the class. The paper was more than 150 pages, with a detailed description
and analysis of the class discussions and readings.

Anthropologists often use key individuals, or "informants," to obtain important "insider" information and insights into a particular culture. In this

instance, my game plan was to treat the practitioners as key informants on the structure and culture of the large law firm. And although I would not be interviewing them directly, their comments and discussion would serve as raw data. My goals were relatively simple. First, I wanted my field notes to serve as a type of "chronicle" or record of the proceedings. Second, I would treat the sessions as data, which are subject to analysis and critique. Third, because I had never worked in a large firm and did not plan to do so, I hoped to give an outsider's perspective and critique of the large law firm.

I prepared a total of fourteen chronicles, each covering a separate class and topic.[5] Before turning to the chronicles, several caveats are in order. I found the process of documenting what happened at each session a daunting experience. Instead of taping the sessions, I opted to take detailed notes. This proved difficult and exhausting and may have hampered my ability to participate. Also, I don't pretend to have recorded everything that transpired. Though I often quoted individual participants, I could not always be certain of the accuracy of my recordings. But I was confident that the quotes represented the essence of what was said by the respondents. Also I do not consider myself an objective, indifferent, detached, or unbiased observer. I know only too well that one's biases and preconceptions color perception. My biases were sociological, ethnographic, and personal. My observations were limited also by not having taken courses in the Law and Business curriculum and by my limited training in law and economics. Finally, my observations were undoubtedly colored by the fact that I entered the class with an unfavorable, or at a minimum ambivalent, attitude toward large firms and the Law and Business curriculum. I entered thinking that I would not enjoy working in a large firm and doubting that they would have me. Rather than corporate law, I was interested in criminal law and jurisprudence and had taken a large concentration of courses in the LSC. After graduation, I hoped to get some experience as a trial lawyer and perhaps teach in a law school.

The First Chronicle: Decline in "Professionalism"

January 20.
The class started with a minor glitch. I went to the classroom to learn that we would be meeting in the staff lounge, which is near the Dean of Students' office. It is a long and fairly narrow rectangular room, not terribly conducive to a seminar type of discussion. People were dispersed; some were sitting

around two round tables at one end of the conference room, others on couches at the opposite end. Professor Gold sat in the middle of the room. I was to his immediate right. It was frustrating because I was apparently outside of his peripheral vision. I had my hand up several times, and he did not notice me. It reminded me of my first semester in law school when Professor Morton would ignore me. Next week we will begin to meet in the faculty lounge. It has to be an improvement.

Despite the limitations of the room and the awkwardness inherent in first class meetings, the class was interesting and we had a good discussion. Professor Gold began by discussing the format for the class. This is the fourth year the Legal Profession Workshop has been offered. In the past, it has addressed a wide range of topics. The class is different this year for two reasons. First, the workshop will focus on a specific theme, the future of the large corporate law firm. Second, in addition to faculty and student participation, a number of practitioners will be joining us and will be actively involved in the class. Given the nature of the theme, the involvement of practitioners seemed essential. Professor Gold listed the practitioners[6] who have committed to participate in the workshop.

In addition to this distinguished group of practitioners, the class will have the participation of a number of scholars who are leading authorities in the field. Professor Max Neiman, on leave from Georgetown School of Law, will discuss his work on in-house counsel and will be a regular participant in the workshop. Cynthia Fuchs Epstein, a sociologist at the State University of New York Graduate School and a leading authority on women and the profession, will talk about her project on women in large New York firms.[7] Marc Galanter, from the University of Wisconsin Law School and a visiting professor at Stanford last year, will report on his research concerning large British law firms. Though the first session focused on the students' role in the workshop, one of the practitioners, Stephen Boalt, and two faculty members, Max Neiman and Bob Gardner, were also in attendance.

The professor proceeded to give the students an overview of the class. The first presenter, Stanford faculty member Bob Gardner, will talk about the history of the large law firm. The next three class sessions will be devoted to supply issues and the structure of practice, including two sessions on "dividing the pie." In session 6, we will begin to look at Professor Neiman's work on in-house counsel. Session 7 will attempt to provide a comparative perspective through Professor Galanter's work on the large law firm in Britain. In session 8, Professor James Rebitzer will present an economic model that seeks to explain, or reconcile, the emergence of the increasing hours spiral with the avowed desire of most lawyers to work fewer hours. The topic of session 9 has generated a great deal of controversy at the Bar Association meeting, the ancillary business controversy or the business of law firms. After the spring recess, we will look at alternative practice structures, women in the profession (session 11), and the devolution phenomenon (sessions 12, 13) or the shift from law as a profession to law as a business. The final sessions will summarize what we have learned and where the large law firm is going.

The topics were important and timely, but there appeared to be at least one glaring omission: the issue of people of color in the profession. I also wondered whether there might be other manifestations of the devolution phenomenon. As presented in class, "devolution" refers to the belief that things were somehow always better in the past and that there has been a change for the worse as law has moved from a profession to a business. I don't deny that this is an important topic, but I wondered whether there might be other forms of devolution. How, for example, has the influx of minorities and women into the profession as students, teachers, partners, and judges affected the devolution process? Is there a sense that things are getting worse because "nonmeritocratic" considerations have emerged in the training (admissions, curricular changes), hiring, and advancement of lawyers in the profession? Do professionals feel that there has been a decline in standards? To what extent is this perception linked to the entrance of women and minorities into the profession?

Professor Gold spoke briefly about the expectations of students in the class. We were to read the material, attend class, and be active participants. He also expected a "product" from the workshop, some sort of group effort or chronicle of what we have done. We would each write the equivalent of a seminar paper that would fit into the larger structure. Although the format had not been determined, the professor's preference would be an anthology or collective monograph, written by participants.

The students, particularly third-year students, got very nervous about the proposal. The concern expressed was that third-year students would not be able to submit their papers by the May 10 deadline.[8] Professor Gold remained undaunted but acknowledged that turning our efforts into a collective project would be difficult. I liked the idea but shared the concern about timing. I feared it might end up being largely a faculty and practitioner effort, with the students playing an ancillary role.

Our first assignment was to read *The Remains of the Day*, a book about "Stevens," the "perfect" English butler, and his declining insular world in postwar England.[9] Professor Gold made it clear that he likes the book a great deal and would feel justified in assigning it for its literary value, even if it were not relevant to the course. The two specific themes that we would focus on are (1) the issue of role morality, or the appropriateness of the professional justifying her conduct solely as an extension of the client, as Stevens did in the service of the lord of Darlington Hall; and (2) the conflict between personal and professional lives.

Remains of the Day is about professionalism and addresses the issue of what defines a real professional. We discussed several examples from the stories told by Stevens's father, who was also a butler. One of the stories focused on a British butler stationed in India who said, "Excuse me, Sir, may I borrow the 30-30?" in order to shoot a tiger that was in the living room. The story illustrates that the professional is always in control, engendering a sense of confidence in those who depend on her. The professional remains cool in the face of adversity and never allows personal concerns to get in the way of professional duties and responsibilities. You can always rely on the professional.

One of the students, Kathy, mentioned that she understood the concept of professionalism but was bothered by the loss of Stevens's humanity. We also discussed the conflict between one's professional and personal life. In the book there is a bizarre scene in which Stevens is washing the feet of one of the guests, as his father lays dying in the butlers' quarters. What were the implications of the book for the attorney-client relationship? What if the client's values were different from those of the attorney?[10]

There were interesting similarities in the treatment of professionalism in the book and the role of the lawyer, but I wondered if we shouldn't have been as concerned with the differences between them. First, the English butler in *Remains of the Day* was an independent entrepreneur, involved in a one-on-one relationship with the client. Second, in my view, the book is as much about social class as professionalism. I made the point in class that in a hierarchical society such as the British system, the only way for a commoner like Stevens to assume the mantle of nobility and to be upwardly mobile is to become an extension of his master. The book is also about property and commodification in the sense that people lose their humanity when they become extensions of their owners. The word *master* itself is interesting and significant . It connotes a relationship of complete ownership, dependence, servitude, and control, as did the status of lord.[11] I wondered how you could have a sense of dignity and yet feel totally subordinate to another person. We ended with a discussion of the tradition of the lawyer-statesman who balances wisdom and the role of lawyer. It is part of the devolution literature, but I frankly could not follow the discussion very well at this time because they made reference to law and economics literature that I did not know or understand.

Based on the first session, it looks like an interesting class. I do have some concerns. First, I do not have much preparation in law and economics. It has been a long time since I took an economics course, and my background and orientation is cultural and anthropological, not economic. I understand that Professor Gold is a leading authority in this area and that he is looking at the large law firm through economic lenses and using rational choice theory. I hope and assume that the class will be open to other forms of analysis because I feel unprepared to assume an economic one. Second, I am concerned about how the three components of the class (practitioners, professors, and law students) will blend. When you have a workshop like this, I think students have a natural tendency to defer to those who are older, wiser, and more powerful than they are. We have assembled an impressive group here. I hope that the students will not be overwhelmed and that they will participate. Professor Gold has set the ground rules, and we are expected to participate. Yet I could sense from the first session that a lot of students were intimidated and reticent to talk. Unlike some law schools, outside of the LSC I don't think that participation and independent thought are necessarily valued or nurtured qualities at Stanford Law School. This is not Harvard or Yale. Though students are generally bright and pleasant, I would characterize them as docile, respectful, and compliant. It seems too often to be a sort of compliant, dull brightness.

The Second Chronicle: History or Folklore?

January 27.
Last week I expressed a concern that the format and the stellar group of practitioners and academics that had been assembled for the workshop might have intimidated the students. Unfortunately, my worst fears were realized. We dropped from having about a dozen students in the first session to only five in the second. The idea of doing a paper for the anthology or collective

product may have scared off most of the students. Only a handful survived. I am not really concerned about having to write a paper. I love to write. Writing is therapy for my solitude. It is still not clear just what we will be expected to do. Professor Gold took the students aside after the class and told us that the idea of doing an anthology or collective monograph is out, presumably because our numbers are so small. I am a bit concerned because I have a pretty good idea of what I want to do for a paper. I would like to keep the journal or chronicle as I go along and have the paper write itself as the semester unfolds. I don't want to begin with a topic in the last few weeks of the semester, and I really enjoy doing the weekly critique. It forces me to pay attention to the dynamics of the workshop as it transpires and to critically reflect on the issues. Without this, they would be nothing more than vague and muddled recollections.

I don't know how to approach Professor Gold. I mentioned to him after class that I was keeping a weekly journal, but he did not respond. I wondered if I should go to see him. It would be important for me to explain that I am trained to do ethnographic field research and that I would like to do an ethnography of the workshop experience. I think part of the problem is that he has a law and economics framework. I don't think economists have much appreciation for fieldwork. Most people in our community wouldn't know what to do with it either. Can you imagine telling your *compas* (buddies) that you are doing "fieldwork" in a class at Stanford? They would probably think you were working on the Farm[12] to pay for tuition.

I have a sense that the good folks in the workshop don't know what to make of me or my questions. Their response reminded me of the discussion in Romo's class about how you handle "strong" comments or comments that are out of line. It is a real business and finance group. I think my questions often are outside their experience or frame of reference, as their comments are often beyond mine. I like it though. It is neat to have a dialogue with folks I would not otherwise have much contact with. But sometimes I worry that my presence in the class may be giving some of them a recurrent sense of devolution of the profession. They must be wondering, "What's this old Mexican doing here anyway?" Is he lost? He doesn't look like a Stanford law student.

The topic this week was the history of the large law firm, and Professor Gardner started off with a brief presentation and guided the discussion. Gardner is a well-respected scholar and legal historian. I think he may be the only one who understands my questions. Before going into the substance of the session, I wanted to comment on what I think is the basis of the disjunction between the workshop participants and me. After grappling with this issue over the weekend, I think the difference is that in talking about the "history" of the large law firm, they are clearly not treating it as an empirical question or problem in the same way that social scientists or historians would look at, say, the history of immigration from Mexico to the United States subsequent to the Treaty of Guadalupe Hidalgo, or the history of Mexicans in southern California.

Law is different. It is not empirical and looks at things from a normative perspective. Because law is a relatively closed, logical system, generalizations are unrestricted by empirical considerations. In law you can conclude that something is true or false without demonstrating its truthfulness or falseness outside of law. It sounds a bit like magic, witchcraft, or hocus pocus, but there are things that are seductive about law. First, as long as you construct a logically consistent system, you can never be wrong. Second, and this is my favorite part, in law you get to make up the rules as you go along. Third, if something does not fit it, you get to create an exception. For example, in law there is the "reasonable man."[13] This is not a real man, or a composite of men, or even an average or typical man. The reasonable man refers to the way that judges or juries believe a person in a similar circumstance would act or, more accurately, how the person "should" have acted. In *Delgado*,[14] for example, *la migra* (INS) went into a factory and conducted a "survey" of workers because they had a tip that undocumented workers might be employed there. The INS refers to them euphemistically as "surveys." I guess it sounds more respectable to say you are doing a survey than that you are conducting a raid. Can you see *la migra* saying, very respectfully, like Stevens, "Excuse me, sir, but we are conducting a survey and wondered whether you might happen to have your documents on you? Would you mind terribly if I asked where you were born?"

During the so-called survey, armed INS agents stood at the exits so that no one could escape, as others walked about questioning workers. The Supreme Court held this was not an illegal seizure in violation of the Fourth Amendment's protection against unreasonable searches and seizures. An initially consensual encounter between law enforcement and an individual can be transformed into an illegal seizure "if, in view of all the circumstances surrounding the incident, a reasonable person would have believed that he was not free to leave."[15] Under these circumstances, however, the Court reasoned that they were not seized because a reasonable person would have known he or she was free to leave. Law is therefore able to use the concept of acts being reasonable or unreasonable without ever defining "reasonableness" or corroborating it empirically. It is like magic in the sense that you can never be wrong.

What is scary is that I was learning very quickly to think like a lawyer and was intrigued by legal scholarship. I had internalized the concepts and vocabulary and could now talk about the reasonable man without a blink. Because of cases involving "battered women," there is now increased recognition of a reasonable woman standard. From *Delgado* and other cases, it is clear that we have yet to develop a reasonable Mexican, or a reasonable undocumented worker, standard.

Professor Gardner started off with statistics on demographic changes among firms.[16] There was a dramatic increase in the number of attorneys at the turn of the twentieth century, followed by a gradual increase until the 1980s, when there was a significant spurt.[17] There was also a dramatic decline in the number of lawyers in private practice and the number of solo practitioners. While in 1948, 61 percent of all attorneys were in solo practice, by 1980 only 33 percent were in solo practice,[18] and today the percentage is even less.

Before the 1880s any firm larger than three members was rare, and those with eleven lawyers were termed "law factories." The senior partner in a firm was usually the "big litigator." In addition to the high-profile litigator, there was a "workhorse" type who took care of the day-to-day business and an apprentice who was being trained. The first large law staffs, it seems, developed around the railroads. Another factor was the merger movement, which occurred roughly between 1897 and 1906. Few companies consolidated, but those that did came to dominate. Another factor that led to the development of the large firm was the emergence of large transactions and the corporate reorganization movement, which required lots of bodies so that corporations could acquire a lot of clients. Recruitment of attorneys became regularized so that firms began to recruit the best students from the top law schools. There was also the emergence of anticompetitive cartels among firms, so that the salaries of lawyers were fixed, and there was an unwritten rule that they would not compete with one another.

It was not until 1967 that "Cravath" (Cravath, Swain, and Moore), a prestigious New York law firm, broke this unwritten price agreement. Prior to this, Cravath set the standard. It was not clear that the laws applied to law. Firms began to use partially meritocratic criteria, but there was still discrimination. Until recently, few Jews were admitted as partners, for example, and most of them were admitted in what have been termed "White Shoe" firms.

A recurrent theme is the rhetoric of decline or devolution. It is interesting that this rhetoric or theme has been a constant one from the beginning. Professor Gardner felt it would be natural to be skeptical of the rhetoric, unless you saw it as a continuous decline in law. The sense of devolution is linked to the perception of a decline in "gentility." The old WASP club of white gentlemen was being undermined. There was the notion that everyone was born a gentleman. What was interesting is that this was seen not simply as a decline in ethnic homogeneity in the profession but as a decline in gentility, a decline in autonomy, an undermining of the view that as professionals we should be above particular constituents' interests. Gardner asked whether these claims had any substance. He, like Professor Gold, believes there have been qualitative differences. I could not help but think about our friend Stevens. I wondered whether there was a parallel between the perception of a decline in gentility in the profession of law and a decline in professionalism in the role of the English butler.

In the past, one company suing another was almost unheard of. Morgan Stanley broke ranks in 1975 and represented "raiders" in hostile takeovers. The mind-set at the time was, "Look at who the raiders were? Their last names are different." Goldman and Solomon were the old Jewish crowd. Chris Huffman, an attorney at a successful investment firm, added that the world of investment banking has changed, so that it's now all transactional.

What I found most interesting is Huffman's discussion of his father. This was the first time that someone said anything about his background or biography. His father was an attorney and practiced for fifty-five years. His father told him, "Even though you will make a lot more money, your practice will be worse in every other respect." His father had the same clients for forty-five years and wondered how you could have more than two hundred partners. Instead of being seen as a counselor, you would be seen as a "cost." Everyone agreed that what lawyers do is very different today than it was in the past. Steve Jackson mentioned that law has moved from a monopoly to a market economy. Publication of the *American Lawyer* and Steven Brill's editorials sent shock waves through the industry. Firms started to advertise and compete, although at first they denied it. This has undermined the relationship of trust with clients.

The ensuing discussion was most revealing and interesting because I began to see these fancy practitioners as individuals with problems and human frailties. Steve Boalt got the ball rolling. He said something like, "I am going to be very candid here, and sometimes this gets me in trouble, but we have a real problem with associates who leave and are very angry and bitter." He added that he believed it was because Cravath sets the norm. The sense that I got from Steve Boalt and Kathleen Fletcher is that those firms where most people make partner are the very ones where folks get most upset when they don't make it. Steve said, "The nicer firms fare worse." Someone asked whether the problem might be that associates are not given enough feed-back. Gardner wondered whether there is a notion that a profession is not supposed to lay people off for business reasons.[19] This reminded me of Stevens, who at the end was trying to maintain the same quality of service at Darlington Hall with a vastly reduced staff. The dilemma is captured when he relates his decision to add another staff person without first getting his master's approval.

Certain themes emerged during the discussion. Rather than one history, there appear to be multiple histories. New York and Washington are important, but they are unique, and we cannot generalize to the rest of the country. What struck me most is the extent to which practitioners in San Francisco see practice in the Bay Area as being different from the New York model. The real shocker for me was the rise in the importance of litigation. I wonder if the masses of Stanford law students realize this. I certainly did not. I am also fascinated by the extent to which the New York model and mystique permeates the law school culture.[20]

I want to close with the issue that I brought up at the beginning. During the class, I only asked one question. In response to Professor Gold's comment that we had two histories, I asked whether this was history at all. I explained that in reading a piece on Baker and Bott's, the Houston firm, I had a hard time figuring out whether it was intended to be historical or folkloric. I guess I felt that the authors of these two pieces "bought into" everything the participants told them. I don't want to appear condescending or cynical but I did not feel that the students or practitioners understood my question. These may be very bright folks, but I don't have a sense that they are well grounded in social science or historical methods. We surely would be suspicious if doctors or morticians did a history of their own profession, wouldn't we? We would expect it to be not only limited but also self-serving. I think that doing a history of law by asking lawyers to assess trends in the profession is like trying to understand the structure of Exxon by interviewing gas station attendants. This may go beyond the insider-outsider debate. I am not sure that these authors are equipped or that they even intended to carry out historical research. I am not saying that their perceptions are not important or interesting. They are. What appears to be lacking is some independent method of conducting archival research by examining letters or records and providing some sort of verification. The danger in this type of historical analysis is that we may wind up legitimating and reinforcing prevailing folklore and firm culture.

The Third Chronicle: "Dividing the Pie"

February 3.

The session today was the first of two focusing on the question of "dividing the pie." Before describing the session, I want to discuss how I am feeling about the workshop. I am having some difficulty in deciding how best to approach my field notes. In the first three sessions, I felt a professional responsibility to take fairly detailed notes, because, as a social scientist, I take what transpires in the session as raw data. On the other hand, the task of taking down everything that happens is daunting, and it is interfering with my ability to participate. I am feeling some tension between the role of observer and that of participant. I am observing, but the professor told us on the first day that he expected the students to participate. I will come back to the issue of student participation. I am not satisfied because I believe that my comments and observations are also important. I need to strike a balance between giving an accurate description of what transpired and my own analysis.

While the law firm was once characterized by organizational stability, it has undergone dramatic change in recent years.[21] Perhaps the most dramatic change has occurred in the way firms divide profits. Specifically, two pillars of traditional firm organization are under assault—the reliance on seniority to divide profits and the "up or out system," whereby one either makes partner after a requisite period of time (normally 8–10 years) or is dismissed from the firm. Moving from a structure in which there were two categories, associates and partners, firms have increasingly expanded to an intermediate tier, which is variously labeled as permanent associate, staff lawyer, nonequity partner, or junior partner.

The changes in the structure of practice raise at least two interesting questions. First, why did the up-or-out system persist when it appears, on the surface at least, to benefit neither the worker nor the employer? It is not advantageous to the firm because it forces employers to get rid of workers who are performing satisfactorily simply because they are not considered ready for promotion. It is also disadvantageous to employees because it denies them the opportunity to remain with the firm without being promoted, an option they surely would prefer over being fired. The authors of one of the readings proposed an interesting answer to the dilemma faced by the firm:

> The puzzle was unraveled by recognizing the dual uncertainty that exists at the time the associate is initially hired. The response to the firm's uncertainty—how to distinguish among a heterogeneous pool of associates—was an apprenticeship period for which the associates were compensated by the promise of partnership for those who met the standards. But this very response created the associate's uncertainty. . . . The up-or-out system serves to bond the firm's promise of a fair evaluation by eliminating access to the firm's principal means of behaving opportunistically: denying partnership to keep the associate working for the firm's account.[22]

The dilemma faced by firms seemed a lot like the dilemma faced by the Stanford Law Review staff. Is there a parallel between the up-and-out system in firms and the Review's extended apprenticeship period? Was the "open" Review policy analogous to the up-and-out system of equal rewards and disincentives based on merit?

There are essentially two models for dividing the pie: lock-step seniority and productivity/incentive. In the traditional model one moves along with a cohort. The model is based solely on seniority, and there are no incentives to produce more than other members of the cohort. Gold related an incident at a conference in which a noted University of Chicago economist, Armen Alshian, commented, "This is an interesting argument, but it could not be true. The firm would surely fail under a system with no incentives." A partner from Cravath stood up and said, "Yes, the pay is the same!" Apparently, Harvard Law School has the same model. Alshian retorted, "But do you have the same offices?" In other words, are there psychic or other types of incentives or rewards?

A number of the partners described how the "pie" was divided in their firms, and in most instances profits are divided according to seniority. I was especially struck when Edward Masters, a distinguished and articulate gentleman and formerly managing partner at Maybury and Foster, talked about his experience. He noted that arrangements for dividing the pie vary by the "culture" and the "personality" of the firm. At Maybury the practice evolved over time.

In developing the new compensation structure, Masters's firm sought to articulate certain basic principles. First, it was a model based on meritocracy, not "lock-step." The model was also one designed to be a "forward-looking way of fixing compensation." They calculated what the firm would make the following year, and everyone received a certain percentage regardless of how the firm did. The partners recognized that there would always be inequities so that all you could hope to attain is what he termed "rough justice."[23] You kept the number of tiers small. This was not a precise or exact model like the one in the reading. If you are going to create a firm as an institution, you have to recognize that various people contribute in different ways, and it would be disruptive to the unit to allocate rewards solely on merit.

I should like to add that there was something very impressive about Mr. Masters. He was clearly older, perhaps in his mid-sixties, dignified, and somehow seemed wiser than the other partners. But what impressed me most is that there was a human dimension to him. When he talked about firm cultures and firm personalities, it felt like he was talking about a family or a fraternal group. Watching him reminded me of Stevens's description of what distinguishes a great butler from a good butler. Early in the book Stevens notes, "it does seem to me that the factor which distinguishes them [the great butlers] from those butlers who are merely extremely competent is most closely captured by this word 'dignity'."[24]

There is an interesting point in the novel where Stevens is embarrassed because Miss Kenton comes into his butler's pantry unexpectedly while he is taking a break from his duties, and she notices that he is reading a "sentimental romance" novel. Stevens resents the intrusion and scoffs at the suggestion that he would actually read such rubbish from cover to cover. He explains that the simple reason that he peruses such works is that it is "an extremely efficient way to maintain and develop one's command of the English language."[25] But mostly he resents the intrusion because to maintain his dignity, "a butler of any quality must be seen to *inhabit* his role"[26] and can never be "off-duty" in the presence of others.

Conceptions of professional values were woven throughout Masters's presentation. His vision of what makes for a successful firm or perhaps a great firm includes the creation of a distinctive culture and personality, an environment that promotes professionalism, mutual respect, and loyalty. Masters added that the fundamental aspects of lawyering remain the same. There is a sense of the quality of what you do, and recognizing and avoiding conflicts of interest. There is also a sense that you don't do anything to hurt the client. But at the same time, practice is organized so that it is a business. It is highly capital-intensive, and there is a strong focus on business management.

Masters felt that focusing on economic self-interest misses what makes you proud of being a part of the organization so that you develop pride and loyalty. Stephen Boalt agreed but was not sure it is inconsistent with self-interest. If you need it, you develop an investment in human capital. Most partners don't have mobility because their human capital investment is specific to the firm. "Age has something to do with it. No one wants you for your last five or ten years," he said.

Before closing I want to comment on what I saw transpiring here today. It was interesting to hear from the practitioners and to have them relate their experiences on how the pie is divided up, the movement toward greater incentivization, and the impact that might have on firm culture and morale. The seminar certainly is unique because it encourages practitioners, academics, and students to engage in significant dialogue. The seminar should provide an opportunity for a free and open exchange among these three elements in the class. I must confess that I was therefore somewhat dismayed by what I perceived as a continual decrease in student participation. There was only one practitioner at the first session (Boalt) when Professor Gold provided an overview of the course and informed us that he would encourage and expect our participation. After that first session there has been virtually no word from the students. I made a couple of comments at the second session, but there were no comments by the students at this session.

I have attempted to raise questions but went unrecognized. In fact, I had several questions that I did not have the opportunity to ask. One of the questions would have been addressed to the young Asian chap, Victor Wong from the Bloom Law Group, who was sitting in for Steve Jackson. Essentially I wondered why there would be a need for such an elaborate distribution system in such a small firm. I also wanted to ask the group whether there would be an incentive to discriminate in hiring on the basis of age. If partners were expected to come into a firm in their mid-twenties, to peak at about age fifty-

four, after thirty years of capital investment in the firm, and a mandatory re-
tirement at the age of seventy, wouldn't a firm view a middle-aged associate as
a risky investment? I asked Boalt this question after class, and he not only disagreed but also seemed uncomfortable with the question. He said, "No, they
would see the experience positively and would treat an associate different
from a partner." I wasn't convinced, and I would have liked to have had the
opportunity to have a more general discussion on this point. I began to gain
more insight into why there might be a disincentive to recruit older people.

I trust there is a logical explanation for the lack of student participation,
but the more I think about Stevens and the traditional English butler, the
more troubled I become with the parallels between the role of butler and the
role of student. Like Stevens, I sometimes feel that we don't really exist, that
we are to be seen but not heard, or that we are there simply as an audience
to witness the exchange between the practitioners and academics. I am aware
that attorneys are by nature aggressive and competitive so that it is hard to
get a word in edgewise when you gather a group of them.

When I went home that night and reflected on the workshop, I could not
help but think about Stevens. I guess the thought of the students sitting
passively listening to the attorneys discussing the firm reminded me of the
relationship that existed between the staff and the great lords who visited
Darlington Hall to discuss pressing world problems. I was reminded specifically of the scene in which Stevens has a dialogue about the concept of dignity with a villager named Harry Smith as he travels through the English
countryside. For Smith, dignity was not something only gentlemen had, it
was something everyone potentially had:

> With all respect for what you say, sir, it ought to be said. Dignity isn't
> just something gentlemen have. Dignity's something every man and
> woman in this country can strive for and get. You'll excuse me, sir,
> but like I said before, we don't stand on ceremony here when it comes
> to expressing opinions. And that's my opinion for what it's worth. Dig-
> nity's not just something for gentlemen.[27]

In rejecting this view of dignity, Stevens relates an incident that he feels
illustrates the limits of Smith's egalitarian conception of dignity. It was past
midnight and his lordship had been entertaining three gentlemen since dinner. When Stevens enters the room to attend to the guests, his lordship asks
him to come forward because Mr. Spencer wishes to have a word with him.

Spencer proceeds to ask a series of weighty questions regarding issues such as whether the debt situation regarding America was a significant factor in the present low levels of trade, the abandonment of the gold standard, and the current situation in North Africa. Stevens is unable to comment and, on each of the issues, responds, "I'm very sorry, sir, but I am unable to be of assistance on this matter."[28]

The gentlemen laugh. Spencer has made his point. He is saying, in effect, our man is unable to assist us on such matters. Yet "we still persist with the notion that this nation's decisions be left in the hands of our good man here and to the few million others like him. Is it any wonder, saddled as we are with our present parliamentary system, that we are unable to find any solution to our current difficulties?"[29] I realize that this is not an entirely fair comparison, but I trust that you will understand why I am troubled by our silence and feel compelled to disclose my displeasure.

The Fourth Chronicle: "Up or Out"

February 10.
Stevens's shadow is still lurking over me. While trying to regain my old writing style, I find myself unwittingly falling back on phrases like "you will no doubt agree." I must be pretty impressionable because I can be influenced by a particular style if I read something. I must be sounding like an English butler with a Mexican accent.

I am anxious to discuss what happened this week because the news is positive. I was encouraged because the atmosphere in the class was different this time. The group seemed much more relaxed and cohesive. Several of the students actually said something. I was happily surprised and feared that I may have been too quick to generalize about the relative passivity of the students. In my view, this was the best and liveliest session we have had so far.

After the summary, Chris Huffman made what I believe was the most exciting comment of the semester, or at least the one that has elicited the most discussion. He said essentially that he believes that the system is based not on economics but on status. He noted that people who are recruited into law are at the top of their class, are very competitive, and are used to getting what they want. In the past, the world was small; there were few partners. "The problem with 'special counsel' is emotional. There are two groups who don't like special counsel, associates and special counsel. We live in a world that is based on status." He mentioned a guy he knew who was appointed special counsel and he could not stand it because it was like he was walking around with a scarlet "S" for "special counsel" on his chest. He did not like it because it was demeaning and he was very aware of the fact that he was a second-class citizen.

I couldn't believe what I had heard but was glad that Huffman had made the point. It was something I had thought about, but I assumed that all of them thought it was all based on economics, so I didn't say anything. His comment made me think about Max Weber's classic discussion of class, status, and power.[30] As long as the analysis was confined to economics, we were only addressing one of the critical dimensions, class. Huffman had now overtly raised the issue of status. What about power? I wondered if we would talk about power. I guess the reading on Skadden indirectly talked about power. I should add that our discussion of market forces and incentivization does not really deal with class in either a Weberian or Marxian sense. As long as economic forces are reduced to talking about market conditions, efficiency, and maximization of self-interest, you are not really dealing with class sociologically. You are not dealing with class in its collective or status sense.

The flip side is that special counsel is a threat to associates because hiring them is more "efficient" for the firm. Hence you have people who may have lower status but make the same money and may actually be more knowledgeable than associates. Huffman added, "It's not necessary for associates (special counsel) because they have to get these people out. Lawyers take themselves seriously. These are people who went to fancy law schools, are very competitive, and expect to make partner. It's not pure economics because it would be more efficient for the firm to keep special counsel."

Cher Davis, a young woman who is a visiting lecturer and who has sat in on most of the classes, said special counsel is attractive to some people such as women who are trying to balance family and career responsibilities. It's attractive because the salary is good and you don't have to put in the hours that you would if you were trying to make partner. It gives them an opportunity to have a career and to pursue a family. I liked this point because it introduced a different perspective—the perspective of the woman who wants to pursue a career without being married to the firm in the way young associates are expected to be.[31]

As I listened to this articulate young woman, I was struck by how different she was from most of the workshop participants. It would have been hard not to notice the gender imbalance in the practitioner and faculty components of the seminar, just as it was hard not to notice the imbalance in those white males who gathered in the insular British world of Darlington Hall to address pressing world problems. Professor Robbins sat in for part of the second class, and the participation of the two female partners has been sporadic. The only regular female participants are Davis and Kit Fletcher, a senior partner.[32] Beyond this and the three female students, it is basically a male group.

What followed proved a fascinating discussion about grades, competition, and the motivation to make partner. Masters felt that this motivation was part of who you are and how you see yourself. "You went to a good law school, had good grades. It's a sign of who succeeds." Pam, one of the students who had a firm job for next year, said that she did not know whether she was looking at this from a skewed perspective but she worked for a firm last year, and she didn't hear anyone talking about making partner. She wondered whether things had changed.

Professor Gold mentioned the competitiveness of the admissions process at elite law schools. Applicants are people who have done astonishingly well at what they have done. They are people who have done well in school, scored well on tests, and have been first in their class. It's an interesting phenomenon. You see it every year with the entering class, when these talented, competitive people suddenly realize they no longer will be at the top. Someone has to be average, even less than average. I was reminded of a Latina student in my class who said that her father and everyone always expected her to do well. Around December of our first year she began amassing outlines for courses and befriending people she thought could help her get better grades. I think she must have been in at least half a dozen study groups. Needless to say, she was devastated by her first semester grades, which were below average.

Masters disagreed with the idea that firms are looking for people who are competitive. They are not looking for people who will compete internally. You don't want people who will be at each other's throats. "They are looking for people who can get along with others in the firm." He asked rhetorically, "How many make partner?" It used to be 20 percent. Boalt added you had to be careful about generalizing from firms like Huller, Erickson and Maybury to other firms. His firm had pressure not to compete. Masters responded that there are competitive types in every firm, and elite firms try to get them.

Professor Gardner said, "People in law are competitive, but they are competitive for grades. Firms don't want ruthless Darwinian associates who want

to win at any cost. People are also selected for cooperation and collegiality."
The ideology of professionalism included the idea that you are all equal.
Someone added that some people go into law looking for security, not com-
petition.

I asked how one could reconcile the emphasis on competition with the
fact that most people won't make it. I also mentioned that in the reading on
the history of the large law firm in the second week, it was noted that firms
were looking for people who were good and bright but not outstanding.
Huffman went back to his initial theme: "It's prestige. It is a prestige-ridden
profession."

Ironically, "the strongest firms are the most elitist." Cravath, for instance,
gets rid of a lot of people. Cravath made a conscious decision not to grow, to
stay small to maintain cohesion, and to pay everyone the same salary. Huffman mentioned one fellow who was fired and who worked for another firm
for about ten years, yet when Cravath contacted him again, he returned. He
thought Cravath was the greatest thing in the world.

Later that night I reflected on the implications of the discussion and my
experience at Stanford. Law was clearly a hierarchical and prestige-ridden
profession. People were status-conscious in the sense that they went to good
schools, wanted to work for top firms, and sought to make partner. But law
was also like a club or fraternity that screened out those who were too competitive or outstanding. They were looking for the lowest common denomi-
nator and, ultimately, for someone who would fit in and not disrupt firm
culture. Someone like my friend Aqueil would disrupt firm culture precisely
because he was outstanding, competitive, and would win at all cost. But perhaps more important, I began to understand what was meant by the phrase
"good old boy." Ironically, although elite schools prided themselves on the
diversity of the student body, anyone who deviated from the norm (white
upper-middle-class heterosexual male) threatened to disrupt firm culture.

Everyone agreed that it was actually cheaper to have senior partners do
the work and that entering associates are overpaid. (Of course, none of them
were entering associates.) I asked whether there was a need to pay associates
more precisely because many of them would not make partner, but my question was quickly dismissed by Huffman. I was still puzzled, then, as to why
firms find it necessary to pay such high salaries for entering associates. What
was the market explanation? It certainly was not that there is a shortage of
candidates. It had to be tied to the uncertainty of not knowing at the outset
who would make partner.

I want to close with an earlier point that I think is important, the male dominance of the profession. What I am really curious to ask, and I may have to wait until we talk about the role of women in the profession, is the extent to which law has been shaped by male values and a male worldview. I recall an article that I read several years ago by the British sociologist David Morgan on the notion of academic machismo.[33] Morgan has a fascinating discussion of how male traits such as aggressiveness and competition are manifested in academia, as they undoubtedly are in law.

The Tenth and Eleventh Chronicles: Alternative Practice Structures and Women in the Profession

March 31 and April 7.
Before getting into the specifics of the workshop, I want to say that I have noticed that certain issues seem to recur. One of them is reconciling traditional notions of professionalism with business considerations; another, lamenting the disappearance of permanent, long-term, trusting relations with clients and a decline in client loyalty. A third issue that has been more covert is changes in the gender composition of the profession and how firms are accommodating the large number of women entering law. We have been dancing around this one and not addressing it directly, but it is simmering. I have already commented on the gender imbalance in the workshop.

We had some interesting dynamics during the Eighth Chronicle, "Working More and Enjoying it Less." Professor James Rebitzer has been studying firms and concluded that people are working more, even though they all say they would like to work less, because billable hours are an index of commitment or "willingness to work." In 1970 only 5 percent of law students were women, and today the figure is at 50 percent. The professor asked how firms would respond to the increasing number of employees wanting shorter hours.

Deborah Robbins, a professor who has studied women in law, responded: "The problem I have with the model is that there are other properties [besides hours worked]. Your model does not take into account variations in quality." Hard work is apparently an index of other traits that are not readily observable. Some women are willing to work for less, and Robbins was "mystified" about why firms aren't more flexible. "I think part of it is the boot camp, the Darwinian mentality in law. Second, people use hours as career commitment. It functions as a proxy for commitment to firm and to the profession. Those who disproportionately drop out are women."

There was nothing terribly radical or surprising in her statement. It was the type of politically correct statement that would normally go unchallenged at Stanford. I was, therefore, surprised by Boalt's response. His face got red and he turned to Professor Robbins. Looking indignant, he said, "I am having a problem here. The interpretations of what happens are being done in such a way that elevates one set of values over another. To say something is 'Darwinian' or 'boot camp' does not advance my understanding." Ironically, the firms that had been most successful had been those such as Cravath that are the most boot camp–like, and firms that were more liberal, and presumably more open to women and minorities, were having a hard time. Boalt was frustrated because he worked for a firm that was trying to accommodate women, and yet these are the very firms that are most criticized because the level of expectations is higher and people are upset when they don't make partner.

I recalled Huffman's discussion of special counsel and wondered whether such a position would be seen as lower status so that people who worked fewer hours would feel stigmatized. Fletcher responded that working part time was not possible for her and that from the firm's perspective it is a very unprofitable way to run a firm in the short run because when one person works part time it increases the "costs" for others. After one of the students, Beth, said that the concern among her classmates was how much money you can make, rather than making partner. Fletcher looked directly at Beth and said, "To be crass. I don't want you to come to M&F for this reason because I will have to stay up all night myself."[34]

During the discussion, it became clear that there was considerable variation in firm culture. Some firms have been very resistant to change. Masters noted that at one point all of the Cravath secretaries were men. But at more progressive firms such as M&F a value is placed on heterogeneity. "Firm culture will always mirror the people in it. You have to have a core set of values to select the best regardless of gender or race. If you want to build a Cravath model, you need lots of money for few partners. But if the goal is to develop good relations with colleagues, you are more willing to do it. One of the problems is that it's things like the *American Lawyer* which define success as profitability." The professor noted, "One story is that being responsive means that you provide the same opportunities to women as men. The view today is that people are different and that firms have to accommodate them."

The young lecturer, Cher Davis, became visibly upset at this point and was bothered by the fact that "lifestyle issues are always defined as 'women's issues.' The dominant model in firms is that of the macho male with women at home."

As I reflected on the tenth chronicle, I realized how much I enjoyed the session and how much I was looking forward to this week's discussion of women in the profession. I liked the fact that Davis spoke up to address the gender issue head-on and that she got upset. I think that when people start getting upset and showing some emotion it generally means that you are dealing with intellectual and theoretical issues that affect them directly. Unfortunately, Boalt was not present. One of the problems with economic analyses is that they make the status quo normative.

The class has evolved over time. We have taken on the characteristics of a group. We all now share a common fund of experiences, we pass the snacks that Professor Gold brings, we greet each other, we sometimes joke, and sometimes we even get upset. I think that the atmosphere is more relaxed and supportive, but the hierarchies remain.

There is a clear hierarchy and division of labor. Gold is the professor. He uses the Socratic method, introduces, synthesizes, and pushes the group to consider contradictions or anomalies. Robbins and Davis are the feminists. Boalt is the litigator, tough, hard-hitting, direct, unabashed, honest, and not at all concerned with political correctness. Masters is the wise, prudent elder, the senior statesman. The students are the attentive audience who smile and listen patiently, although we do interrupt occasionally. Finally, I have found the workshop intellectually stimulating. Though I do not plan to work for a firm, the workshop has provided a rare opportunity to have a glimpse inside the large law firm. We may not always agree, but there is an element of mutual respect.

Cynthia Epstein has done ground-breaking work on women in the profession. She is a middle-aged woman who looks more like a lawyer than an academic. She is carrying out a study of women in large New York firms. This was a fascinating session, perhaps not so much because of the substance of the presentation as because of the quality of the ensuing discussion. There are problems with her study. It is a small sample, limited to New York, and the findings are sketchy. The major findings seems to be (1) women express less dissatisfaction than one would expect, (2) norms are in flux, (3) there are definite generational differences, (4) women are less likely to be supported or encouraged, (5) women, surprisingly, appear to fare better in a meritocratic sweatshop, and (6) women do not always encourage or support each other. Also structures that have special categories, like non-equity partners, general counsel, or part-time associates, may ghettoize women. The gay network appears more supportive of gays than women are of women, so that in the Bay Area having gay representatives on a team is a definite advantage. The generational differences are extremely interesting, as is the issue of the double dilemma experienced by women.

One final pattern that I have noticed is that over the past few weeks Fletcher has emerged as an elder stateswoman. She represents the model of success used by women in a previous generation, but I think she is being accorded respect and deference for her special knowledge and expertise, not so much about law as about women in the profession and how a firm culture can engender diversity. Fletcher is younger, but she has become a female counterpart to Masters, and this has made for greater gender equilibrium. I hope to return to some of these issues.

The Fourteenth Chronicle: Black Corporate Lawyers

April 28.
Over the past two weeks we have been talking about the devolution phenomenon. It was a bit of a letdown after our animated discussions on gender. The first session went over the good ol' days, and we systematically covered some of the themes that constitute the rhetoric of decline. One of the more interesting points that came up is the issue of trust. I assume that because the actions of a partner legally bind other partners, including their assets, like a fraternity (or a gang), you want to make sure that you can "trust" anyone you admit into the club. Jackson mentioned a "rogue partner" in San Diego who got a $40 million judgment against the firm.

Our speaker today, David Wilkins, spoke about blacks in large firms. Wilkins previously worked in a large law firm in New York and is currently a professor at Harvard. This is the first time that we have really addressed the issue of race or ethnicity, though we have talked extensively about gender. I am glad this topic was added because race was conspicuously absent from the initial syllabus. Wilkins, a relatively young, light-skinned

African American who appears to be in his mid- to late thirties, is very personable and articulate. We read an article that he published, which discusses how working for a firm is not necessarily inconsistent with working for civil rights or advancing the status of blacks in the United States. He noted in the article that people of color are too quick to dismiss their counterparts who work for corporate America as sellouts. (What follows is a synopsis of Wilkins's presentation.)

Wilkins is interested in the relation between change and social identity. Most of his friends are black corporate lawyers. Many entered the profession thinking they were going to be like Supreme Court Justice Thurgood Marshall and left feeling like Reginald Lewis. This was the tension that was felt by his generation of black lawyers. What difference, he asked, does integrating blacks make for the style of law that we get? Do blacks practice corporate law differently? Are firms likely to change? Do they change in the direction blacks would want? Are firms likely to change as a result? What are the gender differences among black corporate lawyers? Is it similar to the experience of Jews?

The percentage of black corporate attorneys remains very small, but the percentage of partners has increased slightly.[35] There are various explanations for the low numbers. One explanation is the "discrimination story": white firms don't want to hire blacks. At the other extreme is the "preference story": blacks are not interested in working in large law firms. There is an intermediate, more complex story. The hiring process is impressionistic and entails the use of subjective factors such as speculation, guess, or hunch. These subjective factors work to disproportionately exclude blacks. "Some argue that subjectivity allows for discrimination among people in the middle of the class. Subjectivity allows for stereotyping. There is evidence that suggests that people assume blacks in the middle of the class are worse than whites in the middle of the class. There is less of a tendency to explain away the mediocre performance of white students."

The New York Bar Association has gone to standard goals and timetables. Attrition problems are greater for black attorneys. There are lots of explanations. One is the lack of mentoring. Cross-race and cross-gender mentoring is especially problematic. There are many taboos associated with it. Another problem is that blacks are less likely to have clients referred to them by partners. Some argue for same-gender and same-race mentoring, but this is likely to reinforce stereotypes and marginalize minorities and women. There is a need for more informal mentoring.

Most of Wilkins's data are based on informal interviews. People are very hesitant to talk. Because of the need for confidentiality and the sensitivity of the issues, it is hard to get a representative sample. Also, he is not a sociologist and can't write such a book. "My book will be at the intersection of normative theory and empirical gaps." Professor Robbins noted, "One of the frustrations I have is getting data on black women. Data are grouped. People don't like to talk about it."[36] (She mentioned that the Anita Hill testimony at the Clarence Thomas Senate hearings divided the black community.) "There has been an exodus of black partners who have gone to minority-owned firms. I haven't seen black women doing this."

Generational issues are important. Wilkins's father was among the "pioneer generation" of black lawyers. He went to Harvard, worked for a small firm, and then was hired by a big firm. Wilkins is a member of the second generation, and the current students are the third generation. This generation of black students is more middle class than previous ones.

Wilkins noted, "Some think the only obligation is to do the best job you can. But there are dangers that the more they distance themselves from the black community, this may make things worse." Professor Wilkins sought to illustrate the dilemmas for black attorneys by asking whether you should defend a firm accused of racial discrimination under Title VII. Some of the questions you would ask are whether the claim is valid or frivolous, what type of company it is, and what you are being asked to do and why. There may be cases in which a black person is being brought in simply as window dressing. In making the judgment, you have to consider personal, professional, and group-based or racial identity.

Wilkins added, "The danger is that it can lead to a postmodern dilemma where you do nothing. I am looking to make a statement at the middle level. What are the likely consequences of someone like you [i.e., a black law student] becoming a corporate lawyer? The role of the professional has to account for the fact that this is an important part of the problem." Professor Gold added that he understood the moral responsibility question as being like his mother's stance on any current event or issue. She always asked, "Is it going to help the Jews?"

Overall, I felt this was an excellent session. I liked the way Professor Wilkins framed the issues, and it produced an interesting discussion, although the practitioners were less vocal than usual. I would have preferred a more hard-hitting, no-holds-barred discussion like we had on gender. I think they may have held back on an important issue.

The Last Chronicle: Final Thoughts on the Workshop

May 8.

Rather than summarize the workshops, I have two rather modest goals for my conclusion. First, I would like to briefly examine my own preconceptions about large corporate firms and practitioners and how these were reinforced, altered, or changed by the workshop. In the course of doing fieldwork, we often learn as much about ourselves as we do about the people we are studying. Second, I would like to identify a broad theme that I believe cuts across many of the issues that emerged in the workshop and to discuss it in the context of contemporary critiques of the dominant liberal model in law.

Stereotypes and Misconceptions

I came into the workshop with some fear and trepidation and many misconceptions. One fear that I have already mentioned is that I would be entering an alien world. My interest, after all, is not in the large law firm but in criminal law, constitutional law, and progressive lawyering. Although this was hardly a technical seminar, I often felt handicapped. Sometimes I felt I needed a cram course in law and economics. I felt like a person with limited proficiency in a second language who loses much of the information because his energy is directed at understanding the symbols that are being used, rather than the substance of the presentation. It reminded me of when I first came to the United States and was immersed in an English-speaking classroom without knowing a word of English. I don't know if you can intuit some of this stuff but after a while I began to understand. It also helped that I have a friend who is an economist, and I could occasionally ask him for clarification on certain concepts and issues.

I had to face and conquer my fear of being deficient in this area, and in the end I actually found some of the concepts, like adverse selection and Rebitzer's work, interesting and essential for understanding what was going on in the firm. I also liked Gold's analysis of getting lawyers to act in a way that would be endorsed by clients in a perfect world where they had full information.

A second, related misconception of mine was that all of the participants would be economics or business types. I was shocked when Huffman said, with reference to special counsel, that this is not about economics but about status. Masters told us that this business was "about people" and that you did not need a master plan for everything that you did. When Masters talked about firm culture it sounded like something very personal and intimate. Boalt also consistently articulated a vision of the profession and its decline that was both humanistic and opposed to technological control. Of the practitioners, Boalt reminded me most of Stevens. Like Stevens, he had a consistent view of law and what lawyers do that was clearly eroding before his very eyes. I liked the fact that he was passionate in his discontent.

This leads me into the third misconception. Because I came into the workshop with a monolithic model of corporate lawyers, I was surprised by the diversity that I found. Granted, these folks have much in common. They are middle aged or older (over forty); they are partners in large firms in the Bay Area; they are well paid; most are white; and, with two exceptions, they are men. Despite these similarities, they were fairly diverse. A number of the practitioners are Jewish and would certainly not qualify as WASP or as part of the old White Shoe firm. Although we did not talk about this phenomenon, it wasn't that long ago that Jews were excluded from law schools and firms. It should be noted, however, that the practitioners who participated in the workshop are probably not representative of corporate lawyers, not only because San Francisco is unique, but also because those who opted to participate in the workshop were undoubtedly lamenting the changes that were occurring in law and the movement of law from profession to business.

In the seminar we discovered not only that there are gender differences, but also that there are generational differences among women. This may be an oversimplification, but I believe that Kit Fletcher would fall into the "grandmother" generation and would be more similar to the men, Cher Davis is part of the second generation of women in law (as Wilkins is part of the second generation of black corporate lawyers), and the female students in the class are the new generation. They are not second starters, as Epstein noted, and they are going into law not because it is a lifelong ambition or to make partner, but because the starting salaries are great, and they have a lot of loans to pay, and the perks are good. Where else could a young person, straight out of school and with very little knowledge or experience, earn $125,000 plus and get Knicks or Lakers tickets?

The Meritocratic Ethic and the Dominant Model of Equality

A theme that I observed in the workshop is the tension that exists between meritocratic values, on the one hand, and the need to associate with people we can trust because they share similar values, ethics, and work habits, on the other; the tension between diversity and commonality, and between *Ge-sellschaft* and *Gemeinschaft*.[37] Boalt and Huffman pointed to the apparent paradox—the best firms are the most elitist and, presumably, the least diverse. An additional paradox is that perhaps because of adverse selection, people are probably more dissatisfied at the more diverse and less elitist firms. Fletcher remarked, "Some firms are built around penchant for homogeneity. We value heterogeneity."

Edward Masters captured the meritocratic ethic when he said, "The practice of law is about attracting and keeping good people." On another occasion, Masters remarked that his firm wants to recruit the best people regardless of race or gender. Wilkins made reference to three prevailing explanations for the small number of black corporate lawyers. Two—the discrimination story and the preference story—are, I think, extreme and simplistic. Even if one assumes that some firms don't want to hire blacks and that some blacks don't want to work in firms, neither story is capable of explaining the underrepresentation of blacks. Third, Wilkins proposed that much discrimination is institutional and unwitting and comes into play because the hiring process is subjective, and subjectivity allows for stereotyping.

I agree with Wilkins, but I don't think he goes far enough. There are a number of feminist critiques of law that have important implications for race. These critiques essentially attack the meritocratic model and argue that when there are important differences between groups, as there are between men and women, treating them equally actually works to perpetuate inequality.

The prevailing liberal model in law, and presumably in law firms, promotes a view that defines equality as sameness. According to this model, equality will be attained by treating members of protected groups the same as members of the dominant group. Equality for women will be attained by treating them the same as men; for homosexuals, by treating them like heterosexuals; for blacks, by treating them like whites.

Catharine MacKinnon has been one of the most strident critics of the model.[38] She is critical both of feminists who subscribe to "equal rights" theory and of Gilligan's "different voice" approach.[39] MacKinnon believes that the first view does not go far enough and that the second goes too far in glorifying socially imposed gender differences and terming them "essential." The problem with equal rights is that it permits women to compete in a game with man-made rules in which they are destined to fail. "Why should you have to be the same as a man to get what a man gets simply because he is one?"[40]

The liberal model, on the other hand, is based on the "homogeneity assumption," which holds that there are no "real" or essential differences between the sexes that are not illusory or the product of faulty sex-role stereotyping.[41] Because men and women are essentially the same, once all vestiges of disparate treatment are eliminated, men and women "will achieve equal status through individual freedom of choice and equal competition in the social and economic marketplace."[42] One of the most extreme illustrations of the liberal models is found in *Geduldig v. Aiello*, where the Supreme Court held that the exclusion of pregnancy-related disabilities from a state-administered disability insurance plan was not sex discrimination because "[t]he program divides potential recipients into two groups—pregnant women and nonpregnant persons."[43]

In *Hernandez v. New York*,[44] the Supreme Court similarly upheld the exclusion of bilingual jurors from a petit jury as facially neutral and nondiscriminatory because the prosecutor offered a "race-neutral" explanation for their exclusion. The bilingual jurors were ostensibly excluded not because they were Latino or because they spoke Spanish but because the prosecutor doubted their ability to defer to the official translation of Spanish-language testimony. There was no racial discrimination because the prosecutor's articulated basis for exclusion grouped potential jurors into two categories; those who might have difficulty accepting the official translation and those who would not have difficulty, and "each category would include both Latinos and non-Latinos."[45]

In the last session Wilkins talked about professional identity, group identity, and personal identity. Extrapolating from the feminist critique of the liberal model and from the implications of *Hernandez* for bilingual Latinos, I propose that by adopting the liberal model of equality, law firms work to perpetuate inequality. In other words, treating a white candidate and a black candidate "equally" (the same), or a white associate and a black associate equally (the same), works to produce inequality, to the extent that there are important cultural and group and individual identity differences among these groups that bear significantly on the practice of law.

Wilkins raised the issue of whether a black attorney should represent a defendant charged with employment discrimination and proposed a "checklist" that should be used to decide whether to take a case. There was something about the discussion that troubled me, and I couldn't put my finger on why I was troubled. I was troubled, I think, because the example was based on the dominant liberal model that I have described here.

Wilkins suggested that a black attorney who is contemplating defending a firm accused of racial discrimination under Title VII should consider (1) the type of firm, (2) whether the claim is frivolous or not, and (3) what the attorney is being asked to do. While I am sympathetic to the dilemma identified by Wilkins, and I believe people of color and women should reject being used as window dressing or having the firm otherwise exploit their minority status, the problem with the hypothetical is that it is based on a model where the black attorney must modify her behavior to fit the dominant norm. The problem with this view is that it imposes an additional burden on black attorneys. An additional problem with the model is that it assumes that the racial status of white attorneys is somehow neutralized or nonproblematic.

All of us presumably have a race and a gender, and as lawyers we should use our race and gender to whatever advantage we can. I see no reason why a black or a Chicano/a attorney should not represent a firm accused of race discrimination. The job of an attorney is to be an advocate, not to adjudicate. The decision as to which clients to represent or not represent, moreover, is a firm decision, not an individual one.

I believe that the professional responsibility of each attorney, regardless of color or gender, is to be the very best at what he or she does. Hence if you choose to go into employment law, you must realize that most of your clients are going to be employers that are charged with various levels and degrees of discrimination. If we set up a system where black attorneys have to keep a moral scorecard while white attorneys do not, we are imposing an additional burden and limitation on the black (or Latino) attorney and letting the white attorney off the "moral hook." If whites can defend blacks as well as whites, why can't blacks defend whites as well as blacks?

I am reminded of our friend Stevens again. Once you decided to enter the service of a great household, or even a declining household, you discharged your duties as a butler to the best of your abilities in the service of that household. As a lawyer, you don't always get to pick and choose your clients. I certainly could not choose my client in the Immigration Clinic, and I learned to be a zealous advocate nonetheless. I can't imagine being a great lawyer and only representing people whose values and cultural traits mirrored my own. In fact, a great advocate has to be able to represent people he or she doesn't agree with as effectively as he or she represents others.

People of color and women are bound to be disadvantaged to the extent that the dominant models of what it means to be a great lawyer are based on a standard established by white men. Perhaps that is the greatest legacy that someone like Thurgood Marshall left—a legacy showing how one can be both black and a great lawyer.

One of the ways that the tension between meritocracy and homogeneity gets resolved is by opening up law school admission and firm practice to people of color and women who are most like white men. Professor Wilkins alluded to this when he noted the preference by firms for lighter-skinned blacks. Another manifestation is to recruit middle-class blacks and Latinos who are more like their white counterparts culturally and socially, or to recruit people who claim to be members of a particular racial or ethnic group but are functionally white.

As I reflected on the workshop, I was glad that I had an opportunity to sit in on these conversations by such distinguished professors and attorneys. I have a newfound respect for the complexity of the problems faced by the large law firms and for the humanity and professionalism of this set of practitioners. Despite our differences, I have developed admiration and fondness for them individually and collectively and, like Stevens, feel privileged to have been privy to their dialogue and conversations and to share my reflections and observations. Finally, like Smith in *Remains of the Day*, I hope to have shown that dignity is not something that only gentlemen, or corporate attorneys, have.

CHAPTER ELEVEN

La Noche Triste

In Tacuba, where I grew up as a small child, there was a church near our house, and a square. In the square was a huge old tree that leaned over so much it was almost parallel to the ground. This was the *el Árbol de la Noche Triste,* the Tree of the Night of Sorrows; allegedly, it was where Cortés wept after the Mexicans routed his army as he tried to flee the Aztec capital. Cortés eventually returned to defeat the Aztecs and conquer Tenochtitlán.

I have fond memories of *El Tres,* the house in Tacuba. We called it *El Tres* because there were three houses on the property. As you came in the front gate, the first house on the right was occupied by my mother's brother, *Tío* Roberto, his wife, Adriana, and their two children, Manuel (Macaco) and José María (Chema). The second house was occupied by my mother's sister, *Tia* Margara, her husband the General (Ricardo), and their two daughters, Mercedes (Pete) and Rosario (Chayo). This was my mother's clan, the González-Ochoa. What I remember most is how self contained and insulated we were as a family. I played in the yard and very seldom wandered outside the front gate. Even though there were separate houses, we functioned as a single unit or community, and I roamed freely from house to house.

My parents separated shortly after my dad returned from making the film *Captain from Castille* in Morelia, in the state of Michoacán. I remember that my dad had been gone for a long time and returned with pretty gifts and souvenirs from Michoacán—things made of wood with lacquered painted designs on them like jewelry boxes, ornamental plates and spoons, and a wooden puppet for me.

After my parents split up, my brothers and I stayed with my mother in Tacuba for a short time but eventually went to live with my dad at my grandmother Vita's house in Tacubaya. My mother was reluctant to say bad things about my dad because it's "not good to talk badly about the dead." He was the most *guapo* (best-looking) man she ever saw, he was *bien educado,* and he did not drink or smoke. He had a problem with women, but she said that it wasn't really his fault because women sought him out. He was the love of her life, and she could forgive a lot of things, like his bad temper, his inability to keep a steady job, perhaps even the women, but what she could not forgive was that he would leave us without food or a roof over our heads.

My father was sick. He was a compulsive gambler. He would gamble at anything, with anyone, but mostly it was the horses and poker. He gambled constantly and lost much more money than he ever made. The butcher gave my mother a certain amount of credit until the end of the month, but she had to start taking in sewing at home because she was exceeding her credit.

Once we went to Atlisco to visit my mother's sister, *Tía* María Luisa, and returned to Tacuba to an empty house. My mother had received a telephone call from a neighbor telling her that there was a van at the house and that they were taking the furniture. My dad had lost badly at cards and was forced to hock all of our furniture. "How could you forgive a man who would leave his family without anything to eat to satisfy this vice?"

My mother told me that she and my dad had planned a reconciliation. While we were in military school in Querétaro, she had gone to Chicago and stayed with my dad at *Tía* Terc's house. But she realized that nothing had changed when she saw the ticket stubs from the racetrack all over my dad's room. She went back to Mexico without him, and eventually remarried.

Alfredo's Revenge: LSC Junkie

It is January of my last year and I am sitting in the Saturday all-day workshop for Rick Romo's Lay Lawyering class. A lot of things are the same—Rick,

Roger (the man who videotaped Romo's class), the attorney supervisors, the classroom, and the great food—but the students are different. It's weird, déjà vu. I am taking Romo's class for the second time. I had called Romo in December, near the end of the fall semester, to ask whether there was any room in the class and volunteer to do another placement. There was a void in my life without the LSC. I was especially interested in working with the day laborers. Romo said that everyone had missed me the past semester and if I did the placement, it would help Jessie out. He was in the second year of his fellowship, and there was no one working with him. Romo said he would place me with Socorro, a Two L from Los Angeles and the only other fully bilingual student in the class. We would work with the day laborers in San Francisco under Jessie's supervision.

It was ironic to be working with Jessie because the Day Laborer group had been the most critical of our group the past year. But I liked Jessie and Socorro.[1] I was glad that language would not be an issue in the placement. I especially looked forward to working with them because we were all bilingual.

It wasn't until my last year of law school that I began to understand why third-year students would want to take Lay Lawyering for a second time. During the fall semester, I had taken some valuable courses such as the Immigration Clinic and Employment Discrimination. But something was amiss. Romo's classes had served as my point of reference for the law school experience. Law school simply wasn't the same without Romo. I was torn because I had promised myself that I would not become an LSC junkie. As a Two L, I had resented the know-it-all attitude of some of the Three Ls (see chapter 8). I hoped I wouldn't be like them.

The First Class Meeting

The class is larger than it was last year, and the gender and ethnic makeup is interesting. There are five men and eleven women, and at least nine of the sixteen students are white. Three of the men, including me, are "older." There is one Indian woman, one Chicana, and one Asian. The typical student in the class is single, twenty-four to twenty-five years old, white, and female. Because I have already taken the class and have given a great deal of thought to the issues, I came in to class ready to continue the dialogue that started last year. I realize this is unfair to others. I must approach the class the way that I would if I were teaching it. New and exciting issues are sure to emerge. For now, the previous year's discussion must remain a conversation between Rick and me.

Our first assignment was deceptively simple: prepare three versions of a presentation to our placement group explaining why we are working with the group. We were supposed to determine how much to reveal about ourselves. We began with the Redevelopment group. The first volunteer, Karla, gave a brief introduction of herself and the placement and did not present much substantive information or say much about herself. She said she was from New York, twenty-five years old, a law student, and would be working with an attorney at the Law Project, Cathy Silverman. Rick characterized her intent as going from "thin to thinner to thinnest," because she said less and less about herself in each subsequent presentation. Although her introduction was brief, I liked the way she presented herself: confident, yet modest, approachable, and sincere.

Carmelita was next. She appears to be quiet but has an interesting background and is part Asian and part Mexican. The setting for her presentation was also a Redevelopment tenants' meeting. After the presentation there was discussion about whether one should say that she is from Stanford or working with the Law Project. Two related concerns emerged. One view, expressed by Peter, was that it made political sense to link ourselves with the Law Project. Presumably we want people to know that the Law Project is visible and active in the community. The second view is that Stanford and the notion of being a Stanford law student might put people off. Apparently there is a perception in the community not only that Stanford is an elitist place but also that people from Stanford have a history of exploiting the community. I did not understand why we should hesitate to say we are from Stanford. Though most of us are working through the Project, like it or not, we are Stanford law students. I think it would be somewhat dishonest to try to hide our affiliation with Stanford and the LSC curriculum.

The discussion next turned to how self-effacing Carmelita was. She said she had very little experience and didn't know anything. Rick played devil's advocate, challenging her in a nice way by saying that she had a lot more experience than she gave herself credit for. In fact, both Karla and Carmelita deferred to Cathy, "the Attorney." They seemed to derive their credibility from the fact that they are working with a licensed attorney. I wondered whether one could view such an attitude as a sort of inverse regnancy. The students do not see themselves as superior to the client. On the contrary.

They are excessively humble, but their humility seems to stem from the fact that they are not attorneys. I also wondered how they saw clients. Do clients know anything?

My presentation was the last one of the day. The introduction I gave was not the one I originally intended. I wanted my first presentation to be seductive and regnant. I would appear to be open and personable but would in fact be condescending to the day laborers. It was intended to be "I"-oriented rather than "you"-oriented. I wanted to talk about my background, my education, about how much I knew and how much Jessie, Socorro, and I could help them. I think it was too ambitious and complicated, because I also wanted to do a little Mexican bashing. My second presentation would minimize the "me" and "us" and focus more on the day laborers and what they saw as their most pressing problems. In the third presentation, I planned to ask volunteers from the audience to play day laborers, and I would walk up and begin talking to them. The last scenario was probably the most realistic. My goal was to make the presentations a continuum—from the most to the least directive.

In retrospect, I realize that if there are too many variables in a presentation, the message is likely to get diluted. I had a very complex, ambitious plan, but I did not execute it well. Also, class discussion before my presentation affected what I said. It made me unconsciously focus more on being self-effacing than on how open or responsive I would be to their input. What amazed me about the presentation is that some of the traits I considered negative actually seemed to be working. This prompted me to emphasize them more than I had intended. I couldn't believe that when I was trying to be arrogant and presumptuous, I felt like I had them eating out of my hand. They seemed to like a less humble Alfredo. What I saw as arrogant, they saw as forceful.

So we have returned to Romo's point last year about the gap between our self-conceptions and the external images that others have of us. I feel somewhat ambivalent, perhaps embarrassed, by my accomplishments. Therefore, I tend to say very little about my professional background. Apparently the gap between the way I see myself and the way others see me in this kind of setting is so large that I have a lot of room to be more directive, assertive, and non-self-effacing. Perhaps I am confusing being directive and being immodest. I need to be more directive in this sort of setting; at the same time I realize that one of the reasons I am able to establish rapport with people with less education is precisely because I try to not allow my education to serve as a barrier.

When we talk about the gap between self-perception and external valida-
tion, we are generally talking about people who are viewed much more positively by others than they view themselves. In the exercise, and this was not
planned, I had a chance to see how the audience responded to what I saw as
negative manifestations of my personality. This suggests that what I consider
my negative traits are not necessarily viewed negatively by others. All audiences are not alike, however. The students are not day laborers or homeless,
after all, and it is hard to pretend that they are. Though I had prepared in
the sense of giving quite a bit of thought to what I would say, I always respond to the audience and situation. My discussion about my children and
brothers was not planned, but it felt right. Once I said I had two brothers, I
felt it necessary to say that they were dead, and once I said they were dead, I
felt it necessary to explain how they died. Language affects how we present
ourselves, and you can't always translate things.

For example, if I had made the presentation in Spanish, I would have said
something like, "Tengo dos hermanos pero los dos ya fallecieron" (I have two
brothers but they are deceased). In English, people would normally say they
had two brothers but they died or were dead. This might sound the same, but
it is not. I have two brothers, regardless of whether they are alive or not. My
brothers are as real to me as ever; because I have always had older brothers
it's impossible to conceive of myself as an only child.

I don't feel that exposing one's vulnerabilities in this kind of setting is
necessarily inappropriate. I don't know whether I will talk about my brothers, or about death, when I actually introduce myself to the day laborers,
probably not, but I will do what feels right at the moment.

After my presentation we discussed sexism and machismo. During the
presentation, I was playing with the class by telling them things that I think
many people believe about Mexicans but that they would not expect me to
endorse. Based on last year's experience, I would not be surprised if the issue
of negative machismo and sexism were to arise again. I thought it would be
best for me, a Mexican man, to raise it rather than wait for the problem to
surface. However, during the discussion, Socorro responded negatively. She
felt that it was inappropriate for me to bring up the issue now for two reasons. First, it was unfair to the men because we are assuming it would be
problematic. Second, it was unfair to her, and implicitly sexist, to assume
that she could not handle any situation that may arise.

I disagree. If we view sexism and racism, not as individual attitudes, but
as endemic to society, we should expect it to arise. I am not suggesting that

Latino men are sexist and that white men are not. What I am suggesting is that if we believe that society is sexist, and it is, we shouldn't be surprised if sexism arises in a large group of men and one woman. On the contrary, we should expect it and be prepared to deal with it. The ideal, I think, would be for the problem not to arise but if it does, for the group to regulate itself.

A second issue that came up near the end of the discussion concerned whether people might be offended if someone talked about death in his introductory statement. I believe it was Janet who said she found it interesting that I provided the most detail when I talked about the death of my brothers. Peter added that this was when I touched him because he knew that here was a person who had suffered. Skip, who is white and married to a Navajo woman, said that you would not want to try this with the Navajo. My own response was that if the intent of the introduction was to tell people things that are important to me, then talking about my children and brothers would be appropriate, just like being from New York and twenty-five is important to Karla and being married to an American Indian is important to Skip.

The Placement: San Francisco Day Laborers

In response to public concern about the health and public safety problems created by a large group of men hanging around street corners waiting for employers to approach them, San Francisco established a day laborer program. The program is located in a park in the Mission District and consists essentially of two trailers leased by the city. One of the trailers houses the program staff; the second is a place to be used by the day laborers as they wait for work. The director of the San Francisco Day Laborer Program (DLP) is a personable and energetic man named Geronimo Mendoza.

The basic goal of our placement was to help the workers to organize, or revitalize the Association of Latino Workers (ALATT). In addition to our supervisor, Jessie, there was an advisory committee, composed of lawyers and concerned professionals, that oversaw and administered the day laborer program. A key player in the placement was Rupert Rivera, president of ALATT, which was formed shortly after the program was established. In the early period there was a great deal of enthusiasm among the workers. Though ALATT was now largely defunct, Rivera remained president of the group. There was a long political history, and two rival day laborer organizations emerged from the split. Jessie, Geronimo, and Rupert hoped that with our help ALATT could be restructured and revitalized. We went to San Francisco every Friday to meet with the day laborers.

Though we accomplished a lot in the placement, there were problems. We were unable to separate our work with ALATT from the DLP. Though we were ostensibly working with the day laborers, Geronimo, the executive director of the DLP, was our primary contact person, and he proved to be a charismatic, dominant personality. In addition, because our class members had limited Spanish-speaking ability, we had a difficult time simulating our presentations to the class. We therefore ended up making very different presentations to the class and to the workers. A third, related problem was getting the workers to meet in committees, independently of the ALATT meetings and the DLP. Because day laborers are mobile and many are homeless, it was difficult to get the workers to meet regularly. Even our meetings lacked continuity. For example, the person we had expected to run a meeting would be working. Work was always the priority. But most of the problems were not with the workers but among people in the placement, especially Socorro and me. We disagreed about things like transportation, the fairness of the workload, mutual trust, and commitment.

Commitment and Dignity: Final Thoughts

At the last meeting with the workers, I mentioned to Geronimo that I was sorry that I had to abandon our group (my original subcommittee); Jessie was absent and I was forced to chair his subcommittee.[2] He said that he understood, shook his head, and remarked, "But you know what, it's not fair." I also did not think it was fair. In fact, there were many things about the placement that were not fair.

First, I agree with Jessie that a great deal was accomplished by the workers over the past three and a half months. Yet I feel that we failed because, given what we were capable of doing, we accomplished very little. I also feel that some of the success came despite rather than because of our efforts. I am therefore reluctant to take much credit for their success.

Something happened in the placement—a devolution. I began the placement literally ecstatic. I was happy to be working with Socorro and Jessie and had volunteered to do the placement. I was glad we all spoke Spanish, that the workers all spoke Spanish, and that we did not have to worry about translation. I believed that we each brought something special to the place-ment and would be working together as a team. Jessie did not provide much direction in the beginning. We were confused but were not lacking *ganas* (desire). In the beginning at least, the confusion and lack of direction brought Socorro and me closer together.

Issues emerged early in the placement when Jessie started missing meet-ings. He was late for our first meeting with Geronimo and did not show up for our first scheduled meeting with the workers, a chaotic meeting in which Geronimo took over at the end and established the subcommittees. The problem was that Jessie's role was never clearly defined. A related problem was his ambivalence. He defined himself as a key player and then felt that he could come and go as he pleased. In contrast, I gave the placement high priority and chose to forgo commitments that conflicted with it. In addi-tion, Jessie wore different hats: Hopkins Environmental Fellow, field super-visor, co-participant, and chair of the steering committee that oversaw the program.

Another problem revolved around commitment. Geronimo would say about some event like media training, "nine people signed up for the work-shop and four participated." I was thinking to myself, "Gee, that's not bad, we only got one out of three today in the placement." Geronimo wanted signups from the workers as an expression of their commitment. I knew that we are all very busy, heavily involved people, but when we commit to some-thing, we commit to it, period. Jessie might be the supervisor, but once he defined himself as a co-participant—a choice he made—I had the same ex-pectations of him that I would have of Socorro or myself. His decision to miss this week was particularly untimely because it came at a crucial point, when ALATT nominations took place, and this was his committee.

The reason that our placement group diverted from the curricular plan, I believe, is because we lacked the necessary commitment to implement it. We set up committees, and the committees were supposed to meet during the week, before the general meeting. But we were not willing or able to ac-commodate our schedules to meet with the committees. It may have been unreasonable to expect to make a second trip to the city each week, espe-cially because Socorro, apparently, does not drive. The problem is also a re-sult of Rupert Rivera adding the Mujeres and Amigos groups to the agenda,[3] thereby reducing the amount of time that we have by at least an hour. One alternative that I suggested several times is to hold the committee meetings after the regular meeting. Unfortunately, up to now Socorro has had other commitments, and we generally have to leave before noon so that she can attend another meeting at 1:00 p.m. in Palo Alto.

Another source of tension in the placement was transportation. Placements in San Francisco are difficult because of the distance. They are more difficult when there is only one driver with an old car and when the driver is expected to accommodate his schedule to the nondriver's schedule, rather than the other way around. As I think about it, though, this is not really about transportation; the issue is about having a sense of fairness in the distribution of tasks. This broke down in the placement. It broke down when I began to perceive Socorro's rigidity and penchant for doing things "*a lo mío*" (my way) and when she did a field report on a meeting that did not take place.[4]

The final issue is trust and mutual goodwill. At the March 4 meeting, I discovered that I could not make an innocent comment or suggestion without having to first clear it with Socorro and Jessie. I believe in planning and certainly don't like surprises, but you have to have some flexibility and confidence in your colleagues. Socorro made much of the fact that I suggested we could explore the possibility of inviting an immigration lawyer to a meeting because she thought I was "committing" the other people in the placement. I can't function effectively if I feel that someone is always looking over my shoulder. As a result, the distinction between the committees was completely blurred.

In thinking about the placement and the notion of commitment, I was reminded once again of *Remains of the Day*. Stevens describes the decline not only of the great households but also of his profession. He notes that professionals have to have great dignity and subsume their needs and concerns to those of the client. The professional is always in control, engendering a sense of confidence in those who depend on him or her. The professional is cool in the face of adversity. You can always rely on a professional.

Granted, we are not great butlers and these are day laborers, not English lords, but the day laborers had a lot of dignity, and the concept of professionalism applies nonetheless. Although many were undocumented and homeless and were not paying clients, I defined the workers as my clients. Other than the health and welfare of my children, I can't think of anything that I would give higher priority to than my duty to my clients. For me, not showing up at a meeting is the same as not showing up at court or calling your co-counsel the night before and telling her that you won't be going to court after all. Until we develop this sense of commitment and professionalism toward group work and lay lawyering, we are bound to fall short.

———

I am sitting in my room working on the computer. It is the last day of Lay Lawyering. I am rushing because I need to finish a translation for class and I don't want to be late. Several students are planning to make a special presentation for Romo at the beginning of the class.

My last, self-imposed, assignment for the class is to translate a song called "Amigo." It's a piece sung by Roberto Carlos that captures how I feel. But I realized late last night that the song would be meaningless to most of my classmates because they don't understand Spanish. It's very difficult to translate songs from Spanish to English. The lyrics tend to sound trite or silly in English, and some things just can't be translated because they capture feelings rather than thoughts. But I am doing the best I can.

During my last year of law school, the LSC curriculum came under attack. In fact, from the beginning the curriculum was not fully supported by the administration. It was understaffed, and the bulk of the courses were taught by Romo and Lee. The Lawyering Process course was receiving the most scrutiny. In retrospect, it was ironic. When I took Lawyering Process, there were problems, but now they seemed mild. It was true that most of the people of color felt that we had been silenced, but we did not question the substance of the course, Lee's competence, or the legitimacy of the LSC curriculum. We were questioning the way a specific conflict between a white student and a Chicano student was handled. We were questioning the perceived silencing of students of color by the more vocal white students.[5]

During the second and third years, the criticisms by the students taking Lawyering Process intensified. Professor Lee was on leave, so the course was taught by a visiting lecturer who had been a student in the LSC and was now a successful public interest lawyer. There was consensus that the fellow was very bright and competent, but he was a first-time teacher and it was a difficult course to teach. The concern was that the administration and some of the faculty members who never supported the LSC would use the student criticisms as an opportunity to undermine the program.

There was a flurry of activity designed to promote and support the LSC in the fall. An LSC student meeting was held on November 17, and a larger follow-up meeting with the LSC faculty was held on November 23. The first meeting was attended by about a dozen students and Professors Romo, Bell-Townsend, Associate Dean Thompson, and Lee. The students made constructive suggestions on how to improve the Lawyering Process course and generate more positive student interest in the curriculum. Even the strongest supporters of the LSC, for example, wondered whether it was necessary to have a two-course prerequisite to get into the advanced courses. The second meeting was larger and designed to expose the One Ls to the faculty and the LSC curriculum. Each faculty member made a presentation. In addition, Leo prepared a collage of videotape presentations by students in the curriculum, which was informative and entertaining. Finally, there was a panel presentation by Romo, Bell-Townsend, and Lee titled "My Life in Public Interest Law or How to Survive Law School and Find Happiness in Public Interest Law." Attendance was good, and it went very well.

The prevailing view among supporters of the LSC program was that more students had to be exposed to Romo because he was the senior faculty member and taught the advanced courses in the LSC. Rick worked intensively with a small group of students. These forums were good because they exposed students to the faculty and to students who had taken courses in the program. The students were clearly the best advocates for the LSC.

Stanford law students can be classified into three groups: the mass of students, the "mainliners," who were not taking and would never take an LSC course; the "nibblers," who would sample a course or two in the LSC but would not take more advanced and rigorous courses such as Lay Lawyering; and the "LSC junkies," like Peter, Berta, and me, who were fully committed to the curriculum and took every course they could. As the conflict emerged, the divisions among the last two categories of students deepened.

The attack on the curriculum came to a head during my last semester at Stanford. In January rumors began to surface. Dean West and faculty detractors of the LSC were poised to use the student criticisms to gut the curriculum. The last straw came when we learned that in response to the budget crunch, the dean had apparently asked the key faculty in the program to teach courses outside the LSC. We understood Romo had been asked to teach Contracts, even though he had an agreement with the previous dean when he was hired that he would not have to teach a first-year class. Romo was so crucial to the upper division courses in the curriculum that this move would surely be the death knell for the curriculum.

The students in Lay Lawyering met after class to discuss the problem and develop a strategy. At the meeting we agreed that as supporters of the LSC, it was imperative that we write a letter to the dean, with copies to the alumni, expressing our concern that the LSC was being undermined by the administration. Peter had written a draft letter, but it was admittedly weak. Karla, Skip, and I were asked to work as a subcommittee to write the letter. Because time was of the essence, the letter had to go out before our next meeting. I volunteered to write a draft and meet with Skip and Karla to finalize it. We would share it with Peter or anyone else who was interested, but it had to go out over the weekend. On February 2, a strongly worded letter, which I wrote, was sent to the dean of the law school, Jonathan West, with copies to key alumni who were strong supporters of the law school. The letter expressed "deep concern and dismay with recent events and proposed actions which indicate a lack of support and commitment by the Law School for the Lawyering for Social Change (LSC) Curriculum and the East Palo Alto Community Law Project (EPACLP)." The letter noted that the LSC was recognized as a "unique and innovative" public interest program and detailed the strengths of the program. It concluded with a number of demands, including (1) rescinding the decision to have Professors Romo and Bell-Townsend teach courses outside the LSC; (2) recruiting two new tenure-track professors for the LSC; and (3) providing additional resources for the Law Project.

The Committee to Defend Lawyering for Social Change

The following week we had our regularly scheduled meeting of the LSC Ad Hoc Support Committee. I was late because I had a class. It's hard to describe what happened next. Peter was chairing the meeting and trying to control a large group of angry One Ls who were upset that the letter had gone out to the alumni, although they had authorized us to prepare the letter. The dean apparently went through the roof when he saw the letter and he had cornered Skip, Denise, and Peter, assuming that they were the responsible parties. I wasn't surprised by the dean's response or the attitude of the One Ls because most of them were nibblers, at best. What surprised and upset me is that Skip and Karla were leading the attack on the letter and going through it sentence by sentence. They had approved the letter and complimented me on it. After the meeting, I told Denise, Skip, Karla, and Peter that I felt that I had been set up. What really bothered me was that we had not applied what we had learned in Romo's classes. We had gone into a meeting unprepared and had let the One Ls dictate the outcome. I was disgusted and began to wonder whose side these people were on. I no longer knew who could be trusted.

Later Peter apologized, confiding that he had begun to receive a number of complaints and criticisms from One Ls as soon as our letter was circulated to the Friends of the LSC Ad Hoc Committee. He thought it was important to placate them so that the group presented a united front. But there already was a split between the LSC insiders and the other students.

The meetings of the Friends of the LSC Ad Hoc Committee continued for the rest of the spring of my last year. Because of a class conflict, I did not attend any more meetings, but in April I was asked to draft a response to a memorandum from the dean that presented his vision of public interest law and sought to establish a larger umbrella group of faculty and students to revamp the curriculum. There was a lot of discussion at the April 13 meeting, but no action. After the meeting, the core group of Three Ls met. We were in a bind. We needed to respond quickly to the dean. Knowing the other students would be upset, we agreed to adopt my memorandum and send it to the dean. It would be a memorandum, not from the whole Ad Hoc Committee, but from us as individuals. On April 15 we sent a document with a cover letter from the five students who had taken most, in some cases, all, of the LSC courses. The letter did not mention West directly, but it was a systematic point-by-point critique and refutation of the dean's April 8 memorandum. A couple of days later, Skip, Peter, Denise, and I were invited to have lunch with Professor Lee. He complimented us on the work that we had been doing to support the curriculum. We talked about a wide range of topics. Near the end of the lunch, Lee hit us with the bad news. Romo was resigning. He had accepted a visiting appointment at another university and would undoubtedly be accepting a permanent offer.

The next day, the following memorandum was distributed in our mailboxes:

To: Denise, Skip, Alfredo, Beth, and Peter, April 18, Year Three
From: Jonathan West
Subject: Rick Romo
Dear Colleagues:

By now, you may have heard the unfortunate news that Rick Romo is planning to visit Harvard and that he may well stay there if he receives an offer of a permanent appointment. Word of this will surely get out quickly, and those who care about LSC and the Law Project will under-standably be concerned about their futures.

Under the circumstances, I think it would be desirable to speed up the process of communicating to student and alumni/ae recipients of our March correspondence and particularly to send a memo expressing our joint commitment to LSC and the Law Project.

I suggest that some of us meet today (Tuesday). I am available from 11:30 until 2 (when I have a meeting that includes Denise), from the end of that meeting until 3:30 when we have another event . . . and any time after that event including the evening. Please let me or Judy know when it would be convenient to meet.

Jon

During the long struggle, we had gotten feedback from some of the alumni. A number of them liked our letters and indicated that we had done a great job of keeping pressure on the dean. They felt that we had "West on the ropes" and that we shouldn't let up. The alumni were right. We did have the dean on the ropes. We continued to work with him and eventually en-dorsed a memorandum, which was sent out to students and alumni, in which the dean lamented Romo's departure and affirmed his commitment to the LSC. In the end, we still felt depressed. We might have won the battle, but we had definitely lost the war.

Now I was on my way to say good-bye to Rick. It was a sad day for the stu-dents and for Stanford. What I didn't understand is why I had been affected so profoundly by Romo's departure. Over the weekend, I kept listening to Roberto Carlos and cried every time I heard "Amigo." I seldom cried, except for deaths in my family. Why was I crying over this guy leaving the law school? It didn't make sense. I was lucky. I had taken three classes from him. I was graduating. Why should I give a damn that the One Ls and many Two Ls would never have the opportunities that I had? I didn't know and I didn't understand, but I think it had a lot to do with my brothers.

Sometimes at the height of my alienation in law school I would go driving aimlessly in the Alfredomobile. Once when I had an intense feeling of lone-liness and despair I thought about my brother Héctor: I thought he was the only one who would have understood because he shared my solitude. I kept trying to get in touch with Romo by phone, but all I got was his reassuring voice message: "Hi. This is Rick Romo. I am not in now. Please leave a mes-sage of any length and I'll return your call." He returned the call the next day, and I shared my feelings with him. I think I was affected by his leaving because I had found something meaningful, something that I believed in, and now it was gone. Besides, the idea of law school without Romo was intolerable. I felt like I had lost someone who was stable and unwavering, someone I could trust, talk to, and who might begin to understand my solitude.

The last class was very touching. Denise had a lot of musical talent. She had written a piece for the law school musical with different parts for the students but had withdrawn it because they wanted to trivialize the political message and ridicule Romo. One of the students, Michael, played Romo. He wore a Halloween type of rubber hairpiece with long hair and a receding hairline, like Romo's. The skit was hilarious and had us laughing until we almost cried. It was a wonderful tribute to Romo and the curriculum. After they finished, Romo said, "Okay, who's up?" And we continued with the class as though it was an ordinary day. Near the end of the class, I announced that I wanted to play a tape. I set up my boom box, handed out copies of the translation, and played my song. I cried. Everyone was tearful except Romo.

> "Amigo"
> You are my brother in spirit, truly a friend.
> In every struggle and journey, you are always with me.
> Though you are a man, you have the soul of a child.
> The one who gives friendship, respect, and love.
> I remember together we spent some very difficult moments.
> And you never changed, despite the force of the winds.
> Your heart is like a house with open doors.
> You are truly the only certainty amidst uncertainty.
> In those difficult moments in life, we search for someone
> to help us find the way.
> And the words of strength and faith that you gave me, makes me
>   certain that you've always been at my side.
> You are my brother in spirit in every journey.
> Always greeting me with a smile and festive embrace.
> You share great truths with open phrases.
> You are truly the only certainty amidst uncertainty.
> I can't presume the truth of what I say but it's good
> to believe that you are my great friend.
> I can't presume the truth of what I say but . . .

CHAPTER TWELVE

Return to Kabara

The room is black but the image clear. Brown women dressed in black, bowed heads covered with black shawls. Women carrying candles; chanting in unison, crying, weeping. The room is filled with an eerie, haunting, almost inaudible hum:

> Padre nuestro, que estás en los Cielos
> santificado sea tu nombre . . .
> (Our father, who art in heaven
> hallowed be thy name . . .)
> Santa María, madre de Dios,
> ruega por nosotro los pecadores,
> ahora y en la hora de nuestra muerte.
> (Holy Mary, mother of God,
> pray for us sinners, now and at the hour of our death.)

I wake up in a cold sweat, frightened but relieved. I am not dead! I am back in Palo Alto. It is a recurrent nightmare that I have had periodically since childhood. There is a *velorio* (literally, a vigil over a corpse); black-clad women, surrounding a coffin, mourning the death of a departed loved one. I watch with interest, mesmerized by the haunting rhythm of their chant, at once frightened and consoled by their cries. Then a chill runs through my body as I come to the realization that I am witnessing my own wake. I am dead! The women are mourning for me, or as we say in Spanish, *me están velando.*

It takes a while to realize that it was a dream. I am relieved but concerned about what it means. Is it middle-age crisis? A death wish? No, I doubt it. I've had the same dream for as long as I can remember. Is it linked to an early traumatic experience? I have vague, perhaps repressed memories of nearly drowning in a deep dark hole. My mother told me that when I was about three years old I fell into a well and almost drowned. She was visiting her *tía* in her hometown, Sayula, in the state of Jalisco. I was playing in the yard and disappeared. Everyone looked frantically and it took them a while before they found me at the bottom of the well, moments from death. Later I would have a fear of the water and would be slower to learn to swim than my older brothers. When my dad taught us to swim by throwing us into the pool, I was apparently the only one who sank.

Although my grandfather Alfredo died before I turned two, I remember him vividly. I recall a big man with incredibly thick eyebrows,[1] white curly hair, a large mustache, suspenders, laughing, playing, and lifting me up over his head. My mother said that we lived with my grandfather at the time of his death. Near the end, when he was very sick, he liked for me to crawl into bed and lay down with him. I wondered if I had attended my grandfather's funeral or other funerals as a child and been traumatized by the experience.

———

It has been almost six months since I graduated from Stanford law school, and a year since Mr. Falcón-Guerra's political asylum hearing. I have returned to the Bay Area to finish up the case. I spent a good part of the weekend in Palo Alto meeting with my client, Mr. Falcón, and Mark, the supervising attorney in the Immigration Clinic.

When I think back on the experience of being back in Palo Alto, it's hard to find the right words to describe it. I guess the most appropriate word is *weird*. It was unlike anything I had felt before. It was hard to accept the brutal realization that one could have been so close to something yet so far from it. I had lived in Palo Alto for three years of my life—three important, exciting, grueling, soul-searching years. Yet on my return I felt empty. I felt unconnected to the community, to Stanford, but especially to the law school. I felt like I had never been there and, at the same time, like I had never left. Perhaps the best way to put it is that if it didn't matter that I had been there, it would matter even less that I had left.

I walked the hallways I had walked before; climbed energetically up the stairs to the library; peeked into Rick Romo's office and found a new young professor of color sitting in Romo's chair. I thought, "Do they think that we will be placated so easily? Do they think we'll be content because the law school hired another brown face? I stood in front of the mailboxes, looking in vain for my mine, to the spot where it had been when I left several months before. I knew it wouldn't be there but when no one was watching, I still looked to make sure. I looked for my old locker and found a different name. It was as if all traces of my existence had been erased.

Things had changed. Our Three L mailboxes were now for the One Ls; the Two L students had become third-years; first-years were suddenly important, *chingón* second-years. And there was a new crop of wide-eyed, clean-cut kids with brand-new "Stanford Law" sweatshirts and plastic Stanford Bookstore bags. (I never could understand why all of these people who were Stanford law students wanted to wear "Stanford Law" gear. It was like wearing a uniform in Catholic school.)

As I reflected on it, I realized that things had not changed. Things were the same. Though my name was no longer on the mailbox, or the locker, and Rick Romo was at Harvard, nothing had changed. The hierarchies remained firmly in place. The players had changed, but the game was the same. Several people greeted me and wondered why I was back; some, the One Ls, looked at me like I did not belong. They were right. I didn't belong. I never belonged. What surprised me most is that some people greeted me as though I had never left, the way people had greeted me during the orientation. A woman who works for the Alumni Association, the staff at the library—all of them were very nice but treated me like I was still a student. They seemed very familiar, but it was obviously an indiscriminate, impersonal familiarity.

On Saturday I had to find a room so that we could meet with my client. I was unable to get a key for the SLLSA office, but I remembered that they had conference rooms at the law library. My plan was to introduce myself as alumnus and to ask whether I might be able to use the room, but when I walked into the library and was greeted by a familiar-looking person with a beard, Jim, I knew I was home free. I knew from the greeting that he did not realize I was no longer a student, and so I did what came naturally.[2] I simply asked for a room. He smiled, handed me the key, gave me a folder to sign, and asked to put some sort of ID in the folder. I put in my ID from Super-Duper Video. It was funny. I should add that though security has always been tight at the law library, it is very personal. The staff do not typically ask for an ID, even when you check out a book. I think they pride themselves in knowing who is and who is not a current law student. Besides, Jim was very nice and simply did not realize I had graduated.

———

Oddly enough, I sometimes think a mortician's job is not unlike that of law school staff and faculty. Morticians are trained to be sensitive and empathetic but because the work consists of dealing with death on a daily routine basis, it is by necessity, a transitory, fleeting, impersonal intimacy. I wonder why they called them "funeral homes."

The back room at Gayozo, the funeral home where my brother Alex's *velorio* was held, was a place where the men, especially younger and middle-aged men, gathered. I remember talking there for hours, into the night. We told and retold stories about Alex. As we told the stories, we laughed almost hysterically. My cousin Robertillo was the main attraction. He was the oldest son of my mother's brother, Roberto, and he and Alex had shared numerous adventures together. Robertillo was a great storyteller, almost like the master of ceremonies at a *fiesta*.

No one stopped to explain the purpose of all of this, or said there was a purpose, but it was like a planned event, as we took turns talking and sharing stories about my fallen brother. Storytelling in my family is a team effort; if someone falters or forgets a detail, someone else steps in to correct the story or elaborate. There is a purpose or societal function to this ritual, of course. The stories and anecdotes about the deceased were a belated testimonial and also a roast of sorts. It was almost festive. It was a way of keeping Alex and his memory alive; a way of acknowledging his death by celebrating his life.

It was dawn. We had talked through the night when our laughter was suddenly interrupted by a deep wail, a penetrating scream, like *La Llorona*.[3] It was my mother. She was outside, calling "Alex? Alejandro? Hijo?" Apparently she had heard Héctor's voice and thought for a moment that it was

Alex, that Alex was still alive. We ran outside the room to console her, telling her it was Héctor that she had heard. It had been a bad dream. But I left somehow feeling that she was right. Alex was alive. I still had both my brothers.

Re-preparing the Client

When I agreed to stay on Mr. Falcón's case and to return after graduation, Mark suggested that I arrive a few days before the hearing so that we could practice the direct examination three or four times with the client. I had made a commitment to return; Mark had committed to supervising me and to having a student do an update of the supplementary newspaper materials on social and political conditions in Nicaragua.

Here it was October already. I couldn't believe that it had been almost a year since the initial hearing. I didn't look forward to having to deal with the judge again. I had thought about the initial hearing often over the months and dreaded having to return. They told me to kiss his ass. I had tried but failed. I wondered if I was incapable of kissing his, or anyone else's, ass, because I surely had tried.

The first thing that I did when I arrived at the San Jose Airport was pick up my rental car at Alamo Rental Car. I hated the name. I hated the idea of a Mexican renting a car from Alamo. And I had had a bad experience when I rented a car from them in New Mexico several years back. I had vowed never to use Alamo again. But you couldn't beat the price at $19.50 per day, and so I compromised my ideals, swallowed my pride, and decided to give them another chance. As I arrived to pick up my subcompact, I hoped no one was looking.

I was paying for the trip and was on a tight budget. Other than the Holiday Inn, which is near the campus, there is a shortage of major hotels in Palo Alto. El Camino, south of the campus, is dotted with small, modest-priced motels. After checking at several places, I found a gem of a motel that included continental breakfast—coffee, a prepackaged sweet roll, and fresh tapwater. The motel was small and reasonably clean, but it had the same musty smell as every other cheap motel that I have ever stayed at.

After checking in and unpacking my things, I made several phone calls to see if I could make appointments with some of my old teachers, but I was unsuccessful. I decided to have breakfast at one of the hundreds of cafés in

Palo Alto. I was especially interested in meeting with Richard Cohen. Cohen was one of my professors and had recently been appointed associate dean at the law school, replacing Mathews. Before leaving Palo Alto, I had talked to him about several of the papers I wrote in law school and about the law teaching job market.

My appointment with Mr. Falcón was scheduled for 11:00 a.m. at the Immigration Clinic. I arrived early because Mark had left some recent news clippings and notes on my direct examination on his desk. He had recommended that I go over his comments before I met with the client. The staff, attorneys, and students at the Law Project greeted me warmly—more warmly than I expected and better than I would be treated later that afternoon at the law school.

I had spent the previous week or so preparing for the case, going over the brief, the direct examination, and other materials in the file. Although we had amassed a large appendix of supplementary materials for the first hearing, Mark felt that it was essential to do an update to show that conditions in Nicaragua were such that the Sandinistas still controlled the military and the police and that the government could not control the Sandinistas. We needed, in other words, to establish a nexus between political and social conditions in the country and our client's credible testimony. Mark had gotten a packet of recent, updated materials from the same news service that we used before. Initially, he had committed to having a student do the summaries of each article, but that did not materialize, and about ten days before the hearing he asked whether I could do the summaries. It took me a full day to complete the summaries, but in the end, I was glad that I did because it was a way for me to get immersed in the material once again. I was surprised to see that things had gotten worse and that the country appeared to be in an undeclared civil war. In addition, Mark had wondered whether I could find time during the weekend to translate a few articles that Mr. Falcón had brought in to support the case.

I met with my client until 3:00 p.m. He had gained some weight, but he looked good and, as usual, was eager to get going. We talked for a while before practicing the direct examination. I was surprised at the ease with which we got back into it. I guess it's like riding a bicycle. It's something you don't forget, once you've learned how to do it.

There were still some inconsistencies which I brought to his attention. Mark had heard somewhere that apparently the *turbas,* Sandinista gangs, were no longer in existence. I was instructed to coach the client so that he would say that though the name might not be used anymore, they are still in existence. They are still the same. I don't know where Mark got the idea that the *turbas* no longer existed. Several of the recent newspaper articles mentioned the *turbas*, and Mr. Falcón laughed when I asked whether they were still in existence. Actually, he did not laugh. It was a snide smirk that he used when he thought something was ridiculous or preposterous. He responded with such confidence and self-assurance that you knew the question was silly and off base.

Mark was also concerned about Mr. Falcón's military record. During an earlier meeting, Mark learned that Mr. Falcón had never done his mandatory military service. Mark feared that if the government attorney got wind of this, we could get crucified. In other words, the government could argue that the reason the Sandinistas were harassing Mr. Falcón was not because he was a member of the UNO and opposition efforts but because he had not done his military service. This seemed like a legitimate concern until you thought about it. Why would the Sandinistas wait until after the elections to begin threatening him, since his obligation for military duty had been eight years earlier? Why didn't they harass him sooner? There was also no record to indicate that his failure to serve had been noted by the government or that he had been contacted about it. Finally, death threats were not justified as punishment for not serving in the military. When we asked the client about this, he had a great answer. He said that President Chamorro had eliminated the mandatory service requirement and that people who had not complied with the law had been granted amnesty. Finally, Mark asked me to go over the video of our practice trial to zero in on the questions that Professor Lee had asked during the hearing examination so that we could practice them on Saturday.

We parted and agreed that we would meet the following morning, Saturday, at the law school to go over the direct examination again. This time Mark would interpret, to simulate the actual hearing. Doing the direct examination in English was probably the most difficult and unnatural part of the exercise for me. It was difficult, not because I am not comfortable in English, but because it was artificial talk to my client in English, since he spoke almost no English and he and I always spoke in Spanish.

I arrived early on Saturday morning so that I could get a room for us to practice in. I then walked out to the parking lot to wait for Mr. Falcón. I had given him elaborate directions, he had been to the law school once before, and I knew that he could get around, but I worried nonetheless. I was relieved to see Mark and the client getting out of their respective cars. Mr. Falcón had apparently been waiting for a few minutes.

We went over the entire direct examination, from start to finish, and paused to comment and clarify things. After the direct examination, Mark did an elaborate cross-examination. The whole thing took about three and a half hours but that was okay because the judge had blocked off the entire morning, from 9:00 to 12:00, for the hearing, and we spent a lot of time discussing strategy. We knew that the actual direct examination would be less than an hour. I worried, however, because I remembered the judge's impatience.

Mr. Falcón brought the video of our practice hearing. His little boy had scribbled on the outside of the video in pencil, "*la película de mí Papá*" (my Daddy's movie). When we asked Mr. Falcón whether he wanted to see the hearing examination on the video, he laughed in his inimitable way and said he had seen it at least eight times and knew the questions by heart. I thought Romo would have been proud of our client and our preparation. Mark then proceeded to tell us the areas that Professor Lee had covered in the hearing. The questions focused mostly on the client's marital status (the fact that he was not legally married to his second wife), his military service (the fact that he did not serve), and the genuineness of his fear of persecution (why he didn't just move to another part of the country or complain to the authorities about the threats).

Overall, the direct examination went well, although Mark chastised us for one glaring omission. Not once during the examination did it come out that the Sandinistas controlled the military and the police. This was a crucial point, and we had no chance at asylum if we didn't make the case. Both Mr. Falcón and I insisted that we must have covered it but could not remember because we were so embroiled in the process itself. It was ironic because this was the same point that Mark had made during our trial run for the first hearing. Anyway, we would make sure that this would not happen during the hearing; I had typed a list of key questions that had to be asked. During the hearing, Mark would mark off each key question as it was asked.

Mark's cross-examination was longer and much more detailed than previously. He asked a lot of questions about the military service and about why Mr. Falcón had not moved to another part of the country to avoid persecution. Was Mr. Falcón suggesting that every single Sandinista in Nicaragua knew him and would recognize him? Surely, he wasn't that important or well known, was he? Mr. Falcón handled the questions deftly and was not rattled by what seemed to me a very skilled, aggressive, and spirited cross-examination.

I have to give Mark credit. Though we had practiced until we felt we could do it in our sleep, he was incessant. We would take lunch and go through it again! This time we would practice without interruptions and without a cross-examination. The afternoon session took us an hour. We estimated that the hearing would only take about an hour and a half, including the cross-examination and the judge's ruling.

We took a break and went to the cafeteria to eat lunch. At first Mr. Falcón said that he normally eats a big meal around 5:00 p.m. but that he would keep us company. I was surprised when Mark said that he was buying. I don't know if the client did not have any money, was not hungry, or was embarrassed to have Mark pay for the lunch, but he seemed very reluctant to eat. In part, the problem may have been that he was out of his normal environment and could not read or speak English well. He may also have been embarrassed to admit that he did not have money or could not understand the menu. In any event, Mark insisted, and we had an enjoyable lunch.

We decided that we would not practice again. The next time we would see each other would be at the hearing on Monday morning. We agreed to meet at the court at 8:30 a.m. In the interim, I would translate the most recent articles that Mr. Falcón had brought and bring four copies of the translations and the articles for the file.

Confronting the Silverback

On Sunday morning I decided to move to a motel in the city, overlooking the bay, so that I would be closer to the Federal Building. Although I felt prepared, I spent Sunday going over the brief and the direct examination and practicing my opening and closing. I also went over some important cases. It was highly unlikely that the judge would ask questions about specific cases, but I had to be prepared. But it wasn't all work. I was able to read outside and walk on the path which runs along the beachfront. Finally, I called Mark to check on some last-minute details and questions.

When I thought about the time and preparation that had gone into the case, it was incredible. In talking with Mr. Falcón, Mark had stressed that it would be a tough case to win. It would be a tough case to win because most judges, and probably this one, thought that everything was fine in Nicaragua, after Mrs. Chamorro and UNO came to power. They didn't understand why a member of UNO would fear persecution from the military. After all, UNO was the ruling party. Mark also stressed that if we did not prevail, it would not be for a lack of preparation or hard work.

Mr. Falcón was determined to do his best but realized it would be an up-hill battle. Mark told him that if we lost and he did not appeal, he would have thirty days to leave the country voluntarily before facing deportation. But if he appealed, it would be some time before the appeal was heard. Mr. Falcón wondered whether, in the event of an appeal, we could keep the same *equipo* (team). Mark explained that we could not do the appeal because it would be a conflict of interest; the appeal might be based on a mistake we had made at the hearing. He would be glad to recommend good private attorneys. However, it would cost several thousand dollars.

On Monday morning, I was raring to go. I woke up around 6:00, showered, and took off in my subcompact for downtown, arriving before 8:00 a.m. I wanted to have a cup of coffee and go over my closing one more time. It was strange preparing for the case. I knew it was highly unlikely that I would do the closing, but I had to be prepared to do one. The judge was not likely to ask about specific cases, but I had to be familiar with them or at a minimum have page references for various cases. My opening should be short, Mark said; no more than forty-five seconds. He told me not to ask whether I can do an opening or even call it an opening. He said to just say:

Before we begin the direct, Your Honor, I would like to emphasize three points. First, every one of the death threats and acts of persecution directed at Mr. Falcón as a result of his political beliefs and Anti-Sandinista activities—the forced eviction of his family from their home, and the injuries sustained when chased by a gang of Sandinistas—occurred after the February election won by UNO and Mrs. Chamorro. These threats continued until Mr. Falcón left Nicaragua in December.

Second, the Record will show, and as your Honor undoubtedly knows, the Sandinistas control the military and the police, and the Chamorro government is unable to control them.

Finally, the persecution experienced by Mr. Falcón is as great or greater than was found in cases where the Ninth Circuit has granted Asylum, such as *Aguilera-Cota*, 914 F.2d 1375 (9th Cir. 1990); *Desir v. Ilchert*, 840 F.2d 723 (9th Cir. 1988); and *Artiga-Turcios*, 829 F.2d 720 (9th Cir. 1987).

Traffic was light, and I arrived at the court earlier than expected. I had plenty of time to go over the closing in my head and have a cup of coffee across the street. At 8:30 I headed over to the Federal Building and waited for Mark and the client. Mark arrived at about 8:35, and Mr. Falcón got there shortly thereafter, along with his wife and son. I went over some last-minute details with the client and Mark. There were a couple of minor inconsistencies in the testimony that I brought to Mr. Falcón's attention, and we cleared them up.

One of the things that I had thought about on Sunday was the issue of being deferential. In the first hearing, I had tried and failed. What could I do differently? One technique that I thought of was to imagine the judge as someone else; to think of him as someone I really admired and respected. Just before we went into the hearing, I asked Mark about this technique. He said, "Absolutely, think of him as your father, someone you really respected." It was the right answer but a bad example. I said, "No, my grandfather. I respected him more than my father, although I respected my father."

Mark went to look at the court calendar and returned shaking his head and looking upset. He had some bad news. The judge had scheduled several other cases this morning. We were first, at 9:00 a.m., but other cases followed every half hour after that. It looked like we would not have the entire morning as the judge had promised, unless the other cases were routine matters that were scheduled simply to fill out the calendar.

As usual, the judge arrived late. It must have been around 9:10 a.m. He seemed to be in a jovial mood. He took a key out of his pocket and opened the door to his courtroom. He was wearing a bright sport coat and commented that it looked like he was going to the racetrack today. We went into the court quietly and sat down.

The judge sat down, looked at the file, and asked, "Let's see, what we got here? Is this a continuance?" Mark explained that it was. He then introduced himself and me, and asked if we only had until 9:30. The judge said "Yes, more or less. Since we have it on tape, why don't we begin where we left off. There's no sense starting all over. It's on the tape." We were very agreeable but panicking inside. I hurried to give the interpreter the copy of the terms to help her in the translation. Then I rushed to where Mr. Falcón was sitting and explained that we would continue where we left off and that we only had fifteen or twenty minutes for the entire hearing. I thought about all of the preparation and remembered Romo's statement that you could only improvise if you had planned and were prepared.

It was like the two-minute drill in football. I wished we had practiced doing the hearing as quickly as possible, but we had not. The next fifteen or twenty minutes would be an intense experience. Luckily, I had marked a spot on the paper where we had ended the first time. I was surprised and impressed that the judge had notes. He said, "We stopped when he said that he left Nicaragua because he feared the Sandinistas. . . ." I felt like I was racing through the questions, and I was. On a couple of occasions, I was so anxious that I started asking the next question before the translation. I apologized and put my hand over my mouth.

Mr. Falcón was great. He was self-assured and seemed very credible. The only problem, I thought, was that he was going into too much detail. No one had told me to do this, but I watched the judge and tried to cue in on his responses and body language. The judge did not hide his feelings. At one point, for example, Mr. Falcón was going on and on about all of the things that the Sandinistas had done on November 8, the day he was chased by them and suffered the injuries on his motorcycle. He was explaining how they were engaging in disruptive activities, such as burning buses and government buildings and blocking traffic. I could see that the judge was growing very impatient, and so I rudely interrupted my client and said something like, "Yes, and what did *you* do?" Mr. Falcón caught on right away. He picked up the cue and got to the point immediately. I had to do this a couple of times to keep him on track and to not irritate the judge.

Another problem was that Mark was sitting next to me and continually whispering things to me in my ear during the translation. I had to pay attention to my client's answer, watch the judge's reaction, check for possible inaccuracies in the translation, listen to Mark, and reformulate the question so that I could ask it immediately after the translation. I thought, "Thank God for the translation!" It gave us more time. It gave us the cushion we needed to improvise. As usual, Mark was right on target. The only problem was that I think he tended to ask the obvious. On one occasion, I vetoed it and said, "I think that's clear already." At another point, after Mr. Falcón had been talking about how he feared the Sandinistas, Mark asked me to ask why he decided to leave Nicaragua. This seemed silly. I did not want to ask, but I did, and as I started to ask the question, the judge interrupted me and said, "I think that's pretty obvious."

The cross-examination was not as long as anticipated. Predictably, the government attorney asked about the client's marital status and his wife's immigration status. Mr. Falcón said that her application was in process and had not been concluded. Mark added that they were not legally married and that the basis of her case was totally separate from his. I cringed when the government attorney began to ask about his military service. He asked a couple of questions and went on to something else. It did not take long to see that the government attorney was on a fishing expedition. He would ask one or two questions on a topic and go on. I think the truth is that the government attorney was not well prepared. Mark was pretty sure that he had probably just gotten the file. Even more significantly, I think Mr. Falcón had excellent answers and did not give him an opening. I couldn't believe it when the government attorney said, "No more questions, Your Honor."

The judge then issued his ruling. He began by noting that the respondent had received numerous threats because of the political stance he took against the Sandinistas, that he was visible in his opposition, that his family had suffered injuries, and that he had suffered a substantial scar on his face that was clearly visible. The judge said, "Let the record show that Respondent has a large, visible scar on the left side of his face."

It all sounded great, but I kept waiting for the judge to say, "But . . . ," or "However, ..." I knew that because you can argue both sides of any legal question, I could not assume that the ruling would be in our favor. He never said "But" or "However." It was finally over. I couldn't believe it. We had won! Mr. Falcón had been granted asylum. There was an awkward ten- or fifteen-second interlude during which Mr. Falcón did not realize that it was over or the outcome. I tried to make eye contact with my client and to give him a nod of approval, or a concealed grin, but he kept looking at the judge, as we had instructed him, and then the interpreter. He looked troubled and confused. He didn't understand what had happened. Finally, the interpreter leaned forward and whispered in Spanish that his asylum petition had been granted.

I shook Mr. Falcón's hand as he came off the witness stand, and he moved straight toward his son. He embraced his son and wept unabashedly for several minutes. Mark was busy thanking the judge, signing papers, and putting his things away. I wanted to give my client privacy and went outside to give his wife the good news.

It's hard to describe how I felt. I felt wonderful. It was a feeling of euphoria and satisfaction, as if I had accomplished something important. My return to Kabara proved to be bittersweet. Though I had felt unconnected to Palo Alto and the law school, I was very connected to my client. All of our hard work and preparation had paid off. I was gratified and was beginning to understand why people might want to be trial lawyers. It was an overwhelming feeling of joy and satisfaction.

EPILOGUE

"I Don't Need No Stinkin' Badges"

"We ain't got no badges! We don't need no badges. I don't have to show you any stinkin' badges."

—Alfonso Badolla, in *Treasure of Sierra Madre*

Heroes

I didn't have a lot of heroes while I was growing up. I have vivid memories of going to the matinee in Mexico City on Saturday mornings to watch the exploits of the larger-than-life superhero, El Charro Negro. We also watched *Las Aventuras de Tarzán*. To me, Tarzán wasn't a Hollywood adaptation of the Edgar Rice Burrough's character. Tarzán was *mexicano, indio,* spoke impeccable Spanish, and was the most *chingón* figure *en la jungla* (in the jungle).

After coming to the United States, I discovered that Tarzan was white! I no longer had any heroes, except for my brothers and my dad. Yes, there was Zorro and the Cisco Kid and Cisco's stereotypical sidekick, Pancho, but no self-respecting *mexicano* wanted to be a Pancho or a Sancho. When I saw the film *Viva Zapata,* I was convinced that Marlon Brando had to be Mexican. Anthony Quinn, in fact, was the only Mexican in the film; he won the Oscar for best supporting actor.

In the fourth grade, my school put on a Christmas play. I tried out for a part as one of a group of cowboys who were out in the prairie on a roundup. They were sitting around the campfire talking about how great it would be to be back in town. I was looking forward to being in the play. I had gotten a cowboy outfit for my birthday, with a hat, gun and holster, and chaps. I was disappointed because I wasn't picked to be one of the regular cowboys. I was cast in the stereotypical role of Pancho, a happy-go-lucky *vaquero* with a very thick, exaggerated Mexican accent. In the scene, the cowboys are sitting around the campground, and I had to say stuff in a thick Mexican accent like "When we go back to *de pueblo,* there will bee a *fiesta* and lots of BUI*TI*FULL *señorritas.*" I was a bit of a ham and stole the show. People laughed hysterically when I said my lines. They loved me playing a Mexican but they didn't love me as a Mexican. I didn't know why at the time, but in the end it didn't make me feel good about being Mexican. I didn't understand why Mexicans had to have such thick accents when they spoke English and why they were invariably depicted as swarthy, greasy, unattractive buffoons. I wanted to look like Marlon Brando did in *Zapata,* and I wouldn't have needed all that brown makeup and grease to make me look like a Mexican. I wanted to have a pretty wife like Zapata (who was also played by a white actress). Later on in high school when my hormones started to explode and I got a lot of pimples, I started to wonder whether we really were greasy, since the white kids were not greasy or sweaty like I was.

It has been more than fifty years since the making of *Treasure of Sierra Madre,* and I don't think we have progressed that much. It is a great classic film starring Humphrey Bogart, but the only Mexicans are prostitutes, drunks, and bandits. Mexicans are still largely depicted as bandits and criminals, although now we are gang members or drug dealers, rather than greasy *bandidos.* And even those "stinkin' badges" like a J.D. or a Ph.D. don't really protect us from the racism. We do have more *mexicanos* who are in academia and who are writing about our *cultura* and sharing their narratives, but I am not sure that things have really changed.

We still don't have many heroes or heroines on the silver screen, on television, or in real life. There is a lot of talk these days about "heroes." For me, there are a lot of unsung heroes, like single moms who work the double or triple shift in low-paying thankless jobs and have to be mother and father to their children, or immigrants who put their lives on the line trying to cross the border to the United States and struggle to find a better life for their families. The difference is that the superheroes and role models in this country have always been white.[1] Even "Wonder Woman," who was played by a Latina, Linda Carter, was depicted as white. Whites traditionally played Zorro and the Cisco Kid. Ironically, it is the Chicanos, Blacks, Asians and other people of color who have always been the most patriotic Americans.[2] We were the first ones on the front lines and grossly overrepresented among the casualties of war. I recently went to the Military Museum at the air base outside Riverside and discovered that there was a famous *mexicano* regiment, *Las águilas Aztecas* (the Aztec Eagles), or *el regimiento 201* (201st Regiment) that served with distinction during World War II. *El 201* were Mexican pilots who served during the occupation of Manila and were trained in the United States. At a reception honoring *Las águilas Aztecas* at the military museum in Palm Springs recently, one of the pilots, now a distinguished-looking white-haired man in his eighties, related that when he went out to eat dinner with fellow pilots he encountered "no Mexican" signs in restaurant windows. Although one of the proprietors told him, "No, you are different," he would not eat in the restaurant. He responded, "If you exclude them [other Mexicans], you are excluding me."

El Día de Los Enamorados

I am sitting at my desk at the back of the room. The teacher is talking and the children are laughing. There is a festive mood in the classroom, but I don't have a clue as to what is going on. One of the American girls walks up to me, places a bag on my desk, as the entire class watches, and says with a smile, "This is yours." I return the package and tell her emphatically, "No es mío!" She persists, placing the package on my desk a second and then a third time. I grow more and more frustrated, but she insists and hands the package to me once again. I am determined. I rise from my chair emphatically, walk to the front of the room, place the package on the teacher's desk, and tell her indignantly, in Spanish, that this package is not mine. The teacher smiles and continues with the celebration. I am embarrassed and confused. Humiliated. All of the children are looking at me, laughing, but I do not understand.

I would soon learn about American culture. I would learn that all of the children exchanged little Valentine cards and that some would get larger and nicer Valentines for "special" people. No, I would actually learn that all class members would not get a Valentine from everyone else in the class. I would learn that it was actually competitive, a popularity contest to see who would get the most, and best, Valentines and who would get the least. Some children would buy a Valentine for every single member of the class and one for the teacher.

I feel humiliated by the incident and am motivated to learn English to avoid further embarrassment and humiliation. It seems incredible, but I became fluent in English in about three months. I was very entrepreneurial then, and had become surprisingly popular once I got into school in Oak Forest. I had a large collection of puppets that I had brought with me from Mexico. I decide to stage puppet shows and invite some classmates. I charge a nominal admission fee, ten or fifteen cents. I get a surprisingly good turnout, but some of the children want their money back when they discover all of my productions are in Spanish. They feel cheated, or as they say, "gypped."

When I look back on it, though I may have learned to speak English better than most, if not all, of my classmates and became immersed in American culture, I would never come to feel like an American. Oh yes, they sought to Americanize me by calling me "Al" instead of Alfredo and by pronouncing my name "MY-RAN-DEE" rather than "Mi-ran-dé," but I would always be American in a Mexican sense. I was *americano* in the sense of being *Latino Americano* and part of the continent, though I never felt "American," like hot dogs, apple pie, and all of the other stuff that goes with being American.[3] Don't misunderstand, I participated extensively in American culture. I played Little League, Pony League, adult league baseball, and became an avid White Sox fan. I was a Boy Scout until I earned my Tenderfoot Badge. I lettered in football and wrestling in high school, cruised the A&W Root Beer stand, and attended sock hops and the prom. Yet I always knew deep down inside that I was different from the other children, that I wasn't an "American" because Americans were white. I always knew that I was Mexican. I knew that no matter how hard I might try or how much success I might have, I would never be an American boy. I always knew that I was brown. I always knew in an instinctive way that regardless of my education or accomplishments, I would never be accepted as an American.

It's Valentine's Day again, and I am standing in front of a classroom of young people. It has been a long time since that first Valentine's Day in Oak Forest and several years since I graduated from law school. I'm back where I started a decade ago when I first made the decision to go to law school. I'm older and grayer. I don't know whether I'm any wiser, but I'm feeling good about myself. I'm doing what I love to do. After a stint teaching at the Western Plains School of Law[4] in Plainview, I am back in Riverside, California, teaching "The Chicano and the Law" to undergraduate students. It's a class that I have taught many times before, a class that I could teach in my sleep. Still, it seems like I'm teaching it for the first time. Things appear to be the same, but they are not. I'm a lawyer now, and I have a much more nuanced and complete understanding of the law. I'm looking at the same material in a new way. I'm looking at the world not only as a sociologist but also as a lawyer. I'm a sociologist with an interest in law and social science theories of race and gender but also a lawyer, and I'm discussing cases and integrating law into the readings and discussions. Over the past several years I have combined teaching with a small, largely pro bono law practice. My cases have ranged from divorces and DUIs to domestic violence, child abuse, employment discrimination, and attempted murder. I know that I'm a better and more effective sociology and ethnic studies professor because of my background in law, and I'm also a much better lawyer and law teacher because of my background and experience outside of law.

The topic for discussion today is "The Border and the Law," and we are talking about cases that revolve around "racial profiling," or what I facetiously term "The Mexican Exception to the Fourth Amendment."[5] The Supreme Court has held that you can't stop someone simply because he or she is "Mexican-looking," but it has also ruled that Mexican appearance can be one of several factors that law enforcement takes into account in making a warrantless stop.

I surprise my students this morning when I tell them that it's "el día de los enamorados" and I am going to begin the class by talking about "love." They think I'm crazy because I begin a discussion of racial profiling talking about love. Although love has nothing to do with racial profiling and the Mexican Exception to the Fourth Amendment, it has a lot to with my passion for law and my decision to go to law school. I share the story about my father and how he used to punish us "fairly" and in chronological order, starting with the eldest and ending with me. As the youngest of three boys, I was forced to endure not only my own beating but also the beating and humiliation of my brothers, my heroes, as they were thrashed before my very eyes. It felt a little bit like a death row inmate who had to witness the execution of fellow inmates as he awaits his own demise. I am on a roll, and the class is smiling and watching intently. The students are laughing, but they are laughing with me, not at me. I come in the door to the classroom and dramatically and visually illustrate how my father would come into the house, walking toward us in a menacing manner and simultaneously taking his belt off to whip us. I share how we responded differently to the beatings, with Alex resisting, Héctor enduring, and me pleading and trying to explain and persuade my father not to beat me. I relate how my interest in law and justice did not start when I was in college participating in protests and sit-ins. It didn't start when I was teaching "The Chicano and the Law" at UC, Riverside. It didn't start when I was writing *Gringo Justice* or helping Casa Blanca[6] residents protest police abuse, and it certainly didn't start at Stanford Law School. No, my interest in law and passion for justice started in my family at a very young age, as a child's response to a father who was very unjust and always, always seemed to be above the law; a father who marveled at my gumption in standing up to him and my ability to think on my feet.

In my youth I wanted to be a lawyer but I got sidetracked from that goal and ended up a sociologist and a professor. Now I am all of those things. I'm somehow "double barreled." I reflect on how being a lawyer and sociologist is a lot like being bilingual. It's like knowing and understanding two worlds that should be related but are somehow viewed by inhabitants of each as distinct and impermeable.[7]

I talk about how law for me was like an old, never-to-be-forgotten sweetheart or past love. I tell them how I decided to go back to law school in search of my first love. I also elaborate on some of the things I love about law, to illustrate critical differences between sociology and law. I love law not because it has been fair and just but because of its ultimate concern with fairness and justice. I love law because while the social sciences are empirical and descriptive, law is normative and prescriptive. I love the fact that in law you can say that a case was "wrongly" decided. You can say that it was wrongly decided because it is inconsistent with precedent, because it is unconstitutional, or because it flies in the face of core values or principles of justice and fair play.

Máscaras, Trenzas, Greñas, y Greñudos:
Implications for Legal Education

With the law school experience safely behind me, and my identity and personal integrity intact, I am now free to reflect on my experience and to attempt to draw out some possible implications of that experience for others who might be interested in law or in change and reform in legal education and the legal profession.[8]

Like many other students, I went to law school with idealistic and naive conceptions of law and unrealistic expectations about law school. I went to law school thinking I could make a difference and that I would be able to use law as a tool to reform or change the world and break down societal hierarchies. But these idealistic conceptions and expectations were quickly dashed. I went to law school because I wondered whether my calling was law and lawyering, rather than sociology and teaching and research. I went to law school to become a lawyer, but I came out not only a lawyer but also an aspiring law scholar. I certainly do not regret having gone to law school, for it gave me a different perspective on law school and on law and society. But if I had really known what law school entailed, I wouldn't have gone.

Law school proved demanding, painful, gut-wrenching, but it was also an exciting, stimulating, challenging, and transformative experience. I was profoundly altered by law school, although I was able to salvage the core of my personal and professional identity. I was excited by law and law scholarship. To put it simply: like many others, I hated law school but I loved law. One of the most important lessons I learned from the experience is that the choices I was entertaining were not mutually exclusive, and that you could at once be a good teacher, a good sociologist, and a good lawyer. I learned not only that you can be all of these things, but that the experience in one area enhances your knowledge and competence in the other areas. Ironically, in law school itself, except for the LSC curriculum, I didn't find that my past experience was especially useful or that it gave me any special advantage. In fact, since my various personal, professional, and racial-ethnic identities were firmly in place, the law school experience may have been more difficult for me than it would have been for younger persons whose identities are less fixed. It may have been more difficult precisely because I strongly resisted the boot-camp mentality and the attempts to indoctrinate me and strip me of my identity.

In the final analysis, this book is nothing more than one person's response to the trials and tribulations of law school; an experience that is widely recognized as difficult, alienating, and an assault on one's self-concept and core identity. In the end, I can't speak for anyone except myself, but I hope that my experiences, observations, and reflections not only provide some insight into the law school experience, but also help to shape and reform legal education.

When people ask me whether I liked Stanford, I often respond by saying that it's the only law school that I have ever attended and that I therefore have no basis of comparison or judgment. It's a bit like asking me whether I liked my family, since after all it's the only one I've ever had. But I am firmly convinced that despite differences in prestige, rankings, and physical locale of the 180 or so ABA-accredited law schools, the law school experience has remained remarkably stable and unchanged over the past century or so. Some of the problems and issues I discuss may be unique to Stanford, but most of them are not. I believe that my experiences have broad implications for legal education. My intent was not to write a book about Stanford Law School but to write about the generic law school experience and to share my response to that experience. My intent was to write critically about legal education, not to write a critique and exposé of Stanford Law School. On the other hand, that Stanford is reputed to be one of the most progressive, diverse, and least traditional law schools in the country may give more bite to my critique of law and legal education. For whatever Stanford is, there are surely many law schools that are much more structured, hierarchical, and elitist. Guinier and her associates maintain that "Stanford is distinctive with regard to teaching method and style."[9] A study at Stanford Law School similarly concluded not only that many professors have abandoned the Socratic method but also that "the Dean and many members of the Stanford Law school faculty openly identified with critical legal studies have articulated an interest in creating a nonhierarchical classroom environment, or at least a nontraditional one."[10] If you didn't look very carefully, you might think that Stanford Law School is not elitist or hierarchical. While Stanford may be less traditional and more progressive than most elite law schools, especially with regard to the treatment of women and gays, it would be a mistake to conclude that the law school is not hierarchical.[11]

My experience at the Western Plains School of Law taught me that the less prestigious schools can be as elitist and regnant[12] as the elite schools, or even more so, since they pattern themselves and seek to emulate the elite

schools. Western Plains was a good meat-and-potatoes law school that produced excellent lawyers who served the immediate geographic region. It was
certainly not Harvard or Yale. In fact, it wasn't ranked among the top hundred law schools in the country, but most of the faculty had been corporate
lawyers, dressed in business suits, looked and talked like corporate lawyers,
and were wedded to traditional Socratic methods and hierarchical conceptions of law. The most successful teachers in first-year courses were white
men who were traditional and intimidating practitioners of the Socratic
method. A number of "Hispanic"[13] law students at Western Plains told me
early on how they had been literally shaking in their boots on the first day
of class in Constitutional Law in a section taught by a white male faculty
member who was recognized as one of the top teachers in the law school and
who was a firm practitioner of the Socratic method. While it may be, as
some experts on legal education have observed, that "abusive questioning
styles that once were associated with Socratic methods have largely van-
ished,"[14] Socratic teaching is alive and well and remains the primary method
used to teach first-year law students how to "think like a lawyer."

Rather than encourage open intellectual exchange between student and
teacher, the Socratic method creates the illusion of inclusion and open dialogue when, in fact, it is often no more than a lecture that has been predetermined by the faculty.[15] Gerald López observes, "In the big classroom the
Socratic method looks suspiciously like a set of mini-lectures by the teacher
interrupted by questions that by now no one really expects to precipitate the
kind of critical conversation among students and teacher that many imag-
ined to be the defining strength of legal education."[16] A female law student
at the University of Pennsylvania commented:

> I really resent being an instrument for many—I think it is true for
> many, not all of the professors—for a professor's lecture. I really resent
> feeling like after I am laying out all of this money and putting myself
> under a pretty unpleasant process, that on top of this, I should be
> forced to participate.[17]

In the law school classroom, student comments are always mediated
through the professor so that there is seldom direct interaction or dialogue
among students. As a lawyer, I've noticed that the judge similarly mediates
interactions among attorneys and that great deference is paid to the judge,
just as it is to the law school teacher in Socratic learning. No one ever talks

about this, but it may be that one of the functions of the Socratic method is to prepare students to deal with the hierarchies that they will encounter as lawyers. A co-author of an extensive study of University of Pennsylvania law students, Michelle Fine, observed:

> If law school is "boot camp" to train recruits for equally ruthless law firms, then the success of this institution is brilliant. Silence makes sense, difference has no place, and domination and alienation are the point. Alternatively, if law school is an attempt to engage and educate diverse students democratically and critically about the practice and possibilities of law for all people, then the failure of the institution is alarming. In the meantime, the price borne by women across colors is far too high and their critique far too powerful to dismiss.[18]

Socratic teaching can be a useful way to sharpen one's legal skills and to teach law students how to ask questions and analyze legal issues, but it has drawbacks. I employ an interactive teaching methodology in which, instead of lecturing, I ask a lot of questions and carry on direct dialogue with students. The difference is that I do not intimidate and I do not embarrass students or make them feel they are inadequate or deficient. Although I occasionally call on students, I generally ask for volunteers, and I encourage broad class participation and cooperative learning. Deborah Rhode has noted that, rather than teach one to think like a lawyer, the Socratic method teaches one, at best, to think like a law scholar. It also tends to reinforce the mistaken belief that legal reasoning is a distinct form of reasoning that is qualitatively different from other types of logical or moral reasoning. Rather than teach you that law is indeterminate and that the same set of facts can be used to support contradictory legal outcomes, or that you can render an outcome without making a moral or policy judgment, case analysis and Socratic methods teach you there is an inevitable correct objective result to every legal issue and that legal decisions are cumulative and based on well-founded precedent.[19]

Socratic methods and the large classroom encourage competition whereby the search for knowledge becomes "a scramble for status in which participants vie with each other to impress rather than to inform."[20] They also discourage cooperative learning, which is essential in law practice, and they discourage participation from women, racial and ethnic groups, gays, and others whose cultural background and experience is outside the dominant norm.

The University of Pennsylvania Law School study reported not only that faculty were much more likely to call on and to be more accessible to male students but also that silencing in the classroom was merely one aspect of "a systematically alienating, three-year educational experience."[21] A related problem with legal education is that it remains unconnected to law practice and to the outside world. López has noted that law school is largely about law and "only incidentally and superficially about Lawyering"[22] or law practice. Rhode writes that law students today "can graduate well versed in postmodern literary theory but ill equipped to draft a document."[23] Law school may teach students to "think like" lawyers, but it teaches them almost nothing about legal practice, other than a smattering of courses in clinical programs taught mostly by untenured faculty and considered marginal to the core law school curriculum.

At Stanford, other than in the LSC curriculum and the Immigration Clinic, I was never required to prepare or draft a motion or pleading, and I learned almost nothing about California law. The LSC was a haven from the mainstream law school curriculum and was important precisely because it addressed issues surrounding lawyering and law practice and placed law in the context of race, gender, and class subordination. The LSC eschewed the Socratic method and called into question prevailing hierarchies in the law, legal education, and society at large. Students were encouraged to engage in open dialogue, to develop critical thinking skills, and to challenge regnant conceptions of law and law practice. It offered an alternative for students committed to social justice and to using law as a vehicle for bringing about social change and advocacy on behalf of subordinated communities. Despite the uniqueness of the LSC and the success of the program, in the end it was not supported by the law school administration and is now described by one observer as "defunct."[24] Although the fight to save the LSC exposed internal conflicts and divisions among students, it was significant not only because students banded together in support of the program and successfully exposed contradictions within the law school, but because they showed they were capable of resisting and challenging prevailing hierarchies within law, law school, and society.

If law schools are really committed to diversity[25] and to reforming legal education, they need to self-consciously address issues of race, gender, sexual orientation, and inequality not only in admissions, and in courses that are ancillary to the curriculum, but in the core first-year curriculum as well. The Socratic method as it has been traditionally practiced reinforces a cutthroat, hypercompetitive atmosphere in which some students learn at the expense of others. It reinforces the idea noted by Goodrich, and practiced by my father, that in law, and in life, it is more important to appear right than it is to be right. It helps to breed an environment in which racial and ethnic minorities and women, especially women of color, feel silenced and in which legal problems are treated in a cold, rational, antiseptic way that divorces them from their social, cultural, and economic contexts. Law schools need to seriously question the traditional law school classroom and explore alternatives that encourage cooperative learning, critical thinking, and meaningful dialogue.

The University of Pennsylvania Law School study found that women and racial ethnic minorities were much more likely than other students to report being alienated, intimidated by the Socratic method, and silenced in the classroom. Despite identical entry-level credentials (LSAT and GPA), the study found significant differences in academic performances, with men outdistancing women. By the end of the first year of law school, men were three times more likely to be in the top 10 percent of the class. Women were also much less likely to be selected for law review membership or as members of Order of the Coif (a prestigious law school honorary society).[26] There were also strong attitudinal differences, with first-year women being far more critical of the law school experience. But there appears to be a homogenization or a silencing of women as they progress through law school. "Third-year female students . . . are less critical than their third-year male colleagues, and far less critical than their first-year counterparts." Women are far more likely to enter law school with idealistic conceptions of law and with a commitment to public interest law and social justice. "But their third-year counterparts leave law school with corporate ambitions and some indications of mental health distress."[27] Finally, many women are alienated by the manner in which the Socratic method is used in the large classroom. And women report much lower rates of class participation than men and are much more likely to feel estranged, alienated, and delegitimated. Women often complained that they felt silenced in the classroom both by faculty who were likely to call on men, and by their male counterparts who often jeered or ridiculed their comments. One young woman noted: "Law school is the most bizarre place I have ever been. . . . [The first year] was like a frightening out-of-body experience. Lots of women agree with me. I have no words to say what I feel. My voice from that year is gone."[28]

Margaret Montoya uses the metaphors of masks (*máscaras*), *trenzas* (braids), and *greñas* or *greñuda* (uncombed or unkempt person) to describe the silencing of the voices of people of color and women in the law school classroom. In a manner reminiscent of the so-called brain trust at Stanford, described by my student Cristina, Montoya recounts how she marveled the day one of the white Harvard law students explained the facts and legal issues in the famous civil procedure case *Erie v. Tompkins:* "His identification of the Court's reasoning [was] so precise and concise that it left a hush in the room. He had already achieved and was able to model for the rest of us the objectivity, clarity, and mental acuity that we/I aspired to."[29] Montoya, on the other hand, was silenced in a class of 175 students when she sought to put the experiences of a young Chicana in a cultural and gender context that she understood. *People of the State of California v. Josephine Chavez*[30] was the first case assigned in Criminal Law and involved a twenty-one-year-old unmarried woman who had given birth to a child while sitting on the toilet in a darkened bathroom in the family home, as her mother and her two sisters slept in the bedrooms of the small family home. The legal issue before the court, divorced of its context, was whether the baby had been born alive for purposes of the California statute and was therefore subject to being killed. The class wrestled for three days with complex philosophical questions surrounding what it means to be alive in legal terms but ignored other relevant facts—that Josephine already had had an illegitimate child and that she attempted to hide the birth from her family by wearing a girdle and loose clothing. After listening for three days and wondering why facts relating to Josephine's life were being ignored, Montoya finally mustered the courage to speak up. But she was traumatized by the experience and her comments went outside the normative legal discourse, as mine often did.

Interjecting questions of race, ethnicity, class, gender and the cultural context in which Josephine Chavez's actions were to be judged would have gone against the grain of conventional legal discourse and "would introduce taboo information into the classroom,"[31] for law tends to see issues of race, class, and gender as largely irrelevant to law and legal education. Moreover, Montoya believed that one's right to occupy a classroom seat at an elite law school could be called into question "if one were to admit knowing about the details of pregnancies and self-abortions, or the hidden motivations of a *pachuca*, . . . by overtly linking oneself to the life experiences of poor women."[32] Throughout her law school career, Montoya used her *trenzas*, the braids her mother had taught her to make as a little girl, to retain her sense of difference and dignity while simultaneously seeking admission into the elite world of white culture by demonstrating that she was not a *greñuda*, an unkempt, low-life, dirty Mexican.

Bringing in information about the cultural context of Josephine Chavez's life also would have been taboo because it would have required using Spanish words to contextualize her experience. Montoya points out that in the 1970s, Spanish was still the language of Speedy Gonzales, José Jimenez, and other racist parodies.[33] Telling her story and speaking her truths required that Montoya say "unconventional things in unconventional ways." "Speaking out assumes prerogative" and is an exercise in privilege, whereas "silence ensures invisibility" and "provides protection."[34] Silence serves to mask one's identity and to facilitate entrance into the world of privilege.

Patricia Williams similarly relates feeling marginalized and illegitimate as a black woman at Harvard Law School. Her great-great-grandmother Sophie was sold as a slave to her maternal great-great-grandfather, slave owner Austin Miller, a thirty-five-year-old attorney who raped and impregnated her at the age of eleven.[35] When she doubted her ability to compete at Harvard Law school, Williams took solace in the perverse fact that "the Millers were lawyers" and so she "had it in her blood" to be a lawyer.[36] While taking contracts she also saw the inadequacy of contract law, which was incapable of addressing the experience of those who were property and were, in fact, themselves the objects of contracts.

Throughout the law school experience, I continually felt silenced and excluded. I felt silenced in Civil Procedure because my commentary was ridiculed or ignored, silenced in Constitutional Law because my questions were often outside the established parameters of legal discourse, silenced on the Stanford Law Review because my background and writing experience was not relevant for gaining membership. The students of color and I also felt silenced in Lawyering Process, the initial required course in the LSC, because the white students were uncomfortable talking openly about race and racism. There was also apparently some resentment toward me because I was outspoken and because I had been a professor and was perceived as having an unfair advantage in the class. In law school I encountered hierarchies at every turn: in classroom performance, grades, prestigious clerkships, firm jobs, and law review. Ironically, I also encountered hierarchies in the progressive LSC curriculum that were based on one's position on various boards and student organizations, the number of classes one had taken in the LSC, and one's relationship with our charismatic mentor, Rick Romo.

————

Lani Guinier relates the story of her days as a Yale law student in 1974 when a male law professor walked into class every morning and addressed everyone, men and women, as "gentlemen":

> Every morning, at ten minutes after the hour, he would enter the classroom and greet our upturned faces: "Good morning, *gentlemen*." He explained this ritual the first day. He had been teaching for many years; he was a creature of habit. He readily acknowledged the presence of the few "ladies" by then in attendance, but admonished those of us born into that other generation not to feel excluded by his greeting.[37]

For him, the women in the class were also "gentlemen," a term that referred primarily to men, though it was also perceived as gender, race, and class neutral. "If we were not already members of this group, law school would certainly teach us how to be like them."[38] Learning to think like a lawyer entailed much more than learning the black letter law.

Although the gender and racial composition of the student body at the major law schools in the United States has changed dramatically since the 1970s, law schools have remained remarkably resistant to change. López notes that "legal education regularly resists change—change of any sort" and "calls for transformation of what goes on in this country's law school's somehow get deftly deflected, delayed or diluted."[39]

Perhaps the most dramatic change in the legal profession over the past several decades has been the entrance of women and racial and ethnic groups into the profession. In 1960 a mere 2.6 percent of the lawyers and 3.5 percent of the law students were women.[40] Today, about half of all law students and 20 percent of all lawyers are women. Racial minorities, on the other hand, made up less than 1 percent of the legal profession in 1960 and a little over 4 percent in 1985.[41] Racial minorities made up only 4.3 percent of law students in ABA-approved schools in 1969–70, the first year such figures where compiled, and by 1985–86 they made up 10.4 percent of all law students.[42] In fact, in the anti-affirmative era of the 1990s the proportion of racial minority students in law school actually declined. Soon after the University of California imposed a ban on affirmative action, Boalt Hall had only one black student in its entering law school class.[43] The proportion of women and racial and ethnic minorities in law teaching has been increasing steadily over the past few years. According to a report prepared for the American Association of Law Schools (AALS),[44] in 1994–95, 28.5 percent of all faculty in AALS member schools were women, whereas by 1999–2000 women made up 31.5 percent of all law school faculty. Faculty racial minority representation increased slightly from 12.3 percent in 1994–95 to 13.6 percent in 1999–2000. Today, then, women make up almost one-third of all law faculty, whereas racial and ethnic minorities combined make up less than 14 percent. In 1999–2000, American Indians constituted only 0.4 percent of all faculty, Asians 2.0 percent, blacks 7.1 percent, and Hispanics 3.0 percent.[45] Only about 20 percent of full professors and 10 percent of law school deans are women, and only about 10 percent of the deans and professors are persons of color.[46] In fact, despite the move toward diversifying law school faculty, 82 percent of all women faculty and 88.4 percent of male faculty are white. Interestingly, although there are more men of color than women in teaching, men of color make up a smaller proportion of all male faculty than women of color: blacks constitute 10.6 percent of all women faculty members, but only 5.4 percent of all men. Latino men, similarly, make up 2.7 percent of all male faculty, and Latinas make up 3.6 percent of all female faculty.[47]

Although law schools have become more diverse and inclusive of racial and ethnic minorities, law schools and firms have not changed to accommodate and incorporate these diverse backgrounds. Significantly, law schools serve not only to perpetuate prevailing hierarchies but also to create them. Socratic teaching methods and legal hierarchies have remained relatively impervious to change. Ironically, then, although law schools and law firms have sought to diversify, they continue to homogenize the diverse cultural experiences of the people they admit. A large proportion of women and men of color experience alienation because they enter law school with a commitment to public interest and passionate advocacy on behalf of their respective communities. As one Latino law student lamented:

> The one thing bad about the way I argue now is that I think it's a little bit less passionately. I've been taught [here] that emotion in an argu-

ment is a minus and in my culture emotion in an argument is a plus. And here whenever you present an emotional side of an argument— which I think is just as valid as many other arguments— ... it's instilled in you that if you make an emotional argument then it's wrong.[48]

One of my problems in law school was that it was difficult for me to be unemotional and detached about things that I felt very intensely about. I was often passionate and emotional, rather than objective and detached. People in my family, after all, were emotional. I was taught that feeling passionately about something was a good thing. My decision to enter law school was itself rooted in complex, visceral emotions, which defy rational, cognitive understanding or simple explanations: because I wanted to be an advocate for change but also because my brother's death had led me to to reexamine my life.

"Stinkin' Badges"

During an interview for a clerkship with a U.S. District Court Judge between my first and second years of law school, her two law clerks characterized her as a "moderate" Republican, who was conservative on fiscal issues but liberal on rights issues. They saw themselves as "liberals" and assured me that the judge was a wonderful person to work for. Although the summer clerkship proved an excellent learning experience, it also exposed me to hierarchies in the judicial system.

I shared an office with the other summer clerk, Sandhya Patel, a second-year law student from Santa Clara University Law School. Sandhya was from New York, and her parents were born in India. We discovered we had a lot in common. We were both bilingual and bicultural and proud of our respective ethnic heritages.

Our office, which we called the dungeon, was a dingy place located on the twenty-fifth floor of the Federal Building with bad fluorescent lighting and no windows. It was like a prison without bars. The U.S. marshals maintain security in the Federal Building. At least one marshal was assigned to each floor of the building, and about half a dozen were on duty at the entrance to the elevators on the first floor. Unless you worked in the building, you had to go through metal detectors and might be subjected to additional searches. Employees were given photo identification badges, which clipped to a pocket or lapel. The marshals rotated shifts, although one person was

assigned primarily to each floor. Most of the U.S. marshals were retired police officers, former military, or former Border Patrol agents.

My first confrontation with the marshals took place on my second day of
work. I had run into Sandhya at the entrance to the Federal Building. We
were coming in to work together, and I was carrying a handsome leather
shoulder bag that I purchased in Mexico and used to transport books, pen-
cils, pens, sunglasses, and other materials. As we came through the metal
detector, one of the marshals looked intently at the screen, as though he had
uncovered something important or illicit. He stopped the machine, paused,
and asked in an accusatory tone, "What have you got in there, a Walk-Man?
They don't let you take that up there!" I said, "Look, I don't know what bag
you're looking at, but all I have in there is a constitutional law book." The
marshal responded, "Okay, you don't have to get excited. I'm only doing my
job." I said calmly, "I'm not excited, you're the one who's getting excited. I
just want to get to work." He looked down at me and saw that I had a cup of
coffee in a styrofoam cup and a muffin in my hand, and he informed me,
almost as an afterthought, "Oh, no food or drinks are allowed up there."
Everyone including judges, clerks, and secretaries routinely brought food
into chambers, although no food was allowed in the courtroom itself. But I
wasn't going to the courtroom. I kept my cool and said, smiling, "I see, so
you're going to get punitive with me, huh?" He got nasty. "I will if I have to,
so don't push it!"

Later, as I reflected on the incident, I thought about my brother Alex.
How would Alex have reacted? He would have kicked the guy's ass on the
spot or perhaps waited for him after work, but I wasn't Alex and there were
about six of them and they were armed. I was a law student at Stanford, a law
clerk for a respected federal judge, a would-be attorney. I felt good that I was
able to keep my composure under pressure. The incident was mildly irritating, but mostly it was unreal. A long line had gathered behind us, but I
remained oblivious to the line. People were getting impatient with the marshals and could not understand why I was being detained. Since the metal
detector had gone off, they had me empty everything out of my pockets and
take off my belt. Instead of getting upset or frustrated, I decided to role with
the punches. I moved slowly and deliberately. Most people were trying to
rush through so that they would not be late for work. I figured that if they
were going to give me a hard time for carrying a constitutional law book in
my bag, I would slow down the line and draw attention to the incident. I
slowly emptied my pockets and put my keys and loose change in the con-

tainer. I knew the fact that I did not get flustered or submit to his authority and that I slowed my movements upset the marshal even more.

When we got into the dungeon, Sandhya and I debriefed. She was amazed that I was able to deal with the situation without getting flustered. She could not believe the marshals' behavior, especially the one who gave me a hard time. She was admittedly naive. Her father was a professor, and she had lived all of her life in an upper-middle-class white suburban community in upstate New York.

During the course of the summer, I saw the marshals in action. They never bothered me again when I entered the building, though I got some dirty glances from the one guy on several occasions. On Mondays, when people were sworn in as citizens, there was a flood of people into the building. Most of the people in the long lines were either Asian or Latino. These were the family and friends of people who were being sworn in as United States citizens. It's hard to describe how I felt. I guess I felt a lot of anger and resentment toward the marshals because of the way that they treated these people. Once they realized that we were court employees and saw our badges, they treated us respectfully, but they treated the Asians and Latinos who were visitors like dirt. They treated them, not like people, but like animals who had to be corralled and herded into the building.

The incident over the constitutional law book pricked my memory, and I recalled a nasty encounter I had a long time ago with an INS agent in Lincoln, Nebraska. I told Sandhya about it at lunch. I was a young graduate student in the sociology department at the University of Nebraska. It was during the Vietnam War and I was sitting at my old rolltop desk in the graduate student room. In those days graduate students didn't have telephones and had to go to the main office to take a call. The departmental secretary came to the room and told me I had a call. I went to the main office to take the call and discovered that the caller was an INS agent who was at the registrar's office. He had obtained a list of all of the male students who had indicated on their records that they were foreign born. He told me that he was with the Department of Justice and wanted to know whether I was registered for the draft. I responded, in so many words, that it was none of his business whether I was registered with the draft and that I didn't have to answer his questions. He got irate and said, "Do I have to go over there and get the information from you?" I hung up and went back to work.

I had just sat down at my rolltop desk and started reading when the door to the graduate student room burst open. The secretary opened the door and was followed by a burly man in a blue crumpled suit. She pointed toward my desk and said, "There he is," the way you would pick out a criminal suspect in a police lineup. With a half dozen of my startled graduate student colleagues looking on, the man came at me quickly as if he was about to handcuff me and place me under arrest. He flung a credential in my face. It was a badge with his name, which I didn't get to read before he put it back in his pocket. I asked to look at the badge and slowly inspected it. The badge said Department of Justice, U.S. Immigration and Naturalization Service, and something to the effect that he was authorized to deal with all matters affecting immigrants. I told him I was a U.S. citizen and did not have to show him anything[49] or even talk to him. The encounter probably did not last for more than fifteen or twenty minutes, but it seemed like an eternity. He was relentless, telling me that I needed to show him my draft registration card or he would take me into custody. I felt intimidated and scared but responded with the confidence that comes from knowing you are right. I had my draft card in my wallet, but I wasn't going to show him anything. Besides, it seemed as if there was no probable cause or even reasonable suspicion. If he wanted to know whether I was registered, all he had to do was contact my draft board. He berated me and tried every imaginable intimidation tactic, but I didn't budge. I didn't yell or shout. I just told him, "I don't have to show you anything." Finally, he exploded. He pointed a finger in my face and said, "I've dealt with your kind before. I used to work for the INS in Texas. I've worked up and down the border and know how to deal with you people." This was clearly intended as a racial slur, meaning that he had dealt with a lot of Mexicans, but I was unfazed. He finally stormed out of the door, promising to return. After he left, several of the graduate students shook my hand and congratulated me for standing my ground. I never heard from the guy again. The registrar's office had apparently given him access to student records. I tried to complain to the registrar but nothing came of it, and I was too busy with my studies to pursue it further.

As I left the Federal Building to take my last train ride from San Francisco to Palo Alto that summer, I looked back on the experience with mixed emotions. There was no doubt that I had worked very hard and that the judge and clerks had gotten their money's worth, since I was not simply cheap labor but also free labor. I was able to work on a large number of interesting cases, and I learned more during these thirteen weeks than I had during my entire first year of law school.

Yet as I thought about the summer, perhaps what stood out most in my mind was not the people in chambers or the experience I acquired, but the incongruity between my role as a summer clerk and Stanford law student and my status as a Mexican. We didn't see many Mexican attorneys, judges, or marshals. In fact, we hardly saw any Mexicans at all,[50] although we saw a handful of black attorneys. Mexicans and other Latinos were usually on the other side of the bench: the janitors, the *pro se* prison litigants, the criminal defendants, or the citizenship applicants.

The incident with the marshals might have been minor, but sometimes the little things are important. For me it was important because, like the earlier incident in graduate school, it reminded me that despite my education and fancy degrees, I was still a "Mexican," a *greñudo*. In the eyes of the marshals and the INS agents, the only thing that separated me from these other Mexicans was my stinkin' badge. I came to the sad realization that without the badge, and perhaps even with it, I would have been just another "smart-ass Meskin." But as I look back on this incident and on law school, I also know that my parents and my brothers would have admired the fact that I had faced the challenge and persisted in resisting the hierarchies. I'd like to think that they would have been very proud of the youngest Mirandé, *el Bebo*.

NOTES

Prologue

1. In this book I use the term "Chicano/a" to refer to persons of Mexican descent who are living in the United States. An emerging term, used interchangeably with Chicana/o, is "Xicano/a," which connotes a strong sense of identity with our indigenous past and the fact that we have not been fully accepted as Mexicans or Americans. See Alfredo Mirandé, *The Chicano Experience* (Notre Dame, Ind.: University of Notre Dame Press, 1985).

2. Chris Goodrich, *Anarchy and Elegance: Confessions of a Journalist at Yale Law School* (Boston: Little, Brown, 1991), 11.

3. Ibid.

4. Ibid., 12.

5. John Jay Osborne, Jr., *The Paper Chase* (Boston: Houghton Mifflin, 1971).

6. Scott Turow, *One L: The Turbulent True Story of a First Year at Harvard Law School* (New York: Warner Books, 1977).

7. Goodrich, *Anarchy and Elegance*, 117.

8. Turow, *One L*, 15.

9. Goodrich, *Anarchy and Elegance*, 11.

10. Ibid., 120.

11. Ibid., 16.

12. Turow, *One L*, 5.

13. Goodrich, *Anarchy and Elegance*, 120. See also Margaret Montoya,"*Mascaras, Trenzas, y Greñas:* Un/Masking the Self While Un/Braiding Latina Stories and Legal Discourse," *Chicano-Latino Law Review* 15 (Spring 1994): 1–37, published concurrently in *Harvard Women's Law Journal* 17 (1994). Citations are from *Chicano-Latino Law Review*. I discuss this article at more length in the epilogue.

14. Ibid.

15. In his book about being half white and half Latino, Kevin Johnson discusses his law school experience at Harvard more than twenty years earlier, but the book

is not exclusively about the law school experience. See Kevin R. Johnson, *How Did You Get to Be Mexican: A White/Brown Man's Search for Identity* (Philadelphia: Temple University Press, 1999).

16. My middle brother, Héctor, dropped out of high school and joined the Marines but he eventually graduated from medical school. Although Alex, the oldest, did not attend college, he studied accounting in night school and became a successful corporate executive in Mexico.

17. Rémy Rougeau, *All We Know of Heaven* (Boston: Houghton Mifflin, 2001).

18. Duncan Kennedy, "Legal Education as Training for Hierarchy," in *The Politics of Law*, ed. David Kairys, 3d ed. (New York: Basic Books, 1998), 54–75.

19. Ibid., 54.

20. Ibid.

21. Ibid.

22. Ibid., 55.

23. Ibid.

24. Ibid., 58–59.

25. Goodrich, *Anarchy and Elegance*, 115.

26. Ibid., 111.

27. Ibid.

28. Kennedy, "Legal Education as Training for Hierarchy," 60.

29. Ibid., 59–60.

30. Ibid., 61.

31. Ibid.

32. Ibid.

33. Ibid.

34. Ibid., 56.

35. Ibid.

36. Ibid.

37. Turow, *One L*, 25. For a discussion of how Harvard "set the style" in the use of the Socratic method and the case method in teaching law, see Robert Stevens, *Law School: Legal Education in America from the 1850s to the 1980s* (Chapel Hill: University of North Carolina Press, 1983).

38. Osborne, *The Paper Chase*, 3.

39. Kennedy, "Legal Education as Training for Hierarchy," 56.

40. Osborne, *The Paper Chase*, 68.

41. Goodrich, *Anarchy and Elegance*, 5.

42. Ibid.

43. Richard Rodríguez, *Hunger of Memory: The Education of Richard Rodríguez* (New York: Bantam Books, 1983), 4.

44. Ibid.

45. Ibid., 5.

46. Ibid.

47. Ibid., 3–4.

48. See Cornel West, *Race Matters* (Boston: Beacon Press, 1993).

49. In addition to writing dozens of articles in academic journals, I have published several books, including *The Chicano Experience; The Age of Crisis* (New York: Harper & Row, 1975); *La Chicana: The Mexican-American Woman* (Chicago: University of Chicago Press, 1981), coauthored with Evangelina Enríquez; *Gringo Justice* (Notre Dame, Ind.: University of Notre Dame Press, 1987); *Hombres y Machos: Masculinity and Latino Culture* (Boulder, Colo.: Westview Press, 1997).

50. John Womack, *Zapata and the Mexican Revolution* (New York: Vintage Books, 1968).

51. According to family folklore passed on by my older cousins Betty and Carmela, who watched over me as a child, when I tried to say "Alfredo" it somehow came out as "Bebo."

52. Arthur E. Sutherland, *The Law at Harvard: A History of Ideas and Men, 1817–1967* (Cambridge, Mass.: Belknap Press, 1967), 162–205.

53. Turow, *One L*, xiii.

Chapter One. *El Día de Los Muertos*

1. See Mirandé and Enríquez, *La Chicana*, 87–95.

2. See William J. Adelman, "Illinois' Forgotten Labor History: The Haymarket Affair," Illinois Humanities Council, May 2, 1984, Illinois Issues. Other materials in possession of author.

3. Héctor Javier X. Mirandé, *The Silver Surfer* (1998). This was a collection of Héctor's poems and short stories (some of which were published in his lifetime), published posthumously by The Estate of Héctor Mirandé.

4. Ibid.

5. See Mark Muckenfuss, "Keeping Their Words: Inland Tribes Race against Time in Effort to Save Their Languages," *The Press-Enterprise*, January 17, 2005, A1, A10.

Chapter Two. *Las Mañanitas*

1. Dena eventually graduated from law school and is working for a large law firm in Los Angeles.

2. Octavio Paz, *The Labyrinth of Solitude* (New York: Grove Press, 1961), 47.

3. Ibid., 54.

4. Ibid.

5. Ibid.

6. Alex and the children were killed near Celaya on a road that is notorious for the large number of accidents and fatalities. The highway is dotted with white crosses, each representing a fatality.

7. On silencing, see also Montoya, "*Mascaras, Trenzas, y Greñas.*"

Chapter Three.   One L, Chicano Style

1. *Marsh v. Alabama*, 326 U.S. 501 (1946); 66 S.Ct. 275.

2. Goodrich, *Anarchy and Elegance*, 30.

3. *Swann v. Burkett*, 1209 C.A.2nd 685; 26 Cal.Rptr. 2861 (1962).

4. I have recently discovered that I am mildly dyslexic and that I often transpose numbers.

5. *Gómez v. Toledo*, 446 U.S. 636; 100 S.Ct. 1920 (1980).

6. In Riverside, California, a woman was convicted of second-degree murder for the methamphetamine-induced death of her three-and-a-half-month-old child. Mike Kataoka and Lisa O'Neill Hill, "Mother Guilty in Baby's Meth Death," *The Press-Enterprise*, September 9, 2003, A1.

Chapter Four.   The Age of Innocence

1. *Marbury v. Madison*, 1 Cranch (5 U.S.) 137, 2 L.Ed. 60 (1803).

2. *Regents of the University of California v. Bakke*, 438 U.S. 265, 98 S.Ct. 2733, 57 L.Ed.2d 750 (1978).

3. 468 U.S. 737 (1984).

4. *Simon v. Eastern Kentucky Welfare Rights Organization*, 426 U.S. 26 (1976).

5. *Linda R. S. v. Richard D.*, 410 U.S. 614 (1973).

6. "Latino" is also somewhat problematic because it connotes that someone is "Latin," or European, rather than indigenous, although it is preferred over "Hispanic."

7. Felix Padilla, *Latino Ethnic Consciousness* (Notre Dame, Ind.: University of Notre Dame Press, 1985).

8. "Aunque la jaula sea de oro, no deja de ser prisión."

9. Lucie E. White, "Subordination, Rhetorical Survival Skills, and Sunday Shoes: Notes on the Hearing of Mrs. G.," 38 *Buffalo L. Rev.* 1 (1990): 1–58.

10. An unstated norm in the Socratic method is that the professor is the font of all knowledge. Hence all dialogue is mediated through the professor, and students should not address one another directly.

11. There were also white students, like Peter, who supported and were sympathetic to the students of color.

Chapter Five.   Making the Grade

1. The focus on grades at law school and the assault on my psyche reminded me in an indirect way of how Bruno Bettelheim resisted thought reform and the assault on his psyche in a Nazi concentration camp. See Bruno Bettelheim, *Surviving, and Other Essays* (New York: Knopf, 1979). The control by the guards in the concentration camp was so complete that it extended to every aspect of the prisoners' lives, including control over basic bodily functions like defacation and urination. Prisoners could resist indoctrination only by retaining control over some minute aspect of their lives. As a psychoanalyst, Bettelheim was able to objectify the experience and to retain his sanity by talking with fellow prisoners with a particular purpose in mind and pondering his findings for endless hours as he was forced to perform menial manual labor, and was able to maintain his self-respect by his "ability to continue doing meaningful work despite the contrary efforts of the Gestapo" (52). Bettelheim concludes that the main problem faced by "the author" was to protect his ego, so that if he should ever attain liberty, "he would be approximately the same person" (62).

2. Thurman W. Arnold, *The Symbols of Government* (New Haven: Yale University Press, 1935).

Chapter Six.   "Walk Like a Man"

1. William (Bill) Pierce was a sophisticated and well-educated black social worker who had a master's degree in social work from the University of Chicago and lived in an upscale, integrated area in Hyde Park near the university. He subsequently befriended our family and exposed Héctor and me to a number of cultural events in Chicago. I recall one incident, in particular, when Mr. Pierce took his two teenage daughters and us to a fancy puppet show, an opera sung by huge marionettes. An elegant smorgasbord dinner followed the performance. Héctor must have been thirteen or fourteen years old at the time.

2. At most schools, being associated with law review makes one an object of awe. Turow noted that at Harvard, the words "the Review" were "a constant, if suppressed murmur around us." Turow, *One L*, 66.

3. Ricardo (Rick) Díaz, "Much to My Surprise," *Stanford Law Journal*, May 19, at 4.

4. Ibid., 13.

5. *Stanford Law Review* Senior Staff, "An Open Letter from the SLR," *Stanford Law Journal*, May 19, at 4, 13.

6. Ibid., 13.

7. Lexis is a computer program that can be used to look up cases and references and check cites.

8. *The Bluebook: A Uniform System of Citation* (Cambridge, Mass.: Harvard Law Review Association, 1991). I want to acknowledge publicly that I hated Bluebooking and I am proud to have failed at this enterprise!

9. Turow, *One L*, 67.

10. *Bakke* is the affirmative action case mentioned earlier in which the Supreme Court held that a University of California Medical School program designed to ensure admission of a specified number of students from certain minority groups was unconstitutional. While rejecting so-called quotas, the Court held that race could be a factor in the admissions process. *Regents of the University of California v. Bakke*, 438 U.S. 265, 98 S.Ct. 2733, 57 L.Ed.2d 750 (1978).

11. The *Federal Supplement* reports federal district court opinions, whereas the *Federal Reporter* (F.2d) contains federal courts of appeals rulings.

12. The election for president was held first, ostensibly so that if you were unsuccessful you could seek a second office.

13. Class notes, February 10, Two L.

Chapter Seven.   *Pan y Chocolate*

1. Outdoor sinks where the clothes were washed on one's hands and knees.

2. I have to admit that I took this admonition very seriously and feel reluctant to talk about the class even now.

3. So as not to overwhelm the reader with excessive detail, I have omitted some of the field notes and edited and condensed others, while attempting to retain the "voice" that surfaced at the time that the reports were written.

4. My field placement during the fall semester was with an education attorney, and I focused on special education. The attorney, Robert Woods, was knowledgeable and caring, but he was not well organized. I decided to develop a Special Education Advocate's Manual for the Law Project because I thought it would be useful for students who might work in that placement in the future.

5. Gerald P. López, *Rebellious Lawyering* (Boulder, Colo.: Westview, 1992).

6. For a discussion of the silencing of women's voices, see L. White, "Subordination, Rhetorical Survival Skills, and Sunday Shoe"; Lani Guinier, Michelle Fine, and Jane Balin, *Becoming Gentlemen: Women, Law School, and Institutional Change* (Boston: Beacon Press, 1997), 49–50.

7. For an interesting discussion of genius and improvisation, see Charles L. Black, Jr., "My World with Louis Armstrong," *Yale Review* 69:1 (1979): 145.

8. By "class," I am referring here to the regular Thursday class in which we discussed the readings. The field supervisors and the students who were taking the "field" component of the class, like Berta and Jessie, only attended the Tuesday sessions. The rest of us attended on both days. This made the class somewhat discontinuous because some people were not privy to the Thursday discussions or the readings.

9. *Chingón* is derived from the verb *chingar*, a complex word in Spanish with multiple meanings, especially in Mexico. It is literally an aggressive form of intercourse, or "pricking." *Chingón* connotes a person with power or influence. See Pedro María de Usandizaga y Mendoza, *El Chingolés: Primer diccionario del Lenguaje Popular Mexicano* (México, D.F.: Costa-Amic Editores, 1994).

Chapter Eight.   Sex, Flies, and Videotapes

1. Memorandum of Cathy Bates to Jane Carter and Alfredo Mirandé on Brief Summary and Tentative Timeline for Our "Recent Immigrants" Project (January 14) (on file with author).

2. I had been especially impressed with a paper by Vanessa López describing the farmworker parents' group in Watsonville (discussed later in this chapter). Vanessa was from East San Jose and came from a working-class family. Her paper was thoughtful and passionate. She criticized the ideas in a paper by another student as stereotyping, misgrouping, and underestimating the farmworker parents. López's paper was powerful precisely because she would not, and could not, separate the issues in the placement from her biography.

3. From Field Report #8, March 8.

4. In our group meetings we had commented on several occasions that the class seemed to be focusing primarily on mechanical issues, such as how to transfer information more effectively. See for example Field Report #6, February 22.

5. I did, but my negativity was directed at some class members, not at Jane or Cathy.

6. Field Report #10, March 29.

7. The women in my family, especially on my mother's side, were far from being passive or dependent. My mother's sister, *Tía* Margara, for example, was a large and extremely aggressive woman, and it was not uncommon for her to get into fist fights with both women and men. She carried long knitting needles and often used them as a weapon during confrontations. She also smoked, drank, gambled, and swore a great deal.

8. Ironically, I was the only one of the three brothers who did not drop out of school or become delinquent. Both of my brothers dropped out of high school. Alex came back to graduate but did not go to college. Héctor was a troubled youth. He dropped out of high school in the first year. At age seventeen my dad and his probation officer forced Héctor to join the Marines. When he got out of the service, he settled down, got married, and started working on a garbage truck. Later he attended a community college and transferred to a four-year school. Eventually he graduated from the University of Illinois Medical School. My dad never believed that Héctor would be a doctor. He promised that if it ever happened, he would "walk on his knees to the shrine of the Virgen de Guadalupe," a pilgrimage normally made to thank the Virgen

for miracles. He did not make the pilgrimage. But it was a miracle. See essay on pilgrimage in Carlos Monsiváis, *Mexican Postcards* (London: Verso, 1997).

9. Class discussion, April 22.

10. Ibid.

11. Class discussion, April 1.

12. Class discussion, March 9.

13. Field Report #13, April 19.

14. Ibid.

15. Field Report #12, April 12–16.

16. Ibid.

17. I mentioned this idea on a number of occasions, such as when we first met María Ochoa and Blanca Rosa Pineda of the Mujeres group, at our meeting with Kim Karnes, a legal service provider whom we consulted in the first phase of the project, and when we were planning the workshop at Latino Legal Services.

18. At the beginning of the role-play, the participants asked whether they should speak in Spanish or English. (We had started our demonstration of the role-play in English.) The two white student interns from an eastern private college laughed and said, "English." I told them to use whichever language they felt comfortable in. We did it mostly in English. I was aware that if we had not spoken in English, Jane would have felt left out or would have expected me to translate. (In retrospect, I should have done this.) I blame myself because I did not anticipate this as a problem or take a stand on the issue. It is significant that we assumed that all of the workshops would be in English. It was, therefore, a nonissue.

19. Gerald P. López, "Cleaning Up Our Own Houses" (November 6, 1991), unpublished manuscript. On file with author.

20. In a classic article, Robert Merton notes that we are all "insiders" and "outsiders" relative to particular groups. Robert K. Merton, "Insiders and Outsiders: A Chapter in the Sociology of Knowledge," *American Journal of Sociology* 78 (July 1972): 9–48. For example, a black female student at Stanford would be an insider relative to other law students but, as a woman and as a black person, an outsider relative to white male law students.

21. Kimberlé Crenshaw, among others, has used the concept of intersectionality to show that the needs of women of color are subordinated to those of white women and men of color. When a white man thinks of gender, for example, he envisions a white woman, and when he thinks of race, he always thinks of a black man. In antidiscrimination law, Crenshaw notes, discrimination claims privilege the voices of white women and men of color. The lack of attention to intersectionality marginalizes the unique race and gender claims of women of color. Kimberlé Crenshaw, "A Black Feminist Critique of Antidiscrimination Law and Politics," in *The Politics of Law*, ed. David Kairys, 3d ed. (New York: Basic Books, 1998), 358. See also Angela Harris, "Race and Essentialism in Feminist Legal Theory," *Stanford Law Review* 42, no. 3 (February 1990): 581–616.

22. See, e.g., Aída Hurtado, "Relating to Privilege: Seduction and Rejection in the Subordination of White Women and Women of Color," in *Signs: Journal of Women in Culture and Society* 14, no. 4 (Summer 1989): 833–55.

23. I don't know how many hours I spent transcribing each videotape, but anyone who has ever done transcriptions knows that it is a very slow process. During our debriefing meeting, Cathy fast-forwarded through Latino Legal Services and did not even see the SFLA tape.

24. Class notes, February 10. This was a recurrent issue in the LSC.

Chapter Nine.   Guerrillas in the Mist

1. Mark Levin was the immigration attorney at the law clinic and my immediate supervisor. Professor Jimmy Rae Lee was the faculty member in charge of the clinic and Mark's supervisor. There were two other students in the clinic, Peter, the Catholic priest, and Nicole, a young Asian woman who had worked organizing day laborers before law school.

2. Ironically, Mark was busy, and we had to wait about half an hour for him. This gave the client and me a chance to get acquainted.

3. The names have been changed to preserve anonymity.

4. Mexicans have a different conception of education so that a person who is *bien educada* is one who is prudent, generous, and well mannered and knows how to treat people with dignity and respect. Being "educated" has little if anything to do with formal schooling. I place a greater value on this kind of education, but it is up to other people to assess the extent to which I am or am not educated.

5. One of the most extreme formulations of this proposition is found in Arthur Rubel's *Across the Tracks* (Austin: University of Texas Press, 1966), a classic though not very flattering ethnographic study of a Texas community. According to Rubel, respect for elders and male dominance are the two most basic organizing principles of the Mexican American family so that ideally "the older order the younger, and the men the women" (59). Anyone who has grown up in a Mexican family or has been around Mexicans knows how wrong Rubel is. Yet Latinos do tend to grant elders and men a certain amount of deference and respect, particularly in a public setting.

6. Mr. Falcón said he had four children but that only the youngest, Ricardo Jr., was living with him, and that he speaks English.

7. His wife had filed a separate petition for asylum. Her immigration hearing was scheduled for January.

8. INA § 208(a). While the standard of proof for Withholding of Deportation is a "clear probability" of persecution, the Supreme Court held in the landmark *Cardoza-Fonseca* case that an asylum applicant only needs to establish a "reasonable probability" of persecution, even if it is only a 10 percent chance. *I.N.S. v. Cardoza-Fonseca*, 107 S.Ct. 1207, 1217 (1987). Withholding of Deportation requires

demonstrating an objective clear probability of persecution, whereas the asylum standard is broader and contains both objective and subjective components.

9. I am not usually harsh or judgmental in evaluating people's appearance, but he was my first client, and I wanted to make sure that he made a favorable impression on the court. I also thought that we should not hide the scars because they offered visible evidence of his persecution. In retrospect, I think that I may have been overly concerned, if this is possible.

10. Shepardizing refers to a computer program for checking the judicial history of a case and making sure it has not been overruled.

11. He was accustomed to either having me do it in Spanish or having Mark interpret.

12. It reminded me of talking English with my father. My dad was never very proficient in English, and although my brothers and I usually spoke in English, we always spoke to him in Spanish. We were very comfortable switching back and forth. Sometimes when we were at a social gathering or somewhere where we had to talk to someone who did not speak Spanish, it was necessary to talk to my father in English so as not to appear rude. It was strange and humorous to speak English with my father. He was a different man in English, not as confident, self-assured, or articulate. The image that I have is a person who has a stroke or another condition that impairs their ability to speak. When you are not fluent in a language, you literally lose your voice.

13. In the Criminal Defense Lawyering class the previous year, we conducted a mock trial. I was co-counsel with Peter, and our client was an African American man accused of raping a white woman. That professor also said that I argued with the judge. She was tempted to warn me that she was going to hold me in contempt of court if I argued again. I was not aware that I had argued on that occasion either.

14. One could substitute Edward James Olmos.

15. In fairness to the client, I should mention that they weren't casual jeans but dress jeans. In retrospect, I think I may have been too demanding. Mr. Falcón looked very presentable. I shouldn't have expected the client to dress the way I was dressed for a court appearance: in my firm interview power suit, the uniform worn by all law students on the job market.

16. Lee was kidding, but he mentioned later that the judge said he did not believe in reading the briefs before the hearing because it "biased" him.

17. As it turned out, the first declaration had never been filed with the court. It was, therefore, unnecessary for us to point out the inconsistencies in the two declarations to the court and the government.

18. Mark had suggested that I do this.

19. In fact, it was unlikely that there would be a clinic the next year because the administration was making cuts in the various public interest and clinical programs such as the LSC curriculum.

20. This was Mark's idea. He had gotten a grant from a local organization that felt this would be an important component of the training.

21. I was out of town for a job interview and did not attend Nicole's hearing but everyone said it was very exciting. The government attorney was apparently insistent that Patty admit to having submitted a fake birth certificate or he was going to fight them to the end. Mark and the professor asked for a quick recess, conferred, and agreed to have Patty admit to it. She prevailed.

22. INA § 244. There is a saying in Spanish that may be appropriate here: "El mono, aunque se vista de seda, mono se queda!" (Though the ape be dressed in silk, an ape he remains!).

23. Diane Fossey, *Gorillas in the Mist* (Boston: Houghton Mifflin, 1983), 3–4.

Chapter Ten.   "Remains of the Day"

1. Turow, *One L,* 78–79.

2. My father had taught us that the man, or person, makes the clothes.

3. Entering associate salaries at large law firms in major cities have soared recently and exceed five figures yearly. Because summer associates' salaries are keyed to entering associate salaries, the former have increased proportionately.

4. I wrote several papers in law school that were subsequently published in law journals. See, e.g., Alfredo Mirandé, "En la Tierra del Ciego el Tuerto es Rey (In the Land of the Blind, the One-Eyed Person Is King): Bilingualism as a Disability," *New Mexico Law Review* 26 (Winter 1996): 75–105.

5. Because of space limitations, the chronicles given below are edited and condensed.

6. The names of the participants have been changed, except for two professors who were special guests in the class, Cynthia Fuchs Epstein and David Wilkins.

7. See Cynthia Fuchs Epstein, *Women in Law,* 2d ed. (Urbana: University of Illinois Press, 1993).

8. This actually meant that Three Ls sleep a lot and do not like to write papers in the last semester.

9. Kazuo Ishiguro, *The Remains of the Day* (London: Faber, 1989), 13–14. We were expected to read this book before the first day of class.

10. See the earlier discussion of "Mrs. G" in chapter 4.

11. I have often wondered what it would have been like to have been a lord. In Spanish the word is *don.* I have always had this secret wish to be called don Alfredo or Lord Mirandé but have never attained sufficient land, money, or power to garner such respect.

12. Insiders refer to Stanford as "the Farm" because it was once a farm.

13. For a discussion of the reasonable man, see the prologue.

14. *INS v. Delgado,* 466 U.S. 210 (1984).

15. The Court was using the standard first announced in *Mendenhall* here. *United States v. Mendenhall,* 446 U.S. 544 (1980).

16. For these statistics, see Richard Abel, *American Lawyers* (New York: Oxford University Press, 1989).

17. There was also a decline in the 1940s, but this can be attributed to the war.

18. Abel, *American Lawyers*, 300, table 37c.

19. For an interesting article on downsizing of firms and layoffs, see Erik Cummins, "Fenwick Trims 32 Associates, 15 Paralegals at Cooley, Godward," *Los Angeles Daily Journal*, September 7, 2001, pp. 1, 11.

20. I have been struck by the number of students from New York. In my class we seemed to have almost as many New Yorkers as Californians, or at least they were quite visible. Many faculty members are from New York or have practice ties to New York as well.

21. Ronald J. Gilson and Roger H. Mnookin, "Coming of Age in a Corporate Law Firm: The Economics of Associate Career Patterns," *Stanford Law Review* 41, no. 3 (February 1989): 567–95.

22. Ibid., 594.

23. This was an intriguing concept, one that recognized that there are subjective and imprecise judgments that go into dividing the pie.

24. Ishiguro, *The Remains of the Day*, 33.

25. Ibid., 167.

26. Ibid., 169.

27. Ibid., 185–86.

28. Ibid., 195.

29. Ibid., 196.

30. Max Weber, *The Theory of Social and Economic Organization* (New York: Free Press; London: Collier Macmillan, 1964).

31. During the discussion there was unanimity among the partners that associates tend to greatly exaggerate the number of hours that they are expected to bill.

32. Others attended sporadically.

33. David Morgan. "Men, Masculinity and the Process of Sociological Enquiry," in *Doing Feminist Research,* ed. Helen Roberts (London: Routledge & Kegan Paul, 1981), 83–113.

34. The dilemma for firms is that you want to create an environment that is humane, but you don't want to attract people who are lazy or want to work fewer hours. I think this is what "adverse selection" means.

35. There was no explanation offered by Wilkins for the increase, or discussion.

36. As noted earlier, Kimberlé Crenshaw uses the concept of intersectionality to discuss how in law women of color are obscured by the fact that black women are grouped as "women" or as "black," thus obscuring the intersection and compounded effects of class and gender. See Crenshaw, "A Black Feminist Critique of Antidiscrimination Law and Politics."

37. Ferdinand Toennies, *Gemeinschaft und Gesellschaft* (London: Routledge and Kegan Paul, 1955).

38. Catharine MacKinnon, *Feminism Unmodified: Discourses of Life and Law* (Cambridge, Mass.: Harvard University Press, 1987), 32.

39. Carol Gilligan, *In a Different Voice: Psychological Theory and Women's Development* (Cambridge, Mass.: Harvard University Press, 1982).

40. MacKinnon, *Feminism Unmodified,* 37.

41. Linda J. Krieger and Patricia N. Cooney, "The Miller-Wohl Treatment, Positive Action and the Meaning of Women's Equality Theory," *Golden Gate University Law Review* 13, no. 1 (1976): 513, 538.

42. Ibid.

43. 417 U.S. 484 (1974), 496, n. 20.

44. 11 S.Ct. 1859 (1991).

45. Ibid., 1867.

Chapter Eleven.   *La Noche Triste*

1. The Stanford Latino Law Student Association paired law students with undergraduate pre-law students, and I had been assigned to be Socorro's mentor during my first year at law school.

2. During the course of the placement we had set up three subcommittees, and Jessie chaired the committee focusing on the election of officers. Because Jessie was not at the meeting and we were having the ALATT elections, I opted to work with the ALATT committee to help coordinate the election. I was confident that Geronimo and the other workers could carry on without me in the job development committee.

3. Rupert did this without bringing it up at an ALATT meeting or asking us about the proposal. He simply informed us that for the last six weeks or so of the semester these other groups would be coming, alternating every other week. Mujeres is a Latina group that is interested in domestic violence, empowering women, and conducting Immigration Rights workshops (see chapter 8); Amigos is an Aids awareness group.

4. On Good Friday, we showed up to learn there would be no meeting. We turned around and went home. Rather than "piggy-back" on the next week's meeting, as I did when we skipped a meeting, Socorro wrote a field report on the non-meeting.

5. As I have noted before, not all the white students wanted us silenced.

Chapter Twelve.   Return to Kabara

1. I don't know if this was an exaggeration, but they used to say that my *abuelo* Alfredo could hold a pencil above his eyebrows.

2. In dealing with bureaucracies, I've learned that it's best never to ask whether you may do something, unless you have to.

3. The myth of *La Llorona*, or "Weeping Woman," takes various forms but remains an important part of Mexican folklore, dating back to pre-Columbian times.

In pre-Hispanic Mexico, Fray Bernardino de Sahagún, *Historia general de las cosas de Nueva España* (Mexico City: Editorial Nueva España, 1946), 1:414, recorded that sounds of wild beasts or a woman's cries heard at night were considered bad omens. *La Llorona is* also associated with Cihuacóatl, the patron of the *ciuateteo*, sanctified women who died in childbirth, and "is said to carry a cradle or the body of a dead child in her arms and to weep at night at the crossings of city streets. In times gone by, people knew that she had passed that way when they found in the market the empty cradle with a sacrificial knife laid beside it." Alfonso Caso, *The Aztecs: People of the Sun* (Norman: University of Oklahoma Press, 1958), 54.

In the sixth omen of the eight omens of doom which were said to have been received by the Aztecs prior to the arrival of Cortés, anguished voices, like those of women, were heard in the night air: "Oh, my children, we will be lost! . . . Oh, my children, where shall I take you!" Sahagún, *Historia general de las cosas de Nueva España*, 3:16.

Epilogue   "I Don't Need No Stinkin' Badges"

1. The *Los Angeles Times* reported recently that "Nino," the Mexican Bozo the Clown, passed away. He was seventy years old. He began entertaining Mexican children as *El Payaso* Bozo in 1961 and was forced to change his name to "Nino" after the American film studios sued him for copyright infringement. Other clowns, complete with clown faces, red noses, and the traditional oversized shoes, served as pallbearers in a special tribute to a Mexican hero, Nino, or *El Payaso* Bozo.

2. See Raul Morín, *Among the Valiant* (Los Angeles: Borden Publishing, 1996); Rodolfo Acuña, *Occupied America: A History of Chicanos*, 4th ed. (New York: Longman, 2000), 264–65.

3. For an excellent discussion, and emerging definition, of what it means to be "an American," see Bill Ong Hing, *To Be An American: Cultural Pluralism and The Rhetoric of Assimiliation* (New York: New York University Press, 1997), 174–81.

4. The name of the law school is, of course, fictional.

5. See Victor C. Romero, "The Domestic Fourth Amendment Rights of Undocumented Immigrants: On *Gutierrez* and the Tort Law/Immigration Law Parallel," *Harvard Civil Rights–Civil Liberties Law Review* 35, no. 1 (Winter 2000): 57 101; Mirandé, "Is There a 'Mexican Exception' to the Fourth Amendment?" *Florida Law Review* 55 (January 2003): 365–89.

6. Casa Blanca is a barrio in Riverside with a long history of police abuse and conflict between the community and law enforcement. See Alfredo Mirandé, "The Chicano and the Law: An Analysis of Community-Police Conflicts in an Urban Bar-

rio," in *Criminal Justice and Latino Communities,* ed. Antoinette Sedillo López (New York: Garland, 1995), 87 108.

7. For a discussion of the relationship between law and social science, see Clifford Geertz, "Local Knowledge: Fact and Law in Comparative Perspective," in his *Local Knowledge: Further Essays in Interpretive Anthropology* (New York: Basic Books, 1983), 167–234.

8. I have borrowed the title from Margaret Montoya's article, which used the metaphor of masks, braids, and unkempt hair to describe how she felt silenced at Harvard Law School. Montoya,*"Mascaras, Trenzas, y Greñas."*

9. Lani Guinier, Michelle Fine, and Jane Balin, *Becoming Gentlemen: Women, Law School, and Institutional Change* (Boston: Beacon Press, 1997), 49–50.

10. Janet Taber et al., "Gender, Legal Education, and the Legal Profession," *Stanford Law Review* 40, no. 5 (May 1988): 1254.

11. That a few Stanford faculty were associated with Critical Legal Studies (CLS) is not surprising, for the CLS leadership was made up of elite white male faculty at the top law schools. Critical Race theorists have been critical of the CLS lack of attention to race and gender. See, e.g., Richard Delgado, "The Imperial Scholar: Reflections on a Review of Civil Rights Literature," *University of Pennsylvania Law Review* 132, no. 3 (March 1984): 561–78; Harlon L. Dalton, "The Clouded Prism," *Harvard Civil Rights–Civil Liberties Law Review* 22 (Spring 1987): 435–47.

12. This is a term used by Gerald López to describe the prevailing traditional, hierarchical view of law and law practice whereby the attorney is viewed as the source of all knowledge. Gerald P. López, *Rebellious Lawyering: One Chicano's Vision of Progressive Law Practice* (Boulder, Colo.: Westview Press, 1992).

13. I call them "Hispanic" because the Mexican-origin students at Western Plains referred to themselves as "Hispanic," although except for their drawl they certainly looked like Mexicans to me.

14. Deborah L. Rhode, *In the Interests of Justice: Reforming the Legal Profession* (New York: Oxford University Press, 2000), 196.

15. Gerald P. López, "Training Future Lawyers to Work with the Politically and Socially Subordinated: Anti-Generic Legal Education," *West Virginia Law Review* 91, no. 2 (Winter 1988–89): 312.

16. Ibid.

17. Guinier, Fine, and Balin, *Becoming Gentlemen,* 49–50.

18. Ibid., 76.

19. For a critique of *stare decisis,* the idea that law is cumulative and based on precedent, see Kairys, *The Politics of Law,* 1–20.

20. Rhode, *In the Interests of Justice,* 197.

21. Guinier, Fine, and Balin, *Becoming Gentlemen,* 74.

22. López, "Training Future Lawyers," 321–22.

23. Rhode, *In the Interests of Justice*, 185–86.

24. Kevin R. Johnson, "Celebrating LatCrit Theory: What Do We Do When the Music Stops?" *U.C. Davis Law Review* 33, no. 4 (Summer 2000): 776.

25. For a discussion of issues of diversity in legal education, see ABA Commission on Women in the Profession, *Elusive Equality: The Experience of Women in Legal Education* (Chicago: ABA, 1996); Linda F. Wightman, Law School Admission Council Research Report series, *Women in Legal Education: A Comparison of the Law School Performance and Law School Experience of Women and Men* (Newtown, Pa.: Law School Admission Council, 1996); Deborah L. Rhode, "Whistling Vivaldi: Legal Education and the Politics of Progress," *New York University Review of Law and Social Change* 23 (1997): 217; Guinier, Fine, and Balin, *Becoming Gentlemen*.

26. Guinier, Fine, and Balin, *Becoming Gentlemen*, 41.

27. Ibid., 48–49.

28. Ibid., 28.

29. Montoya, "*Mascaras, Trenzas, y Greñas*," 24.

30. *People v. Josephine Chavez*, 176 P.2d 92 (Cal. App. 1947).

31. Montoya, "*Mascaras, Trenzas, y Greñas*," 20.

32. Ibid.

33. Ibid.

34. Ibid.

35. Patricia J. Williams, *The Alchemy of Race and Rights* (Cambridge, Mass.: Harvard University Press, 1991), 418–19.

36. Ibid., 418.

37. Guinier, Fine, and Balin, *Becoming Gentlemen*, 85.

38. Ibid., 81.

39. López, "Training Future Lawyers," 306.

40. Marc Galanter and Thomas Palay, *Tournament of Lawyers: The Transformation of the Big Law Firm* (Chicago: University of Chicago Press, 1991), 39.

41. Ibid.

42. Ibid., 39–40.

43. See Andrea Guerrero, *Silence at Boalt Hall: The Dismantling of Affirmative Action* (Berkeley: University of California Press, 2002). See also Nancy McCarthy, "A Year as 'The Only One' at Boalt," *California Bar Journal*, February 2003, pp. 1, 7.

44. Richard A. White, "Statistical Report on Law School Faculty (American Association of Law Schools, 1999–2000)," Table 1B. Pamphlet published by the American Association of Law Schools.

45. The term "Hispanic" includes anyone with a Spanish surname or whose ancestry is linked to Spain and excludes those without Spanish surnames. It therefore includes Spaniards, South Americans, Cubans, and others who would not necessarily qualify as "disadvantaged," or what Justice Stone termed "discrete and insular" minorities who are in need of special protection by courts. See Stone's opinion in note 4 of *Carolene*

Products, perhaps the most famous footnote in the history of constitutional law. *United States v. Carolene Products*, 304 U.S. 144 (1938).

46. Rhode, *In the Interests of Justice*, 192.

47. R. White, "Statistical Report on Law School Faculty," note 12, Table 1B.

48. Guinier, Fine, and Balin, *Becoming Gentlemen*, 53.

49. I had recently become a naturalized U.S. citizen. I now hold dual citizenship.

50. I recall only one case in which one of the U.S. attorneys who came before the court had a Spanish surname.

ALFREDO MIRANDÉ

is professor of sociology and chair of ethnic studies at the University of
California, Riverside. He integrates his teaching and research with a
limited, largely pro bono law practice, specializing in criminal law and
employment discrimination.